FRAGMENTATION

The Memories of the
3rd Platoon of I Company 260th Regiment
65th Division

Written by Joe Windham

First Edition

**Biographical Publishing Company
Prospect, Connecticut**

FRAGMENTATION

The Memories of the
3rd Platoon of I Company 260th Regiment
65th Division

First Edition

Published by:

Biographical Publishing Company
95 Sycamore Drive
Prospect, CT 06712-1493

Phone: 203-758-3661   Fax: 253-793-2618
e-mail: biopub@aol.com

All rights reserved. No part of this book may be reproduced or transmitted in any form or by any means, electronic or mechanical, including photocopying, recording, or by any information storage or retrieval system without the written permission of the author, except for the inclusion of brief quotations in a review.

Copyright © 2005 by Joe Windham
Seventh Printing 2023

Copyright © TXu1-238-776, April 12, 2005 by Joe Windham

PRINTED IN THE UNITED STATES OF AMERICA

Publisher's Cataloging-in-Publication Data

Windham, Joe
Fragmentation : The Memories of the 3rd Platoon of I Company 260th Regiment 65th Division/ by Joe Windham
1st ed.
P. cm.
ISBN 9781929882397 (alk. Paper)
1. Title 2. World War II personal accounts 3. U.S. Military stories
Dewey Decimal Classification: 940.53
Library of Congress Control Number: 2005938526

ACKNOWLEDGEMENTS

I wish to thank the people that helped me in writing my book.

First, Mary, My wife of 56 years. She was my proof reader, critic and inspiration, always telling me how good my writing was. I accused her of prejudical treatment.

Ellsworth Cunningham, My Platoon leader who sent me a copy of the notes he had kept.

Carol Park, daughter of Steve Rakosi, A deceased Platoon buddy that was a gargantuan collector of memorabilia. She copied most of his collection and sent it to me. These things were invaluable to my research.

Harry Rice, who was with my best friend, Dayne Simmons when he was KIA. Harry was also severely wounded at the time. His correspondence and telephone conversations helped refresh my memories of that time and place.

Jack Zinaman a Platoon buddy that sent me many reminders of our combat experiences and also sent me a book containing a Chronology of The Third Army's advance across Europe. This saved me valuable time in my research.

Robert Cardinell, Historian, 65th Division Association.

George Haber, Historian, Deggendorf, Germany.

FRONT COVER: Photos top left: Ellsworth L. Cunningham; top right: Joe Windham author, VE Day plus 2 in Austria; bottom: Ellsworth Cunningham and Joe Windham reunited after 58 years in Biloxi, Mississippi.

DEDICATION

This book is dedicated to T/Sgt. Ellsworth Linwood Cunningham, who was my Platoon leader throughout the war. I served as Platoon Messenger, which kept us usually in close contact. His greatest concern was for the men of the Platoon. He always did the dirty work. He placed the grenades through the windows and the satchel charges against the Pill boxes, while we covered. He was always the first to reach the wounded. He would hold them while they drew their last breath, and give comfort to the ones that were waiting for the litter bearers. When communication broke down and there was more than one task, he always took the most dangerous and leaving for me the easy one. We were Blood Brothers, not because of our blood, but because of the blood of our buddies. This he would transfer to me as we lay huddled together, after the battle, trying to keep warm.

If it had not been for this man, I am sure that I would not have had these sixty years since. Fifty-six of them married to the love of my life and enjoying the things that our three children have brought to us.

Sgt. Ellsworth L. Cunningham received the Bronze Star for Valor, was recommended for a Battlefield commission, but due to shoddy paperwork, he never received it. To me, it went beyond military. He was a Prince!!!

There is one great thing you men will be able to say after this war is all over and you are at home once again. And you may thank God for it. You may be thankful that twenty years from now when you are sitting by the fireplace with your grandson on your knee and he asks you what you did in the great World War II, you won't have to cough, shift him to the other knee and say, "Well, your Granddaddy shoveled shit in Louisiana." No sir! You can look him in the eye and say, "Son, your Granddaddy rode with the great Third Army and a son-of-a-bitch named Georgie Patton."

Third Army speech
May 31, 1944.
to the men of General Gerow's
Sixth Armored Division
in England

FRAGMENTATION
By Joe G. Windham

I Co. 260th Infantry

This story is about the highlights of my twenty-nine months spent as an infantry rifleman. All of my battlefield experience was with the 65th Infantry Division 260th regiment company I. Of this time and with these men of the third platoon of "I" company I discovered the true meaning of comrade. I worked almost forty years on the same job after the war. I was a member of organized labor, walked the picket lines with brothers, and fought all the battles that working men have to fight. I never once got that feeling of brotherhood that I felt while I was with the men of "I" company 260th Infantry.

My army life started forty-nine days after my eighteen birthday, four months before I was to finish high school. My school principal told me he would give me enough credits to get my diploma or he would help to get a deferment. My reply was, "I will go on into the army and get it over with." How many times did I think? "Big mistake." Getting it over with had too may definitions.

Being from Mississippi, I entered the army at Camp Shelby, Mississippi. (I can hear boo's as I sit here.) From Shelby I went to Camp Blanding, Florida into the I.R.T.C. (Infantry Replacement Training Center.) Replacement training, the worst idea ever conceived by a four-star General.

When my seventeen weeks of training was finished I was sent to Fort Mead, Maryland for an "overseas" assignment. When I stepped up to the door of that black hole known as the "Repple Depple" I was met by an officer who informed me that my orders had been changed, that due to a new law, no eighteen year old draftees would be sent into combat zones. My first lucky break, saved by public opinion. My new orders were to go to Camp Shelby, Mississippi and report to "I" company 260th Regiment of the 65th Infantry Division. My second lucky break, back where I started from fifty miles from home. While on the train from Ft. Mead to Camp Shelby I met Dayne Simmons, from West Point, Mississippi. We were comparing assignments, we discovered we both were assigned to the same company. Third lucky break, I had a friend going in.

Simmons and I reported to the C. Q. at "I" Company on a very hot day in July, 1944 we were told by the C. Q. that the company was out in the field and that they would be back around five, and the brass would assign us then. He gave us the first orders that we would receive from "I" company, "Hang around until the brass shows up and do not leave the company area." About five we heard the sound of Cadence being counted. We looked up from our seats on our duffel bags and watched as the company swung into the company area, they were called to attention with their backs to Simmons and me. We were seated on our duffel bags against the wall of A barracks in the shade trying to keep cool. We were facing all the brass and noncoms as they went through the routine of dismissing the men. After the dismissal we were beckoned by the C. Q. to come across the company area to where he and another solder was standing. As we approached I could see that the soldier was wearing the chevrons of a First Sergeant. Simmons and I were told by the C. Q. "This is First Sergeant Harrell, he will take care of you." Sergeant Harrell was about fifty years old, regular army, with a permanent scowl on his face. His first words to us were, "do you have orders stating you are members of company "I" 260th Infantry 65th division?" We said yes, then he asked us why we kept sitting on our duffs when the company was called to attention. I stammered that I guess I was not thinking, this answer made his face turn another shade redder. He told us that would be the last time I would say those words while I was under his command in "I" company. Then he told us to follow him to meet the old man before he got away. He took us to the company office and introduced us to the company commander, Capt. John Batts. A former high school principal from Kentucky, who was a great leader and always thought of his men first. After our introduction to the Captain, Sgt. Harrell looked over our orders, then took us to where the third platoon was billeted and he introduced us to Staff Sgt. Ellsworth L. Cunningham, third platoon guide. After a short discussion between Harrell and Cunningham, Simmons and I were told that he and I were being assigned to the same squad in the third platoon. I remember thinking, "this old regular army man knows what he is doing." He let us know who was in charge, won our respect and loyalty in less than thirty minutes.

The next four months of my time were spent making new friends and taking "advanced training." This consisted mostly of what was taught at the IRTC, in Blanding, Florida. The difference here was welding a group of men into a fighting force unlike at the IRTC where men were sent off to join a fighting force of total strangers. A new environment with total strangers in a battlefield situation almost never produced desired results. I believe the powers that be began to recognize this, and in 1943 started to form new divisions, train the men together, send them into battle together, relieving whole divisions instead of leaving a division in battle and replacing the casualties.

The men of my company were made up of a diverse group. Mostly from New England, New York, Pennsylvania and a few from the other states. The men were diverse ethnically and education wise. The education of our platoon ranged from a twenty-nine year old father of four, who could neither read or write, to college graduates. Most of the college men came from the army's trimmed down (ASTP) Army Specialized Training Program. These men, America's best and brightest, made up the nucleus of the 65th Infantry Division. Most of the noncoms in our platoon were from this group. Before coming to the 65th Division, my idea of an infantry division was that it would be made up of men that had no particular skills, and thus was relegated to the infantry. This may have been true at the beginning of the war when there was a shortage of man power in all branches of the services in all departments.

As the war progressed, the casualties among the infantry were much higher than anticipated, especially among the noncoms and junior officers. This shortage of front line troops, led to a high rate of infusion into the newly activated infantry divisions the men from the trimmed down ASTP program, the 65th was one of these divisions. I believe the men from ASTP was the catalyst that made the 65th the great division that it turned out to be. The thing that impressed me most about the 65th was how little regional difference existed between the men of the 65th compared to the men of the IRTC at Camp Blanding.

The 65th had been activated about a year before my arrival, most of the members had been together since the activation. The difference in their attitude toward each other was so much better, compared to the men I had trained with at the IRTC.

The training with the 65th was hard, but at times it was enjoyable, because of the comarada that existed among the men. Training, for the most part consisted of discipline, physical conditioning, and how to attack that dreaded enemy, V.D.

In October 1944, I was chosen to be the platoon runner for the third platoon, I was replaced on the B.A.R. team by my friend, Dayne Simmons.

In November 1944, I broke my right foot and was confined to the hospital at Camp Shelby until mid December when Capt. Batts, my company commander came by the hospital and informed me that he had to bring the company up to strength by the end of the month for an overseas assignment. He asked if I would like to come along with the company instead of being sent to a repple depple depot. Capt. Batts said he would bring me back to the company and give me light duty (K.P.) until we shipped out. I agreed to go with the company.

While in rehab at the hospital in Camp Shelby, I met some of the most unforgettable heroes of the war. I was privileged to be billeted and take rehab with the famous 442nd members who were wounded in Italy. There was one man that I took special notice of, he was just under five feet tall, weighed a little under one hundred pounds and his right leg was off just above the knee. I was amazed at his balance on one leg, he could stand and hop for hours and never sit down, especially in the barracks while shooting craps against a foot locker. Why I never wrote the names of these heroes down I will never know, unless I thought being eighteen I would never forget a hero's name. As time marched on I found out "big mistake" you are lucky, if after fifty-eight years you can remember your own name.

On December 28th, only five weeks after my nineteenth birthday, my company, "I" company 260th Regiment 65th Division, boarded a troop train headed for Camp Shanks, New York and overseas duty. There was a lot of mixed emotions on the train, some men were happy, especially the ones that lived in the New York area. They were looking forward to going home one more time. There were lots of gung-ho and let me at them attitude, but I felt that most of it was fake. Me, I felt bad, I was going away from home, had that homesick feeling that a kid of nineteen plus five weeks can get knowing that carrying an MOS 745 you were not heading for a picnic.

We arrived at Camp Shanks on December 30, 1944. The ground was covered with snow and the snow was covered with black soot, we Southerners figured it was fallout from New York City. Being from Mississippi I had seen snow a few times but it never stayed long enough to turn black.

When we pulled onto the siding of Shanks. It was drizzling rain and the day was cold and gray. The men from the New York area were all excited, for me it was depression city. I started to get that knot in the pit of my stomach that I would become so familiar with in the days to come.

After being told by some noncoms from transportation not to leave the train until told to do so. We sat on the train what seemed like hours watching officers and noncoms scurrying around outside, going over papers and maps, pointing in all directions, doing that hurry up and wait thing that the army is notorious for. Finally our platoon guide, Sgt. E.L. Cunningham came into the car and informed us that we were to assemble outside the car and we were going to march to our new billets in company formation. That would take about thirty minutes, and that our duffel bags would be brought by trucks to the company area. This brought on a loud cheer from all the men. We usually had to wag those bags it was under one hour marching distance. I suppose they did not want to get anyone wounded on the snow and ice, and had to call on the "Repple Depple" before we reached the war zone.

When we finally arrived at our cold tar-papered barracks we were glad that these were our temporary home. Things were going downhill, one was beginning to think that by the time we reached the combat zone we would be glad to be there. Bad thinking, no amount of bad treatment can prepare you for the initiation into combat.

The next ten days we spent preparing our equipment for overseas shipment and taking some last minute training, except January 4th and 5th, these two days the men were given passes to go into New York City if they so desired. Most of the men from the New York area had been going in to visit families almost every night since we arrived at Shanks, even though we were on restriction. Everyone showed up in the morning so no harm done. I was given a pass to go into New York on the 5th. I went along with Jasperson, a member of my squad, who was from Minnesota. New York was quite a sight for a Mississippi farm boy who had never seen anything taller than a pine tree. We took the tour of the New York Empire State Building, Radio City Music Hall, we checked out the Stage Door Canteen, and of course ended up making Jack Dempsey's and a few more bars. By 2:00 a.m. we were pretty well under the influence, we decided since we had to get a cab, catch a ferry, take a train and end up on a bus in order to get to our company area at Shanks, we had better start moving if we were going to make reveille. We made it, but bad news greeted us. This was the day we were to go through the gas chamber and check for leaks in our gas masks. Gas chambers are tough when you are operating with a hangover.

On January 6, 1945 we were told that we were on high alert, that everyone was restricted to the company area and we could be shipping out at any time. Some of the men from the New York area did not take the restriction too seriously and managed to slip away for one last visit with their families. They were right. The next couple of days were spent checking equipment for correct shipping numbers and identification labels, but mostly just lying around fielding rumors about where we were headed. There was not one hot spot on the globe that was not mentioned.

On January 7th, we found out that some officers from our company were being transferred. "I" company ended up short one officer. My platoon, third platoon, ended up without an officer platoon leader. T/Sgt. Hilton was put in charge of the platoon. S/Sgt. E.L. Cunningham was moved from platoon guide to platoon Sgt., and S/Sgt. Raymond Smith was made the platoon guide. This new arrangement did not seem to bother any of the men, guess they figured there were worse things to worry about.

On January 9th, we were told that this was the day that we would be boarding a ship, by this time tomorrow we would be at sea. Shortly after noon we were told to strip our beds, fold the mattress over, place the pillow on top of the mattress, turn in our linens and then fallout into the company street with all our gear, that we would not be coming back into the barracks. The trucks would be picking us up soon to take us to the train that would take us to the port of embarkation. This turned out to be another of the army's hurry-up and wait deals. After standing around in the snow and ice for almost three hours the trucks arrived and took us to the train station. There it took a couple more hours to load the train and move out. When we arrived at the port it was almost midnight. As we looked out onto the docks we could see two columns of soldiers slowly moving toward the front of the train. We were told to get our gear and fall out on the dock and to fall in at the end of the column and follow it. As we slowly moved along with the line we were served coffee and doughnuts which tasted pretty good since we had not eaten since noon. I had not thought too much about eating all day, anxiety has a way of suppressing one's appetite. After about an hour of moving along with the line I could see the front of the line was disappearing through what appeared to be a large door in a wall, as we drew near we could see that the door they were disappearing into led into the biggest ship I had ever seen. Neither the top, bottom or either end was visible. They way we recognized this was a ship with lifeboats that were visible on the partially revealed deck above the door and little streams of water being pumped from small holes in the side of the ship.

We were met at the ship by our company commander, Capt. John T. Batts and First Sgt. Harrell. We were formed up into company formation, everyone was present and accounted for. Within a short time we began going through the door after crossing over a very short gang-plank, straight into the bowels of the ship, not at all like I had pictured it in my mind's eye, going up the gang-plank waving to the crowd, more like "a thief in the night." They were sticking to that slogan, "loose lips sink ships", and at that moment I was glad they were.

By the time we were moving on board the ship, the 10th of January had arrived and the strain of the long day was beginning to tell on us. The calls from some of the wise guys, who had boarded the ship earlier, using that old military phrase, "you gonna be sorry", were met by some instructions from us as to where they could go. We struggled down several sets of steps, more like ladders, until we reached what they told us was D-deck aft. We then moved into a compartment filled with what appeared to be bunk beds made from canvas stretched inside metal frames. I was intrigued by the locking system on the door of the compartment. The inside had a simple handle while the outside had a large wheel that operated tumblers inside the door to lock and unlock it. This locking arrangement did nothing to improve my slowly rising feelings of claustrophobia.

We received our bed assignments and were given our meal tickets from Sgt. Hilton. We were told to use our blankets and sleeping bag liners as our mattresses and covers, but to be careful about zipping yourself up in the sleeping bag that you could be thrown from your bunk by rough seas and not be able to break your fall. By this time I was thinking maybe I will tie myself in bed by the neck. The bunk beds were stacked three high, naturally I was assigned the one in the middle so I would catch hell from both sides whenever I moved.

Finally, around 1:00 a.m., January 10, 1945 we had finished our bedding assignments and were told to get some sleep, that we would be pulling out pretty soon. We were among the last to board the ship. After a short rumor session about our destination, which ranged from Alaska to the Suez Canal, things quieted down and I suppose most everyone fell asleep, I know I did. It had been a long day. I hardly remember the ship moving out in the wee hours.

We were awakened after what seemed like a short nap by the voices of the noncoms yelling, "hit the deck and get ready for chow, stand by your bed until we come for you, we will go as a group to the galley area and have breakfast." I am thinking we have some smart noncoms already speaking the navy lingo. Me, I am still trying to figure out the connection between latrine and head and where they told me it was before I went to sleep.

About an hour later the noncoms returned and told us to follow them to the mess area and be sure and bring our mess gear. We moved through the chow line, receiving our chow in our mess kit and our coffee in our canteen cup, then moving into the dining area. The dining area consisted of long lines of chest-high dining tables with a rim around the top edges, no chairs, everyone stood to eat. At the end of each table against the bulkhead (wall) was fastened a large garbage can. As I looked over the dining area where other troops were still eating, I wondered why the garbage cans were so popular, most of the troops seemed to be standing around them. It did not take long to find out why it was called mess. Every meaning of the word, as defined in Webster dictionary, was represented here. Sea-sickness was raising its ugly head, the rolling of the ship was not compatible with the food. It soon became evident that the popularity of the garbage cans was due to the regurgitation that was going on. The troubles of others were soon forgotten after I set my food on the table and tried to eat standing. I found that I was badly in need of two more arms and hands, one to hold on to keep from falling, one to hold my mess kit to keep it from sliding away and mixing with other peoples food or worse, one hand to prevent my coffee from turning over, and another to hold my fork. Being a rifleman from the 65th Division, I had learned the art of improvisation well. I managed to savor every crumb and drop and walk out with my head high, while a large part of the other diners seemed to be losing theirs to the garbage cans.

After breakfast we reported back to our sleeping quarters and after a brief orientation class we were told that we could go top side and look over the ship and see the ocean, which I had not seen yet. As to what I had seen on the ship, it was all below the water line. I could tell by the sound and the condensation collecting on the bulkhead by my bunk. After being told to be back in our sleeping quarters by 1000 hours that we were going to have a meeting to work out some details. That word detail has raised its ugly head.

For this farm boy from Mississippi to see the ocean for the first time from a ship with no land in sight, is as poignant as it gets. There were ships all around us of every description, some were going in all directions, I was informed that they were Navy destoyers and destroyer escorts protecting us from enemy submarines. With the vast amount of water that I was surveying, I still did not feel that safe. After watching the ocean roll for awhile, we began to check out the ship, it was much larger than I expected, a four stacker. I had always heard that a ship with four stacks was a very large one. The rumor was that our ship was the Flagship, that all the brass was on our ship. We were in the center of the convoy protected by all the other ships around us. I am thinking they are telling the troops on the other ships the same story to hold down anxiety.

When we returned to our quarters, all the noncoms in our platoon were waiting for us with papers in hand. Sgt. Hilton, our platoon leader, briefed us on the ships rules. Everything must be kept clean, smoke only in designated areas, keep all aisles and passageways clear, all equipment must be kept in place. He pointed out how and where to get PX rations and he told us the procedure for getting into sick-bay and where it was. Sgt. Hilton also informed us the hours of blackout and that we were never to throw anything overboard. After these instructions and all the elaborations that go with them we were turned over to our platoon sergeant, Sgt. E.L. Cunningham who was in charge of the details. Sgt. Cunningham first asked for volunteers to keep our quarters clean. Getting none, he then appointed a few. He then said he needed about fifteen good men to work in the ship's galley. I saw a few eyes roll but no show of hands. I am thinking pots and pans, then my mind slowly turned to food and how close I would be to it and maybe I would not have to eat in that hole where I had eaten breakfast. Before I regained control, my hand shot up into the air. I looked around, at the most there were about three arms up the rest were drafted. After the details were all assigned Sgt. Cunningham took the galley detail, sixteen of us in all, to the galley and introduced us to a petty officer whom he said would be in charge of us as long as we were on this detail, then he left. The petty officer (I can't remember his name) told us right off, what our job was going to be. He said, "you sixteen men will be totally in charge of the disposal of all garbage and trash that comes from the dining area and the galley." There was total silence for a few seconds then a shuffling of feet and low voices repeating "garbage." I was standing up front, I did not turn around to face the men, I was too busy thinking about those garbage cans in the mess area and what I had seen going into them. The petty officer gave us time to let the message sink in, then he told us that it will not be so bad, that we would see, and keeping busy would help us to fight off sea-sickness. He also said the chow would be better for us. He explained what our duties would be, there were to be two shifts, eight men on each shift, we were to work seven hour shifts and the first shift would come on at 0600 hours and work until 1300 hours. The other shift would work from 1300 hours until 2000 hours. He told us that we would be totally in charge of the service elevator, which ran from the top deck to the very bottom of the ship. There was a place on the top deck where we would store all wood and cardboard until it could be thrown overboard after dark. Nothing would be thrown overboard during daylight, that they wanted at least ten hours between the time it was thrown overboard and daylight in case it was spotted by Germans. At the bottom of the ship, we were told there would be two men in charge of the service elevator. One on each shift, that no one would be allowed to use the elevator except our ships officers on top deck. They would be recognized by their uniforms and name tags. The petty officer told us he was going to dismiss us, that we would return to our quarters, have a meeting, divide yourselves into two equal groups, select one man from each group to operate the elevator, decide which shift would work, inform Sgt. Cunningham of your status and all of you report back here to me at 1300 hours ready to work. This afternoon I will have some ship's personnel here to instruct you in where and how the work will be done.

At our meeting we selected Tony Castagliola and Howard Stern to be the elevator operators, a gentile and a Jew both from Brooklyn, they were also to be responsible for getting the men together to be at work on time. We then lined up and counted off, odd men on morning shift, even on afternoon shift. I ended up on morning shift with Howard Stern in charge.

We returned to the galley where the petty officer and two other navy men were waiting for us. The two men first took us through the galley to show us where the trash and garbage pick up places were, they then took us through the dining areas where the garbage cans would be picked up and informed us that all garbage from this area would be taken to the bottom of the ship and disposed of there. We then took the elevator to the top deck and there we were shown the place the trash would be stored until thrown overboard. We took the elevator to the bottom of the ship. We departed the elevator and were led through the door that was directly across from the door of the elevator. Inside this door was a room that contained only one item, that appeared to me to be a giant commode from the description we were getting that was what it was. The navy men had another name for it, but I can not recall what it was. The container was about five feet tall and looked as if it would hold about two hundred gallons. We were told that we would pour the garbage from the garbage cans into the container until it was almost full. Then they showed us a lever at the bottom of the container that opened a valve that would let the contents run into the ocean. The catch was that it had to be opened at the proper time so that the contents would not be blown back into the room and onto the operator. If the ship was rolling with the wave action the valve was to be opened at the bottom of the roll so when the ship lifted up, the contents would be pulled out into the ocean. If the reverse happened the man who opened the valve would be responsible for the clean up. The sailors gave a demonstration of its operation. Then we returned to the galley. The second shift went on duty and we of the first shift returned to our quarters.

Being a garbage handler has its rewards. We ate in the galley workers dining room, we had better food and ate from trays instead of mess kits. Sometimes the stewards would give us cups of ice cream that was reserved for the ship's officers. After observing the clean-up detail, which had the job of keeping our quarters clean, I sure was glad I volunteered for the galley detail.

Most of our free time was spent on the upper decks. Shooting the bull and watching the ocean roll, sometimes it was so rough you would have to look up to see the tops of the waves when sitting on top deck. Having never seen these forces of nature before, I was completely awed by it all.

By the third day at sea, sea-sickness seemed to have become an epidemic among the troops. When the wind was blowing, one learned to stay away from the open decks as there was more than surf being blown across them and showers were hard to come by on this boat.

It was either the third or fourth day, we were informed that the ship we were on was the S.S. John Erickson, a former Norwegian luxury liner. As we were able to explore more of the ship, there was evidence everywhere of its former glory. There were the fancy bars with their heart-breaking, "closed" signs still intact. There was a theatre that still had its curtains and chandeliers, and an olympic size swimming pool made of different colored tile, but was now filled with mattresses.

On January 15th, I had not experienced any symptoms of sickness yet, but I began to feel an old bug-a-boo of mine returning. A boil was forming on the back of my neck, caused from an infected hair follicle. I had been down this road before, at Camp Blanding, Florida. There I was told by the medical staff that the cause of the infection was the rubbing of the short clipped hair on my upper neck by the collar of my uniform fatigue shirt. When I discussed this problem with the medical discharge board I was told my only option was to grow a longer neck. I said I would try, but sadly that steel pot they gave me to wear on my head seemed to stunt the growth.

If anyone has ever suffered the pain of an emerging boil, they know what I was going through. It is the only thing that fits that old adage, "can't touch it with a powder puff."

The morning of the sixteenth, while getting ready for work I noticed that the swelling around the boil had intensified to the point that it was readily touching my shirt collar. I sought out our platoon medic, Lloyd Coy. He placed a bandage over it and told me to come to him after work and together we would go to sick-bay and find out if they could help. I told my friend Howard Stern what was going on, he seemed genuinely concerned and he told me to run the elevator that he would handle the garbage cans. This day was the beginning of a growing friendship between a New York Jew and a Mississippi Protestant. Following my work shift I returned to my quarters where I was met by Coy who took me to sick-bay. I then signed in and wrote down my problem. I was told to go outside and fall in at the end of the line of green men that were holding on to the railing waiting to get in. While there I found out that the Navy had that same hurry-up and wait attitude that the Army has. They also had the same caste system that the Army had, no officer that entered the door to sick bay returned to fall in line. After what seemed like hours I made it into sick-bay, where I was met by a young man in a uniform so white it hurt my eyes. He asked me what my problem was. After I told him, he reached up ripped the bandage from my neck, then started poking and mashing at the back of my neck. While doing this he would ask me if that hurt. I don't know what he thought those deep knee bends I was doing were for. He then opened a door and called out and two other sailors came into the room. After they all had their turn at poking and mashing, they held a conference. They then told me it was a boil but it was not ready to be lanced. It would probably be two or three more days before it would be ready. Then they gave me some aspirin to take for pain and told me to take it easy and to return in about three days.

The next three days were routine. I ran the elevator, the boys took care of the garbage, Coy changed the bandage on my neck twice a day, always saying that is was not ready yet.

On January 19th, we of the garbage detail were informed by the galley Chief petty officer that our tour of duty with him would end at 2000 hours the next day. The 20th of January, that we would probably would be pulling into port soon after then. He wished us good luck and said that he would see that "garbage masters" would be entered into our military record.

Before we left the ship there was a debt we felt we owed to one of the waiters that served the food to the ship's officers. There were two of them, they worked alternate days. Each day after noon at about our shift changing time, they would take a cart filled with ice cream in paper cups up to the officers mess. One of the waiters always brought enough for each of our crew to have one. The other waiter said he could not do it. So we named him "Snot", which he resented to the point that he never spoke to us. We worked out a plan that members of my crew would hang around in the galley area until he showed up to take the ice cream up. Tony Castagliola was to hang around with the crew and was not to relieve me until the waiter showed up with the ice cream. I was to keep the elevator at the bottom until the light came on for me to come to the galley deck. If the plan worked, the waiter would be waiting at the door with his cart when I arrived. He would push his cart onto the elevator, Tony would step up and tell me he was relieving me. I was to say "good, how about dropping me off at D-deck, my neck is killing me." The four men of my crew after hearing me, were to say "drop us off there too." We were then to proceed up and just before we reached D-deck, Tony was to turn off the lights in the elevator, the four men were to fill their fatigue pockets with ice cream. Tony was to stop at D-deck, the four men were to run out the door. Tony and I were to remain on the elevator asking each other what happened. The plan worked to perfection except there was more ice cream on the floor than in fatigue pockets, this was not about ice cream anyway. The waiter raised hell, said he knew the robbers were part of our work crew and he was going to turn us in. Our answer was, "go ahead, maybe they will fire us and send us home." We never heard anything about the incident.

Early in the morning on January 21st, 1945 there was lots of excitement aboard the S.S. John Erickson, there were rumors that there had been enemy subs in the area of our convoy last night, also we would be pulling into the harbor of Le Havre, France any time now.

The English Channel was living up to its reputation of being a rough, foggy and cold place. We were almost into the harbor before the City of Le Havre came into view. There was lots of cheering and applause coming from the men on the ship as the harbor appeared out of the mist. Even though I will be glad to shed this ship, I am thinking, "Out of the pan and into the fire."

The Le Havre Harbor was a mess. There were parts of sunken ships protruding everywhere. The ships could not get into the harbor, they were being off loaded onto smaller boats and landing craft, then ferried to land.

We were told to return to our quarters, get our gear together and prepare to disembark. I had Coy to check and bandage the boil on my neck one last time. It had now gotten to that throbbing stage. He took care of it and told me he thought by tomorrow it would be ready to lance. Then he told me he thought it was turning into a carbuncle. There seemed to be three heads forming. Just what I needed at this time!

I suppose the unloading of the ship was in reverse order to the loading. Our Battalion was among the first to disembark. If you have never unloaded from a rolling ship onto a pitching landing craft with all the gear that the Army had issued, you and a three headed monster riding on the back of your neck in freezing rain and snow flurries, you have not reached your pinnacle yet! I thought this was mine, but I found out in a short time that it was not. "There is always something!"

It took about fifteen minutes to reach the shore aboard the landing craft. There were about four to six inches of snow on the ground and bitter cold. After about an hour, Company "I" was finally assembled and accounted for. We were then told to move toward some cattle trucks that were being pointed out to us. We stumbled over to the trucks, carrying and dragging our gear, having a hard time through the snow. Especially after not yet having lost our sea legs.

The trucks we were told to board were called cattle trucks on the farm in Mississippi. They were semi's with stake bodies open at the top. I had never seen Army trucks like these before. I am sure they belonged to them. They were painted that beautiful olive drab. The loading of the trucks was a slow, torturous process, every name on the company roster had to be checked off. Finally my name was called, having ridden a cattle truck before I knew to get to the side so you would have something to hold on to. At last we began to move. I thought I was cold while the truck was standing still, it really got cold after it started moving. As we moved along, the throbbing on my neck stopped. Either the pain in my hands and feet had overridden the pain in my neck or the boil had frozen. As we rode along through the small towns, the children would run up near the trucks and yell for candy. Some of the men managed to throw out a few bars. If they had known what was in store for them, they would have held on to the candy.

It was getting late in the afternoon when we pulled into an open field with little snow covered mounds scattered around. In the distance we could see what appeared to be tents. We were ordered to unload. We all began to wonder why we were unloading so far from the tents. When we asked we were told that we were not unloading too far away. Then they pointed to the mounds of snow and told us our tents were there under the snow rolled up. They said we had to put them up and bring in the canvas cots that were under the other pile of snow, so that we would have a nice bed to sleep in tonight. Twenty cots to the tent. We were told that the tents were twelve man tents, but twenty men would make it more cozy.

After about an hour of mass confusion it was finally decided who was to do what. Then we were told to take a thirty minute break. They pointed out a tent about three hundred yards away that was of a different architecture than the others. They told us that was the latrine if anyone needed to use it. This surprised me, looking at all the little green holes in the snow I thought we were standing in the rest room. The latrine was new and well furnished. A fresh dug trench, nice big rolls of toilet paper, a neat pile of lime, a stack of fresh dug earth and a brand new shovel. Man did it make you feel proud to know they had all these good things waiting for us. They only forgot one small thing--food! We had not eaten since breakfast. We were informed that the kitchen could not be set up in time for the evening meal. That it would be morning before we had a hot meal. We were told they were trying to get, K-Rations issued to us for the evening meal. It did not happen for us. We heard that part of the battalion received them.

Where the tents were to be positioned had been staked off before our arrival by the Post Engineer. There were also men from that group to assist our men in the raising of the tents.

After all the details had been assigned, the company was formed up again, ordered to open ranks, place your gear in front of you, stack arms, and then the men that had not been assigned to a work detail were dismissed, and told to stay clear of the work area, but to be back in two hours ready to form up behind your gear and move into your new home. I was one of the lucky men to be selected to stand guard over the men's gear. I was having to walk continuously to keep circulation going in my feet. Not having eaten anything since breakfast my energy level was falling fast. With the cold feet and hunger pains, the throbbing boil at the back of my neck had almost become a non issue. Coy came by and checked the boil and put a new bandage on the boil. He said he thought it was ready and that first thing tomorrow morning, after breakfast he would work on it.

Darkness comes early in central Europe. In January by 1600 hours nighttime had arrived. There were a few lights in the area, and with the reflection from the snow, there was sufficient light for the tents to be erected.

The next three hours I spent standing in the snow. I tried to deflect some of my pain by trying to rationalize what was happening here. Was this part of the training program? Are things as really screwed up as they seem? This has to be part of some grand design, if not, I don't want to be around when shots are being fired to compound the confusion. At this late date I don't think I have any choice in the matter.

About 1900 hours, the off duty men began wandering back into the area, they were griping about being hungry. Some of them wanted to go to where their gear was and retrieve candy bars. We had orders not to let them. So we did not. We got all the cat calls and guff. For example, "what you going to do shoot us? You have not been given ammo yet." We gave the standard answer, "we are going to take names and kick asses."

Finally, at about 2100 hours, Capt. Batts showed up with the other company officers and First Sgt. Harrell. The officer, from the Post Engineers who was in charge of the tent raising, came over and reported to Capt. Batts that the living quarters were ready to be occupied. We were then told to fall in behind our equipment. After an orientation speech about Camp Lucky Strike, that the cause of our quarters not being ready was due to the unexpected influx of troops from the Battle of the Bulge, and that the influx was also causing the shortage of food due to the change having to be made in the shipping arrangements. There was to be only battalion mess for the next few days, starting at 0600 tomorrow. Meals would be served to the companys in alphabetical order, starting with A company at 0600 hours. Each company will be notified when their time comes to enter the line, also that we will be notified later at what time lunch and dinner will be served. Trying to go through the chow line with any other company besides his own, will be dealt with, severely.

Then came what we were all looking for. The sleeping quarters assignment times. Each platoon was assigned two tents. The platoon leaders took control of their respective platoons. S/Sgt. Cunningham led our platoon to the front of our two tents where he called the roll. After roll call the squad leaders took their squad inside for bed assignment. 1st Squad and half of 2nd Squad in the first tent, the rest of 2nd. Squad and the 3rd. Squad in the second tent. I being platoon runner and belonging to no squad was assigned the last cot, which was located at the right rear corner of the tent. Sgt. Hilton was in charge of the number one tent and Sgt. Cunningham the number two tent. Inside the tent the lighting was terrible. One could hardly see the cots lined up on each side of the tent. The source of light was a couple of small battery operated lanterns. We were told that we could use our flashlights if necessary, and tomorrow we will have electric lights. Down the center of the tent between the two rows of cots was an aisle approximately six feet wide that ran from the door to the tent to the back wall. By the Army's own destination the tent was "a squad tent." It was written right on the tag hanging from the wall. There were twenty cots, ten on each side, and there were six inches between each cot.

As each man was assigned a cot he was asked to stand at the foot of it with all his gear in front of him. While the men were raising tents and pulling guard, Sgt. Hilton and Sgt. Cunningham were at a meeting. They were learning the rules and regulations that we had to live by while we occupied this fine establishment. Sgt. Cunningham started out with the house rules first. Nothing was to be placed in the aisle. Tomorrow two wood heaters and a rifle rack would be placed in the aisle. The linen arrangement for the cot would be the same as it was on the ship coming over. After you got what you would need for the night you would place your duffel bag beneath your cot, and not to worry about it getting wet because of the snow. It will not get warm enough in here tonight for the snow to melt. We would have to sleep with our rifles. The rifle racks would not be in place until tomorrow. We might as well get use to it. We probably would be sleeping with it a lot, soon enough.

Sgt. Cunningham started telling us about the rules and regulations of Camp Lucky Strike. They covered everything, from what uniform to wear while running to the latrine at 0300 in the morning to the protocol for visiting Generals. Sgt. Cunningham noticing that some of the men were asleep, and the rest were suffering from attention deficit disorder, said "what the hell, get some rest. I'll explain it in the morning." With those words we crawled into our sacks, snuggled up to our rifles, and fell fast asleep.

For me it was more like a coma than sleep. It just didn't last long enough. After about three hours, I awoke with uncontrolled shaking with a chill caused by the fever from the boil, and the snow beneath my bed. After a couple of hours of this, I knew that I had to get help. I could feel myself slipping into delirium. At about 0700 someone came into the tent and informed Sgt. Cunningham that we were to be ready to enter the chow line at about 0800.

Man, I was never so glad to see daylight come in my entire life. I called out to Cunningham, he knowing of my condition, came over immediately. After I told him what was going on, he said that he would send medic Coy over right away. Coy arrived a few minutes later with a couple of other medics. He removed the bandage and asked me if I was able to walk. I told him yes so he told me to slip on my shoes and come outside to where there was more room and better lighting. Once outside the medics gathered around "oohing, aahing and probing." Coy said he thought it was ready. He took an instrument, some gauze, a towel from his bag, and told me to bend my head forward. He then placed the towel across my shoulders and reached up with the instrument and I barely felt the touch to the boil. I heard Coy say, "Damn!!! I believe everything in him is coming out". The relief was immediate. I felt and acted like a dog whose master had just returned home after being gone all day,

My appreciation knew no bounds.

After Coy thought the draining was sufficient, he informed me that he was going to sprinkle some sulfa powder on it, bandage it good, and give me a couple of pills. Coy instructed me to take after them at breakfast this morning and to take one after dinner this evening. He also said from now until tomorrow morning spend as much time in the sack as possible. I needed to drink lots of water and that he would check on me this evening. I could see the battalion chow line out in front, stretching out for about three hundred yards to my left and ending up at a rather large tent. There appeared to be about five hundred men in it. They were all stomping their feet in the snow and trying to keep them warm and each one had little puffs of steam coming from their nostrils. I am thinking, "no way" there is no way that I will be able to survive that line. I then went back into the tent. All the men were awake. There was a lot of griping going on about what was happening with the mess. Sgt. Cunningham was telling everyone that chow was optional that we could stay in bed if we wanted to. The griping continued. Some were saying they would rather starve than freeze. Others were saying that if we stayed here without heat we would starve and freeze. It ended up about half staying. Sgt. Cunningham and Stern came by to see how I was doing and if I needed anything. I asked Cunningham about the water. He told me he would have five gallons in the tent before noon and that the Post Engineers were to install lights and a heater today. Stern told me if I would take all my clothing out of my duffel bag, spread them over my cot, place the blankets over them, place the sleeping bag on top of the blankets, and then pull the ends of the blankets over the bag, that most of the cold was coming from beneath ~ the snow. He was right. I ate one of the two candy bars that I had found in my bag. I drank what water was in my canteen and slept all day, except for a couple of mad dashes to the latrine. Thus I started a phenomenon of Camp Lucky Strike that remains a mystery to me until this day. What caused every man to awake at least twice every night and having to immediately urinate. One learned to keep his raincoat and boots handy. The uniform of choice while running to the latrine were long handles, unbuckled boots, and a raincoat. At night in our tent there was always someone going to or coming from the latrine. On the outside they would join the steady stream of men with jingling boot buckles but later on when the snow began to melt the sloshing of ankle deep mud was added. That made for a weird sound as I lay in bed wondering what was going on back home with the "Mississippi Mud."

I awoke sometime in the afternoon to bright lights. I could see the new rifle rack and the Post Engineers had one heater almost up at the front of the tent. The men were asking how we were to heat this thing. The Engineers added, that was not their department and for the time being we were to get only one heater. There was not a noncom in the tent. When I asked where all the brains were I was told that Sgt. Cunningham was at a company meeting and all the other noncoms were conscripted to work K.P. This one I could not figure out unless they thought they could intimidate them with the threat of a bust from rank. Whereas there was nothing left for the lowly dog face to endure. Or just maybe they wanted them to be fed well. One thing I learned, is not to try and make logic out of what was coming down through the Army's chain of command. You just take it and accepted the consequences, good or bad. The Army called it discipline, but I often heard other definitions for it which in my weak moments I would catch myself nodding in agreement. Especially with the one referring to poultry.

Sgt. Cunningham came in telling everyone to get ready to fall in line for dinner since they were only serving two meals a day. Most of the men, having run out of candy, decided they had to "sweat the chow line."

There was a lot of griping about it being crowded enough without, "a damn cold heater sitting in the way." Cunningham asked me if I was going to try and make it to chow this evening. I told him that

Coy was coming by later to change the bandage on my neck, and that I was going to skip chow tonight. I had one candy bar left and I would try and make it to breakfast tomorrow morning.

I awoke on Jan. 23 feeling much better health-wise but the hunger pains had taken over. It had been forty-eight hours since I had eaten a meal. I was still wearing the same clothes that I was wearing when I left the ship. Except I had added a pair of socks trying to keep my feet warm. Some of the men were trying to shave with a little ice water which they had in their helmet and some shaving cream. I sure was glad to be a blonde kid with a small amount of stubble on my chin. Cunningham came into the tent telling us it was time for us to get in line for breakfast. He said that we were getting coal for our heater today. This brought on a cheer from the men. It had been a long time since we had anything to cheer about.

The chow line stretched for almost a half mile. The snow along the chow line had been trampled on so much that it had turned into solid ice. It was making it difficult to stand. Especially in a hunger weakened condition. I kept thinking how ironic it would be if the 65th Division's first casualty in Europe was from a broken leg caused from slipping in a chow line. After standing in the chow line for almost two hours, I was within twenty feet of the servers when I heard them yell out from the kitchen to send out more bread. The answer was that they had run out of bread and to give an extra spoon of eggs to the men instead. Going through the line I received two serving spoons of powdered eggs, one tablespoon of grape jelly, and a canteen cup of black coffee. You had three choices of where you wanted to eat, standing in the snow, squatting in the snow or taking the food back to your tent. I chose squatting in the snow. Mainly because it was near the three garbage cans that held the cleaning fluids for mess gear that we had become so familiar with while enjoying bivouac. I squatted down in the snow carefully placing my coffee and mess kit on it. I took my trusty spoon from my pocket, mixed my jelly and eggs together, gulped them down, started to lick the mess kit and thought I had better not. After remembering the lecture we had about warm damp skin and cold metal, I also figured Coy would not be happy if I came into the tent with a mess kit attached to my tongue. Especially after the ordeal with the boil. I reached down for my coffee. The heat from the cup had melted the snow beneath it, partially turning it over. Spilling all but a couple of swallows I drank what was left. I then threaded the handle of the mess kit through the canteen cup and spoon handles. I walked by the three garbage cans marked wash, disinfect and rinse. I was dipping my mess gear in each one. I noticed when I walked by the group of cans marked "garbage here", there was no garbage. As I staggered back to the tent I kept thinking my calorie count was on the debit side. Before leaving the tent, my stomach was telling me the same thing.

Back at the tent things were looking up. I was told that Cunningham had taken my friend, Howard Stern and some more of the men to get coal for the heater. Things were looking better. Funny how the conversation had changed in the tent. In just two days it had gone from women to food. The few candy bars that some of the men had left were selling for twenty dollars a bar which was over half of my monthly take home pay. (pardon the pun.) It was amazing to watch the men with candy struggle with their greed and hunger.

While listening to the men wrangle over candy, I came to the conclusion that my feet should take priority over my hunger. They had gone from being extremely cold and painful to having no feeling at all. I climbed upon my cot, removed my shoes and socks, and began vigorously rubbing my feet. Slowly the feeling and pain came back. There was no source of heat anywhere. I sat on the cot in the yoga position, pushed my feet up my pants leg, against my calves, and slowly they began to warm up. I found a clean, dry pair of socks and slipped them on. I crawled into my sleeping bag and fell asleep.

I was awakened a short time later by loud abusive language that was coming from the front of the tent. It was Cunningham and the coal brigade returning with their ware. I asked Stern what all the fuss was about, and he told me that when they arrived at the coal pile he thought they had made a mistake and had ended up at Fort Knox. You could not see the coal because of all the guards surrounding it. Sgt. Cunningham had to go by a table where an officer and two noncoms were seated. Give the name of his outfit, the number of the tent he was in charge of and what type of containers he had brought to transport the coal. Cunningham told him he had brought six men with two steel helmets each. He said the officer gave him a look of disdain and told him to send one man up. He added, that until further notice we were to receive only two helmets full a day. The recommendation was that we should use it in the evenings just before going to bed. After the speech by Stern I walked over to observe our prize. As I looked, I thought "Fort Knox hell." I believe they went by the horse barn. Being from Mississippi I had never seen coal pressed into little balls before. It was almost time to sweat the chow line again, (pardon the pun) so we decided to wait until after chow to start the fire in the heater. We knew then our feet would be extremely cold.

My second meal at Camp Lucky Strike consisted of one serving spoon of what they called goulash. It was placed on one side of my mess kit and on the other side they placed a gob of butter and one piece of bread. There was a large bulbous aluminum pitcher that a Sgt. poured into my canteen cup, what he had the gall to call, coffee.

After returning from chow, everyone was excited about starting a fire in our new heater. This turned out to be more difficult than we had anticipated. We had no kindling. Someone suggested lighter fluid, but smarter heads ruled that idea out, we were probably saving the tent and several casualties. We finally raked up enough paper and cardboard to start the coal burning.

After we got the fire going good, we poured the day's supply of coal on to it. We were determined to try and get warm for the first time in four days. We placed cots around the heater as best we could to try and accommodate all twenty men. It was quite a sight to see forty feet sticking out toward a two foot square heater. It felt good in spite of the smell. We sat around for about two hours belly aching and bemoaning our fate. We all knew that we were very lucky, that one month sooner and we could have been a few miles north of here at the "Battle of the Bulge" and suffered some real pain.

The fire had burned down. I noticed that the heat from the heater had turned about a three foot circle of ice around it into mud. It was going to take a lot of trips to the coal pile to melt all the snow in the tent. We all put our shoes on and made that last trip to the latrine before lights out. Before turning in, everyone made sure their boots and raincoat was placed where they would have quick access to it, because no one escaped that early morning "Lucky Strike Trot" to the latrine. That French water sure had something about it. Fifty years later when I noticed that famous french water appearing on retail shelves across the U.S.A. I wondered who the hell thought of this. I knew that whoever it was never had to take that "Lucky Strike Trot."

On the morning of the 24th, they had opened up more mess tents. The quality of food remained the same. The only difference, you spent less time in the chow line. After breakfast we were informed by Cunningham that we were having our company formation at 1000. Capt. Batts had a few things he wanted to talk to us about. The time came, everyone was present and accounted for except two men, who were being treated for frostbitten feet. The Capt. started out by apologizing to us for the problems we have encountered, but when on to explain that the problem was caused by the unexpected turn of events during the December German counter-attack. He said shifting men and ammunitions around was not a big problem, but changing the routing of food and personnel supplies was a logistics nightmare that may get worse before it gets better. That statement brought out a low moan from the men. Capt. Batts addressed the frozen feet situation. He said orders had come down from Division Headquarters, that the men were to pair off and each man would be responsible for helping keep his partner's feet warm. That the most effective way to do this was to place your partners feet beneath your arms at the arm pits, and to rub them to help the circulation. Everyone's eyes immediately looked down at the feet around them. I looked at Stern and he gave me a little nod. We both had rather small feet. I did not want to get stuck with someone who wore a size fourteen shoe. The process would probably work in reverse. I would end up with frostbitten arm pits. The Capt. promised that in a couple of days every tent would have two heaters, and if there were any trees growing in France our small amount of coal will soon have a wood supplement if the shortage of coal was not solved. Mysteriously, a couple of days later, wood started appearing in the early morning hours inside the doorway of "I" company tents. Since it was against Army regulations to cut wood for heat in France, I figured someone had made a deal with the French Underground. I believe that almost everyone with the 260th Infantry that was at Camp Lucky Strike at that time, understood my thinking on this.

The next few days were spent having early morning formations, standing in chow lines, receiving very little food, short sessions of calisthenics, short marches into the French countryside, trying to keep your piece from rusting and griping about the food and cold. During this period, the cold situation improved slightly, but the food problem remained the same. Sgt. Poage, an assistant squad leader from our tent who was on permanent K.P., decided to help alleviate the hunger in our tent by confiscating a gallon of peanut butter and a loaf of bread from the kitchen. Back at the kitchen someone had snitched on the snatcher. Just when we were enjoying our ill-gotten gains the higher-ups stepped into the tent and seized the evidence, removing three stripes from each of Poage's sleeves. The men did not protest from fear of choking on peanut butter. After the incident we wanted to nickname Poage "peanut" but he disagreed with us. He stood six feet four and weighed two hundred and twenty five pounds. We decided to agree that peanut did not fit him.

The first weekend at Camp Lucky Strike, I believe it fell on January 27th or 28th, some of the men in our tent were out exploring the camp when what they found along the east side of the camp was a highway that ran from Le Havre into eastern France. Next to the highway was a huge parking lot that was used by the Red Ball Express drivers to park their trucks. Next to the parking lot was a large area with several large tents. The men said that there was a wonderful aroma coming from this area. After further investigation they discovered a huge kitchen with a large serving area and two big dining tents. They found out this was what the Army called a "transient mess." They served meals to the Red Ball drivers and other military personnel traveling to and from the war front. Our men decided they fell into that "traveling to the front category," so they fell into the chow line, picked up their trays, silverware and china and received the largest, most tender, the best cooked steak they had ever eaten. They had all the trimmings plus cherry pie. (Their words). They noticed while eating, all the Red Ball drivers brought their mess gear in with them and when they left they would go back through the chow line, fill their mess kits and take some food with them. What a discovery!! The men could hardly wait to return to the tent to give us the good news. After a discussion among the men in our tent, we formulated a plan to take advantage of our new discovery. First each man was sworn to secrecy, so as to prevent the whole division from showing up at the transient mess and no one getting to eat. Then we decided that each evening while the company was in the dinner chow line, ten of the men from our tent would take mess gear, hide it beneath their clothes and head for the transient mess, eat and return under the cover of darkness with meals for the other ten men. This plan worked to perfection and we used it until the food problem was solved within our division. Amazing how soon the conversation returned to women after acquiring enough food. We never knew if any other members of the division discovered the "transient mess." If they did, the number was limited and they kept the secret as well. There was never a large scale attack on the "transient".

After a few days of sunshine and with the help of thousands of feet, the area within our compound was becoming a quagmire. Something had to be done. The small amount of training we were getting turned into work details.

The Post Engineers laid out the walkways, leading to the different facilities within the battalion area. There were three work details, one to shovel the mud from the laid out walkways, down to the hard surface, a detail to remove and haul away the mud and dirt, and there was another detail we called the helmet "brigade." This crew used their helmets to transport crushed rock from a rock pile that was being continually replenished. (France had more rocks than coal) The rocks were placed in the dug out walkways. The projects progression and appearance was stunning. In a couple of days and with about three hundred men, we had changed the area from moonscape to landscape. Everyone seemed proud of their contribution to the building of Camp Lucky Strike. It also was a great boost to the morale of the men not having to wade in mud everywhere they went. Especially in the wee hours of the morning when doing the "Lucky Strike Trot."

As the days wore on, the conditions at Lucky Strike improved. We had company mess and the quantity and quality of food had gotten so much better that we no longer had to supplement our diet with food from "transient mess." The tent had two heaters and the coal supply had increased to the point that the heat in the tent had melted most of the ice beneath the cots. Training increased, as the days wore on, with longer marches through France's small towns and countryside. There were hours of lecture, mostly on the dangers of slipping out of Lucky Strike at night, and being confronted by the dangerous French women.

During the last days at Lucky Strike I tried not to think much about where I was going, but where I had been and wonder about small things. Like wondering how and why they came up with the name of Lucky Strike for this place. My mind wandered back to the first days of the war. Before I was drafted. All the news and advertisement was about contributing to the war effort. I remembered the advertisement on the radio and in all the magazines, placed there by R.J. Reynolds Tobacco Co. They stated that "Lucky Strike Green had gone to War." They changed the color of the Lucky Strike cigarette pack from green to white. They replaced the foil the cigarettes were wrapped in with paper. Their statement was that the green paint and foil was their contribution to the War effort. As I looked out over the camp I understood about the foil, but did the green paint have anything to do with all the "Olive Drab" I was gazing at.

Finally on about the 23rd of February, the rumors were that our movement to the front was imminent. As we moved among the troops talking about the movement there was braggadocio on some lips. But most eyes showed a worrisome look. I also noticed that the ones that were raring to get started were not wearing cross rifles on their collars.

The word came down on February 25th to have our gear ready to move out at a moment's notice. After breakfast on February 27th, we had company formation. We were told that as soon as we finished lunch, which would be at about 1200 hours, everyone would fall out and stand in front of their tent with all of their equipment. At 1200 hours all of "I" Company was standing out along the walkways we had worked so hard to build. It was obvious that everyone was ready to get the Lucky Strike experience behind them. This time there was no "hurry and wait." The powers that be, were there with papers in hand. We were told to gather up all of our equipment and move to the truck loading area. This was the same place we had unloaded from, when we arrived here. As we arrived at the trucks, everyone was present and accounted for. We were then told that we were being trucked to a small town about thirty minutes away. There we were to be loaded on a train and be moved to the east. As the trucks pulled away from Lucky Strike, I felt that wave of nostalgia and that knot in my stomach that I had felt when I departed New York. I thought about that old adage pertaining to "things getting worse.

After about a thirty minute ride we arrived at a rail siding that was near a small town. On the siding tracks were about fifty Railway boxcars. We were told to unload from the trucks and move to the side of the road next to the boxcars. All the cars had their sliding doors open and you could see hay on the floors of each car. The trucks moved out. The Company was then formed up along the road next to the boxcars. We were instructed that these boxcars would be our transportation to eastern France, and that it would take about twenty hours. We were told that the boxcars were called "forty and eights." The name was derived from World War I, when they designated to transport forty men or eight mules. Looking at them, I figured these were used during that war. Once again the roll was called and we climbed into the boxcars. I was surprised at how small the boxcars were, once we were inside. Thank God they did not put forty men inside, only about half that. Our company was one of the last to load. I was in the fifth car from the end. The reason I remember this is, the coupling broke on our car sometime during the night and the last five cars came to a halt. While the rest of the train moved on. I was hoping that they would not miss us, but no such luck. They came backing down the track towards us after a few minutes had passed. The French crew that was operating the train seemed unsure as what to do. After a few minutes of discussion and finger pointing, one of the men went to the front of the train, returned with a tool box, went to the last boxcar to remove the hook-up from the rear of the car and replace the broken one on our car with it. After about an hour we were on our way again. About daylight the train came to a stop. We had pulled onto a siding near some town. We were told to have a short break to smoke and use France's rest room facilities which turned out to be the good earth. I was glad the French were not as restrictive with their sewerage systems as they were with their wood and coal. After the rest stop we loaded back on the train and road into a railyard inside the city. (I can't recall the name.) We were told that we would be there for about an hour. The train had to take on water and fuel. While there we could break out our K-rations and have breakfast, but not to wander away from the rail yard. While we were waiting a Hospital train pulled along side of us. The train consisted of Pullman type cars, all painted white with big red crosses on them. The train came to a stop by us. GI.'s started getting off the train. Some were in uniform, some in pajamas, and some in a combination of both. There were some of them on crutches with one pants leg pinned to their waist. Others were walking with one shirt sleeve pinned to their shoulder. The medics helped one off in a wheelchair that had part of his right leg and his right hand missing. The one thing they all had in common was their youth. If they had possessed all of their parts, they could have been mistaken for some high school football team.

We asked them where they were headed and they told us England. From England, the ones with the missing limbs and million dollar wounds were going home to the U.S.A. When we asked them what hospital they were coming from? They told us they had made them all! From the aid station to the field hospital, then into some French hospital that was being operated by both the French and the U.S. Army. The men wanted to know where we were headed? We told them we did not know. Our only information was "the front." They wanted to know what kind of outfit we were? We told them we were an Infantry Company. The soldier in the wheelchair said he was a rifleman and he was wounded the first of December in the Hurtgen Forest. He went on to say that the Siegfried line had not been breached yet, if where we were going was anything like the Hurtgen Forest, we were headed "straight into Hell." Just what I needed to hear, with that knot in my stomach growing larger with every mile. After about fifteen minutes of the wounded men telling us how it was up there they loaded onto their train and started to pull away. As they did, someone on the train opened a window and yelled at us "you'll be sorry," we knew it was coming. But this time, for me, it sounded different.

After about an hour we were told to board our boxcars and for the hundredth time we were warned about smoking in the boxcars and catching the hay on fire. After traveling most of the day on

February 28th, we arrived at what we were told was the Lorrain District of France, in a town called Kandage. There we loaded onto trucks and took to the outlying villages where we were billeted in private homes and other available shelter.

The next week was hectic. We were checking equipment, being told what we could and would be allowed to take into combat. The first thing to go back into the duffel bag was the overcoat. It would be left behind. Everyone cheered that decision. The G.I. overcoat was a great example of the inferiority of the winter clothing that the American fighting men had to wear when fighting in the winter cold of Europe. It weighed almost five pounds dry, and three times as much when wet, and in sleet and rain it was impossible for one man to carry. Only then it be used to cover a foxhole. The footwear was not any better. It's a tribute to the American foot soldier, that he survived the winter of 1944-45 with two good feet. The German soldiers winter clothing were far superior compared to ours. This became obvious when German prisoners were taken, they could stand for hours in the snow without any discomfort, while their American guards were continually stomping their feet, and had to be relieved every couple of hours to warm their feet.

One item of clothing was optional. The wool knit cap, worn under the helmet liner, it could be worn, but never without the helmet liner. The reason given for the restriction was that the Germans, when on patrols at night, always wore long coats and bib caps. The standing orders in some sections were to assume that any silhouette that appears with these identifying features were the enemy. I chose to keep my wool cap because cold air circulated freely beneath the helmet liner. After we packed everything that we were not going into combat with into our duffel bags, which was to be stored, we had left: one tent shelter half, one G.I. blanket, two pairs of socks, one set of underwear, a small shaving kit with razor, toothbrush and soap.

The blanket was folded once and on the folded blanket you placed all the forenamed items. You then rolled them up in the blanket, ending up with a blanket roll about three feet long. You placed the blanket roll onto the tent shelter, half folded the shelter, half over the blanket and rolled it into the shelter half, so as to keep the blanket and contents dry. After rolling you took one tent rope and tied each end of the rope around each end of the roll. Leaving enough slack so that it could be slung over your shoulders and carried bandolier style. Combat dress would consist of the following: underwear (shorts and tee shirt), long handles (top and bottom), wool shirt O.D (optional), fatigue pants and shirt, field jacket, gloves and muffler (optional), combat boots with two pairs of socks, digging tool, cartridge belt with first-aid pack, a canteen and cup, knit cap (optional), helmet liner and steel helmet. Everything must be G.I. We were told never to wear any civilian clothes or German military gear, to do so may present a problem, if captured.

About the third day at Kandage, the word came down that General Patton would be at Division Headquarters and would speak to the officers, noncoms and other available members of the 65th Division. On the day of the big speech our platoon leader Sgt. Hilton was preparing to go to the front (Saarlautern, Germany), for orientation, so he told our platoon sergeant to take a couple of men and go find out what the Man had to say. Sgt. Ellsworth L. Cunningham, our platoon sergeant, picked squad leader Sgt. Kendoll and me, the platoon runner to go and listen to "The Man." Being warned that General Patton was a stickler for wearing the correct uniform, we retrieved our O.D.'s from our duffel bags. We dressed up in Class A with neckties and helmet liners. We were off to see the General.

We were told to be at Battalion Headquarters at 10:00 to board trucks and go to Ennery, a small village where 65th Division headquarters was located. It was just a short distant from Kandage. When we arrived at Ennery everything was spit and polish. There were more MP's wearing white gloves and shiny helmets, than you could shake a stick at. They directed us swiftly to the parking area and pointed out an open area where a crowd was gathering. They informed us, that was where the talk from the General would take place. As we approached the crowd, which was smaller than I expected, we could see an imposing figure standing at one edge of the crowd and surrounded by a lot of brass. There was no mistaken General Patton with his shellacked helmet liner, shiny boots and a pair of pearl handle revolvers strapped to his hips. He looked exactly like all the pictures I had seen of him in the newspapers and news reels, except he appeared much taller in person. There was no waste of time, at the appointed hour, 1100th hour, General Stanley E. Reinhart, Commanding General of the 65th Division, introduced General Patton to the crowd. General Patton began by welcoming us to the war, which he described as the greatest movement of troops and supplies that the world has ever seen. His theme was about new combatants entering in the fight. He talked about not getting pinned down by small arms fire. That was what the Krauts wanted, so that they could throw the big stuff on your ass while you were stopped. He said you must keep moving at all times in a fire fight, always forward, and do not forget what the rifle was for that you carry. You fire it in battle, we have plenty of ammunition, you don't have to have a target to fire at. The sounds of battle have a psychological effect on the combatants. The old saying "wait until you see the whites of their eyes" is bullshit. Besides their eyes are not white, they are yellow. He said the biggest problem we have with new combatants in battle was to get them to fire their weapon. The General went on to say, that we have had men to participate in pitch battles close up with the enemy for hours, and after checking their rifles found that they had not fired a shot. The general then dove into the subject of taking prisoners. He said that there was a time when the taking of prisoners was an objective usually to obtain information, and there is a time during the lull of battle that prisoners might surrender without causing a problem. But always remember in the heat of battle and when operating short handed, that the taking of prisoners is not a priority.

The general told us he was not recommending lining prisoners up against a wall and shooting them. That would be murder. Good soldiers died before they reached the wall, and that he considered the Germans good soldiers. He talked a lot about the dress code of the Army, and that we should always adhere to it. That we are representatives of the greatest country in the world, and should always look the part. After a few superlatives about our commanding officers, the history of our training program and our fine appearance as we stood at rest listening to his orating, with the words of God bless, good luck and have a good war, ringing in our ears. We were dismissed.

The next couple of days were spent cleaning and checking equipment and placing everything in our duffel bags that we were not taking into battle, so that they could be stored. On the 6th of March we had company formation and we were told that this was the day that we had spent all those months and years training for. We believe we got it right. The good in all of this has been to work with, and to get to know such fine men. The journey has been great, but as we all know war is one of those few objectives in life where the journey is more enjoyable. You know, as Infantry, you are the eye of the storm. But never forget that you have a great support system that stretches out three thousand miles behind you. We were restricted to the area and told that we would have another company formation at 1700. We would be issued ammo and shortly after that, we would be moving by truck up to the front.

The next few hours was a time of reflection. I always felt that I would never reach this point. That somehow it would be over before I arrived. What was my hurry? Why did I not seek a deferment to finish high school? If I had taken a different approach would the outcome be any different? Or is life like some people believe, "What will be, will be?" It's too late to look back. The fact is, "I am here." Although I really don't want to be. All that is left now is your faith in God and that he will answer a Mother's prayer. If this happens I will be home!

That evening, the Mess Sergeant and his crew did a superb job in preparing a hot meal for us. We were told to eat all we wanted, that this would be the last hot meal for awhile. The thought ran through my mind, that this could be the last hot meal for some--period. How true this prophecy turned out to be. The Mess Sgt. told us that the mobile kitchen and supply trucks would never be far behind. That we would be getting hot meals from time to time, and that cold rations would always be available. He then told us when we finished eating to go by the supply truck and draw one days supply of K- rations, to take with us to the front. After drawing food rations we were then issued live ammo for our weapons and told that there would be other weapons and ammo available when we arrived at the front. We drew our ammo and we were told to return to our quarters, get all the gear that we were to take into battle, and fall into company formation wearing and carrying the gear as previously instructed. We are going to have one last inspection. The Company was called to attention, then to open ranks, and parade rest. Capt. Batts, our Company Commander, Sgt. Harrell, our First Sgt., and the platoon leader of each platoon, took an inspection tour of the entire Company. Each man came to attention as the Capt. stepped in front of him, without saying a word, Capt. Batts looked each man in the eyes, and with his right hand grasp each man by his left shoulder, and then moved on to the next man. After the inspection, Capt. Batts told us to take care of ourselves and our buddies. To always trust our junior officers and noncoms, and not to worry about the big picture. That our war will always be directly in front of us. Tomorrow this time you will be combatants. Tonight we will relieve men that are holding a position that was taken last October. In a few hours we will be arriving there. All the details have been worked out. You will be briefed upon your arrival by the party being relieved. The Captain then told us to take from the ammo we had drawn and load our respective weapons. From now until the end of the war our weapon will be part of us. It will go where you go. It has a replacement guarantee until the end of the war. Take care of it and it will take care of you. We will be leaving in a couple of hours by truck, so do not leave the area. He then dismissed us.

The trucks showed up at about 2200 hours, a cold misty rain had begun to fall. Everyone put on their raincoats and we loaded onto the trucks. After about an hour we began to move. We were traveling under blackout and the movement was painfully slow. There was a lot of stopping and starting. The darkness was almost total. One could barely see the blackout lights on the rear of the truck ahead. For the first few miles no one spoke, then a few whispers started up among the men. Even in the darkness you could feel the tension start to build up, especially with us cigarette smokers. After a while this voice came out of the dark, "anybody want a cigarette?" This helped break the ice and the men started conversing, which helped everyone to relax. We were not thinking about this being the first of many nights to come and that we would be living under blackout conditions. I often wondered why the Germans did most of their counterattacks just before daylight; after we smokers had not smoked all night. Didn't they know we were ready to kill anything. After thinking about it, maybe their counterattacks were led by smokers. Anyway, there was some hellish fights that started about dawn.

Shortly after midnight we began moving into some weird light, similar to moonlight. We were told by the truck driver that this was artificial moonlight being made by powerful searchlight beams reflecting off the clouds. He said it worked well with cloudy nights, like tonight, but on clear nights it was not as efficient. I don't know why we were not told to expect this by our superiors.

Suddenly, we came over a ridge and the land sloped downward into a broad valley. In the distance you could see scattered fires burning. As we drew closer to the fires we could see the outline of buildings. Further on we could see that we were entering the outskirts of a city. As we moved on into the downtown area we could not see one building that was not damaged or destroyed. There was a peculiar musty odor that I had not smelled before, but I was to smell that many times in the days ahead in most of the bombed out towns and cities through which I passed. My deduction was that the smell was coming from the centuries old buildings that were being ripped apart, and exposing elements that had been trapped all of those years. My wondering about the smell was cut short by the trucks coming to a halt. Up ahead we could see shadowy figures walking towards us. They were stopping for a second at each truck. When they arrived by us, one of the figures was our platoon leader, Sgt. Hilton. He had been here a couple of days for orientation on the positions and objectives that we would have. Sgt. Hilton told us to unload from the trucks and stand aside until after the trucks had gone. The platoons of "I" Company were then lined up along the road in numerical order. Then we were told that each platoon would be leaving at ten minute intervals. We were to proceed in columns of two, starting out with one column on each side of the road, and soon we would be narrowing down to one column because of conditions. We were to travel at intervals as far apart as our vision in the lighting conditions will allow, never losing sight of the man ahead of you, to do so may be fatal. The area is heavily mined, and if we came under artillery fire, hit the ground and stay as close to your position as possible. Use your trenching tool and don't panic, because there is no place to run to. If it happens, it probably won't last too long. The ten minutes were up and Sarge said "lets go."

We were accompanied by a noncom from the 26th Division. He said he knew the layout well, that he had been here about six weeks, and that it would take about forty minutes to reach our positions if everything went well. There were not too many sounds of war as we moved along, except for a few shell bursts far off to our right, and a little closer in to our front. The artificial moonlight was working real well against the cloudy overhead, helping the men to keep safe intervals. After about a thirty minute walk, we came to a halt. Looking ahead I could see that we had stopped at the foot of a rather large bridge. The word came down that this bridge crossed the Saar River. We would be waiting here for five minutes before crossing, to give the platoon ahead time to increase the distance between us. Shortly after we had crossed the bridge we were halted again. Sgt. Cunningham, our platoon guide, came back through the columns informing us to form one column to the right of the street. After about a couple of hundred yards further down the street, we turned right, single file, into a trail that led us between and through bombed out buildings, around shell holes and over broken concrete. After a few minutes we were stopped again. Sgt. Cunningham came back through the columns informing us that we were coming to a wide street. We were to cross one man at a time, and that there would be a man at the crossing to tell us when to cross. We found out later that this street was the famed "Burp Gun Alley." This crossing had caused many "Dog faces" to say a prayer before dashing across.

Each man ran across the street, entering a door on the opposite side. We were told that it would be impossible to get that many men across this street in the daytime. We moved through the buildings along "Burp Gun Alley" for about a half a block. We came to an opening in the floor with steps leading down into a cellar. Half the men of our platoon were directed into this cellar. A half block further down was a door beneath a stairway that led into another cellar. The remaining men of the platoon entered this cellar. The door at the bottom of the stairway was covered with a G.I blanket. The inside of the cellar was dimly lit with candles. Near the door there was a chair and small table, on the table was a candle and a map. Standing nearby was a Staff Sgt. and three other men from the 26th Infantry Division. The Sgt. looked over each of our men as they came through the door. We had a B.A.R man in our platoon, named Frank Blubaugh. He was a large man who stood about six foot four inches and always had a smile on his face. He was well liked by everyone. On our way here, when riding on the truck, Frank had complained about being cold. So he unrolled his bedroll and took out his O.D. shirt and put it on beneath his fatigue jacket. When he unfolded the shirt a tie fell out. He said when he would put the tie on it would help keep him warm. Frank walked through the door of the cellar. The Sgt. from the 26th who had about a two month growth of whiskers and hair, was covered with candle soot and dirt, and his hands looked as if he had been making mud pies, and they were shaking. This man's eyes showed the strain of his being in an almost constant battle since joining the 3rd Army in September. His battles through the Lorrain of France, then up to the Bulge with Patton, to help turn the tide there, then back down to the Saar Valley. In January he moved into a Bridgehead across the Saar Valley and has been under constant bombardment since.

The Sgt. looked at Frank, took a double take, and asked him where he thought he was going, "to a parade?" Frank answered that it was General Patton's orders to wear a tie with an O.D. shirt. The Sgt. replied that he would not have to worry about Patton seeing him up here. He said that he had been hanging around this cellar for two months and the highest ranking officer he had seen was a Second Louie. He said he had seen a captain once but he had to go back to company headquarters to find him. After this introduction, he told us to listen up, that he had information to pass on to us before he left. He said he wanted us to listen carefully, because what he had to tell us might mean the difference between living or dying for you, and your buddies. The Sgt. went on to say, "First of all I want to tell you where you are. You are in the city of Saarlautern, Germany."

Now I will tell you what your situation and objective is. First, when you crossed the bridge a few blocks back, you crossed the Saar River which runs north and south through the city of Saarlautern. This crossing took you into a small Bridgehead on the east side of the river. This Bridgehead was forged last November by the U.S. and French forces. It has been held ever since by various U.S. Forces. We of the 26th Division being the latest, have been here since January. The battle line in this area runs along the west bank of the Saar River except for the Bridgehead that the 260th Infantry, as of this moment, has just finished taking over from us of the 26th Division, you of "I" Company being the last to move into place. The Bridgehead that the 260th will occupy on the east side of the Saar is wedge shaped, with the base of the wedge running along the Saar River for about eight city blocks and extending into the city of Saarlautern for about the same distance, ending in a point of about two blocks wide. This point is now occupied by the third Battalion of the 260th Regiment of the 65th Division. On your right will be the 259th Regiment holding on the west bank of the Saar, due to a bend in the river your right flank will be partially protected by the 259th, except a couple of blocks at the point of the Bridgehead. On your left the 261st will be holding the west bank of Saar, leaving the left flank exposed. The enemy, roughly holds the territory on three sides of the 260th. This, being the beginning of the Siegfried Line, the Germans are well trenched. You will be able to observe some of their fortifications from vantage points throughout the Bridgehead.

The cellar that you are now in lies beneath a former three story building. It is now about a story and a half. This building faces east and sits on a street that we call Burp Gun Alley. This street in front of you is no man's land for about three blocks to your left. After that, it is held by the Germans. To your right, the street curves back toward the Saar River where it is protected by the 259th and 65th Recon. The buildings across the street from you are held by the Germans. They are approximately thirty feet away.

They come and go to these buildings by using trenches and tunnels leading from the bunkers that are part of the Siegfried fortification. Top-side here, between the cellar door and the door that leads into the street, there is a light machine gun, set behind sandbags, covering the building across the street. There are two doors in that building, about eight feet apart. Occasionally a Kraut would come out one door, fling a potato masher across the street toward our door, then run back into the building through the other door. They have seldom gotten one through our door, and never over the sandbags. This machine gun, positioned by the cellar door, is an outpost that is manned twenty-four hours a day by two men. These men guard the cellar plus report on any activity that goes on across the street. Also when daylight comes you will see a dead German soldier lying next to the building across the street. He has been there since the last of January, when he walked out into the street early one morning, firing his machine pistol in all directions. His life was cut short by a thirty caliber projectile. We figured he had gotten hold of some bad Schnapps. We never understood why they never retrieved his body since he fell so close to their door. So we took it for granted that they had booby trapped his body to get some enterprising Grunt, that would try to retrieve the machine pistol that was still slung around his neck.

The Sgt. abruptly stopped his banter. He laid his pointer on the table, which he had been using to point out places on an area map. Which we could not see in the dim candlelight, and could hardly make out the outline of the map. The Sgt. checked his watch, got serious and said, "look we have to be out of here by 0300 hours, and I still have to get my men in front our outpost. It will take a full squad of your platoon to man the outpost that will be assigned to you. Pick a squad and let them follow my sarge here. He will lead them into position, brief them on what their responsibilities are when they arrive, and he will then bring my men back to here. The relief for this outpost will be worked out by your platoon leader. While I am waiting on my men to return, I will finish my briefing.

Out front in the middle of burp-gun alley you will see a G.I. steel helmet. I know you will be wondering why it is there. About a month ago a patrol was sent out by a Division from across the river into enemy territory to try and capture prisoners to be interrogated. The patrol never returned or was ever heard from. Except one man came running across the street towards us in the middle of the night and was killed by friendly fire. You can't be too careful around here at night. Out back of the building is a railcar with a few railcars scattered around. Underneath one of them was a couple of dead enemy soldiers. They were there when we arrived here. I know you feel like you are in a precarious situation, and you are, but actually you have a few things going for you. You know exactly where the enemy is. When the shelling is going on, the enemy is so close that you do not get any of the big stuff, for fear of causing casualties among their own troops. You are mostly hit with mortar fire and an occasional "88." You will be hearing those terrible sounding "screaming mimis," but their sound is worse than their bite and most of them will be going across the river. Also when we go on the attack to breech the Siegfried line, you will already be across the Saar, and as you have been trained to know and will find out soon for yourselves, that crossing a river into enemy territory is never any fun. Your greatest danger is from a counterattack, which we think will not happen because we occupy an unfortified position next to the Siegfried line. They know if they drive us out and occupy our position, all hell will rain down on them with our big guns across the river. But take nothing for granted. You never know what they are willing to do or sacrifice. So always be ready.

The Germans usually counterattacked around daybreak. They know that we know this, so they play this little game with us. They start their artillery barrage about an hour before daybreak. They know we are wondering if this is the day. They have done this every morning since we have been here. So we go on alert two hours before daybreak every morning with every man. We suggest you do the same. You might as well be on alert because you are not going to be able to sleep with all the noise going on. Your greatest danger along this line, will come from mortar fire, snipers and an occasional short round from outgoing mail.

The mortar's are the worst. Any movement observed by them will bring down those, almost silent, killers. The snipers, they usually move into position during the night and stay hidden until a target presents itself. Sometimes, depending on their location, they will stay hidden all day until dusk, pick their target, then escape under the cover of darkness, A place that is safe today, may not be safe tomorrow. I see my men are ready to go. One last thing, this little piece of real estate was paid for with blood. Hold on to it. The 26th is still going to be in the third Army, so we will be hearing about you, good luck. After the Sgt. left, there was total silence. I looked up and no one was moving. Everyone seemed to be looking down at the floor. The only thing moving was the shadows of the men dancing on the walls in rhythm with the flickering candles. The knot in my stomach doubled in size. Finally Sgt. Hilton told us we could unroll our blanket, roll over and try and get some sleep. We would all have to be up in a couple of hours and that the alert started at 0500 hours. He said don't scatter your gear and keep your rifle and ammo. handy. Remember if you snore loud enough for the guard at the door to hear you, he has orders to come in and wake you.

I unrolled my bedroll, rolled up in the blanket using spare clothes for a pillow and tried to sleep. Some of the men slept pretty well but I don't sleep to well on concrete in stressful situations. The first night on the front is about as stressful as it gets. After a few fitful doze offs, the guard on the cellar door came in and told Sgt. Hilton it was time to go on alert. I suppose no one was sleeping, because all heads popped up at once.

Everyone put on their cartridge belts and helmets, rolled up their bedrolls, picked up their rifles and sat down against the walls. We did not have to wait long. At 0530 the big stuff opened up going across the river. Our boys across the river answered back with heavy stuff going over us into enemy placements along the Seigfried line. Then the mortar shells started falling around us. Coming from our left, a steady stream of machine fire passed by our building, and from our right flank our boys from anti- tank would send rounds of 57's up toward the burp guns emplacement. Burp-Gun Alley was a two-way street. You could hear the screaming-mimis when they left their emplacements. They got louder as they came towards you, screaming overhead to land along the river to our rear. After about ten minutes everything stopped, except for an occasional burst of machine gun fire coming down Burp-Gun Alley.

After the shelling, Sgt. Hilton checked for communication break downs. All telephone lines were intact. We found out that this was a rare thing that over half the times after a bombardment the telephone lines would be severed. Keeping telephone lines open was a never ending job. I hated this because of my job as platoon runner. To this day I believe my job was easier than spending those long hours on an outpost. But I never saw any foot soldiers job that would be classified as easy. After checking with Company H.Qs, Sgt. Hilton told us we were to remain on alert for a couple of hours. Then the off duty men could try to get some sleep. In the meantime he and Sgt. Cunningham would work out a schedule for reliefs on our outpost. There was not much sleep going on. Everyone was anxiously awaiting daylight to go topside to see what we had gotten ourselves into. As we waited, the shelling became sporadic. Most of it arcing overhead, with an occasional mortar round landing in our vicinity.

Shortly after 0800 Bobby Spicer, who was one of our men on the outpost above us, stuck his head through the door and told us it was daylight and did anyone want to see our new home? Everyone stood up. There was about a squad of men left in the cellar. Sgt. Hilton told us that about half to go up at a time, look around and do not move around too much, then return in ten minutes and let the others take a look. Being near the door, I was first out. When I reached the head of the stairs I took a few steps, looked around and was shocked. The total devastation in every direction. The Sgt. from the 26th had drawn a good picture of our surroundings, but there was no way to describe the destruction. You had to see this in order to grasp it. Everywhere you looked, told the story of what had taken place here in the last four months. Most of the buildings had only partial walls left standing.

The buildings along Burp Gun Alley appeared to be in better condition than the surrounding buildings, giving credence to the Sgt.'s briefing about the closer the combatants, the less heavy shelling you receive. The holes blasted through walls, leading from one building to the next along burp-gun alley, spoke to the fierceness of the fighting it took to clear this side of the street. The rail yard out back was filled with shell holes of all sizes. The large ones were filled with water, giving some indication that not any large shells have fallen here since the securing of the Bridgehead. There were hundreds of small pot holes telling you that dropping mortar shells was a popular sport around this part of town. Looking left, northward up burp-gun alley, at about a distance of 200 yds. where the street entered German held territory, the street was covered with little wooden boxes, called Shu Mines. We were told that they contained about a quarter pound of T.N.T. that exploded when stepped on, causing all kinds of problems for the one doing the stepping. This I can attest to through later observation. Starting from where the street was mined, you could see where the Germans had dug trenches across the street so that they could move from the bunkers on the east side of Burp-Gun Alley into the area they occupied on our left flank. This was the area from where our Battalion received most of its harassment. Mostly from mortar fire and snipers. We also found out later that the machine gun emplacement, that the street was named after was on this, the west side of the street.

Across the street from us the dead German Soldier lay on his stomach with his head almost in a door way. There were two doors, about eight feet apart, in the building across the street from our cellar door. From these doors, on rare occasions, an enemy soldier could pop out quickly and try to toss a potato masher grenade into the door of our building before we could react. He seldom was successful in getting the grenade through the door. If he did, it rolled harmlessly up against the sand bags inside our door. Looking through the large hole that was blown in the back of our building, you could see the bodies of the two dead German soldiers beneath the railway cars that the Sgt. from the 26th had told us about.

We returned to the cellar, so that the rest of the men could look around. Sgt. Cunningham and Hilton had the schedule made for the relief of the outpost that our platoon was responsible for. The schedule worked out so that there was always a squad of men resting in the third platoons two cellars. Stern and I were assigned the outpost by our cellar door. We were to be relieved by Squad leaders and assistant squad leaders, when available. This was not bad duty because there was always someone hanging around the cellar door who couldn't sleep and was willing to pass off time in a friendly card game, or a bitching session.

Our first day at the front was rather quiet, with an occasional short mortar barrage in our area. Late in the afternoon we were jerked into reality when word came down that "I" Company had suffered its first casualty, Pvt. Nelson, from second platoon had just been killed by an enemy sniper while he was going to the Company Command post to pick up supplies. In order for the men from the third battalion to pick up supplies they had to cross Burp-gun Alley about two blocks to the right of our position. After Burp-gun Alley passes our position it makes a gradual turn to our right rear, leaving only half of the east side of the street in the Burp-gun operators field of fire. When crossing, one had to exit and enter the street through doorways, this allowed only one man to cross at a time. The first man was always relatively safe, if there was more than one they always got a burst. Crossing from the east side was more dangerous because the doorway on that side was in the gunners field of view. To lessen the danger, we would cross in the evening twilight to obtain supplies and return under the cover of darkness, except in emergencies. Our ordinance usually came to us at night by Special Forces and were placed in designated places that we had easy access to. Designated ordinance for special operations was brought in as close to the beginning of the mission as possible and removed as soon as possible. If not used or if there was an excess, this was done because of the extra danger they posed and to cut down on waste. I cannot say enough good things about the Special Troops of the 65th. Division. They did an extraordinary job under some of the most trying conditions imaginable.

The nights in the Saarlautern Bridgehead were the worst. They were long in this area of Europe. In March darkness comes around 1500 and lasts until about 0900. The artificial moon was a big help on cloudy nights, but its effect was limited on clear nights. Stern and I usually manned the outpost by the cellar door from around midnight until about 0530, when the full alert was given. This period was relatively quiet. Communication between us was limited to whispering in each other's ears. The biggest problem we had at this time of night was with the feral cats. Except for us and the Germans, they were the only living things in town. They would come out at night looking for food. I think their main diet came from licking out the C ann K ration cans that the GI's had discarded. In the middle of the night, when your senses are primed, there is nothing that will raise your hackles like the movement of a tin can. There is nothing as fast as a cat that recognizes the sound of an armed fragmentation grenade coming his way. We never had one cat casualty inside the Bridgehead that I was aware of. The few men that were brought by our outpost, suffering from shell-shock were never heard to say anything about shells, but I did hear some murmuring about cats.

The days that followed became almost routine. Everyone awake at 0530 and hunkering down when the shelling started a few minutes later. Stern and I were working our outpost from the cellar steps with only our eyes above floor level. While in this position it dawned on me that this must be the way that the Kilroy art began. After the shelling stopped and it was ascertained that there was no counter-attack under way, almost everyone came topside breaking out the sterno cans trying to get the water in their canteen cups warm enough to dissolve the coffee powder that came in small sealed packs in C and K rations. Of all the dozens of items that I carried in my fatigue pockets, the two most treasured were the packs of coffee and that tiny can opener developed for the military. This to me was the greatest invention of the war. That beat the hell out opening cans with a bayonet. This little opener quickly became extinct, after the arrival of the pull-tab can. It died a hero.

On March 12, you could tell that things were about to change. Special Forces started bringing up ordinance in greater quantities. Items like pole charges, satchel charges, bangalore torpedoes, concussion-grenades and primer cord.

Around 1600 Stern and I were awakened to relieve the outpost. Topside there was a small room next to the outpost where we kept our meal rations, water and Medic Coy kept his extra medical supplies. Stern and I checked out the supply room to find out what was on the dinner menu. K-rations again, cheese, crackers, that crumbly chocolate bar, the one that when you gave it to the French kids they threw it back at you. The K-ration also contained that great pack of lemonade powder with the instructions on the side instructing you to "just add water". This great tropical drink was just what a man needed here in the Saar Basin with the spring thaw coming on. While checking out our dinner, we noticed that while we were asleep, someone had left us some goodies. There behind the 10 in 1 rations boxes, lay a pole-charge, a satchel-charge, a bangalore torpedo and some primer cord. Just what we needed. Explosives stored nearby waiting for an 88 shell to come in on top of it. When we asked Sgt. Hilton about the ordinance, he told us that the 260th was sending probes into enemy territory after midnight to try and make contact with the Germans. That the entire 3rd. Army was expected to make an assault any day to try and breech the Seigfried Line. The probes by 260th would start at midnight. They would be conducted by the 1st and 2nd Battalions. We of the 3rd Battalion would hold our positions.

Shortly after 2400 the 65th Division Artillery from across the Saar River, opened up with a barrage that was landing about five hundred yards to our front. Meanwhile the probes moved across Burp-gun Alley into enemy territory. We of the 3rd Battalion took up covering positions on the west side of Burp-gun Alley, but the probes drew no fire as they crossed the street. After about fifteen minutes the shelling came to a halt. The Germans did not answer with their artillery. It became very quiet in our area. Around 0300 we saw flares light up the sky about four hundred yards to our front. Then there came the sounds of small arms and mortar fire. The probes had met the enemy. Shortly after 0300 word came down that the three divisions on the 65th's left flank: the 94th, 80th, and the 26th on March 13th. 1945 at 0300, had started an offensive to breech the Seigfried line.

At 0500 on March 13th, the 1st and 2nd Battalions of the 260th attacked out of the Bridgehead with limited objectives. The main purpose of these attacks was to try and prevent the Germans from moving men and materials to the north, in opposition to the 94th, 80th and 26th's offensive. Meanwhile on the 65th's right flank, the 70th Division of the 7th Army was preparing to cross the Saar. Their objective was to capture the city of Saarbrucken.

The frontal attack out of the Bridgehead by the 260th managed to advance a few hundred yards, but was driven back by strong enemy resistance. The enemy on our left flank never wavered. They were operating from bunkers within the Seigfried Line by means of trenches, tunnels and by extensive mine fields. The rumor was that the decision had been made to wait for the main assault on the Seigfried and try to out-flank and cut off this position because of the potential of our suffering heavy casualties if an all-out attack was attempted. This later proved to be a wise decision.

After March 13th, business picked up in the Bridgehead. The shelling by the Germans into the area became heavier and more frequent. It was no longer mostly mortar. There were a lot of 88's coming in since the enemy had pulled back, and the shelling no longer posed a threat to their own troops. There were sounds of motorized vehicles being moved around inside the German sector. The clanking sounds coming from the track vehicles were especially ominous and seemed to double the size of that knot in my stomach. The rumors were flying. Some were saying the Germans were preparing to counter-attack. Some said they were moving out, and others said the sounds were coming from the self-propelled 88's being moved into position.

The next four days were marked with intensive shelling from both sides. The 260th making regular attacks into the enemy lines with limited objectives, always meeting strong enemy resistance and then falling back into the Bridgehead. The enemy seemed to think the main assault from the 65th would come from the Bridgehead. Meanwhile the three divisions, on the 65's left were having great success with their attacks on the Seigfried line. It was reported that they had achieved all their objectives. We of the 260th felt that we had achieved our objective of preventing the enemy from moving men and materials to the point of the original attack of the Seigfried line by the third Army.

As the shelling increased inside the Bridgehead, so did the casualties. The 88's were particularly devastating when slamming into the partial standing brick walls. Brick and parts of brick would fly in all directions, sometimes for hundreds of yards. Believe me, nothing gets your attention like part of a brick bouncing off one's steel helmet. Most of the casualties were caused by flying debris. For example, one rare warm afternoon the sun was unusually warm. The only sounds of war was the steady stream of American bombers flying overhead going deep inside of Germany to unload. Sgt. Rakosi, Stern and I found an out of the way wall, that the sun was shining against. It was a really warm spot. We decided to sit next to the wall and remove our shoes and socks and let the sunshine warm our feet, especially since it had been many days that they had seen daylight. We were sitting there half asleep, when a mortar round dropped in about one hundred and fifty yards to our front, throwing a few pieces of small fragments our way. After a few seconds had passed I heard Rakosi say "look a here!" He was pointing toward his big toe from where a slight trickle of blood was coming, "I do believe I got myself a purple heart, let us find Dr. Coy and get this terrible wound dressed and verified." I can't remember whether he received a purple heart or not.

On March 15th, Sgt. Cunningham informed me that he and I were moving the ordinance that was still in our store room to a room on the other side of the cellar door. It was more accessible than our store room. While moving it, we decided we would move a couple of boxes of 10 in 1 rations over to the same room, to have for breakfast the next morning. Sgt. Cunningham informed me that around 0300 tomorrow morning, a combat patrol was being sent out by the 260 Reg. and they were going to pickup the ordinance, then cross Burp-gun alley from our position into the enemy's territory. Cunningham said that Stern and I would be on duty at the cellar door at that time and that he would be on the telephone in the cellar. The guard at the regular Burp-gun alley was to call him when the patrol crossed the alley and he would come up from the cellar and inform Stern and me that they were on their way and to help clear out the ordinance. Shortly after 2200 Stern and I were awakened after a short nap and told it was time to relieve the men on the cellar door outpost. I took up position behind the machine gun and Stern sat on the top step to the cellar, it was unusually quite. I was getting sleepy, so I moved a short distance to where Stern was. I sat on the floor with my lower legs and feet dangling into the cellar door below Stern. I figured a whispered conversation would help to break my sleepy cycle. It did not work. I remained sleepy and my dangling feet, with the circulation cut off were sound asleep. I decided if I stood it would help, so I moved onto the cellar steps below Stern and took up my old "Kilroy" position. Standing helped but sometimes a man can doze on his feet. At about 0200 I was jerked out of my trance by the unmistakable sound of a tin can being rolled around. The sound was coming from the room where Sgt. Cunningham and I had placed the ordinance. I heard Stern moving around, then I heard that sound that a fragmentation grenade makes when it arms itself. Stern had pitched a grenade into the room where Cunningham and I had placed the ordinance. This room Stern and I had thrown many grenades into, to chase cats away. I can not tell you how many things went through my mind the few seconds it took for the grenade to go off. I will tell you the first thoughts, but the next ones are private. It had a lot to do with that telegram being sent home to Mama. My first thought, I did not tell Stern we had moved the explosives, the grenade was going to land in the middle of the ordinance causing an explosion that would bring the entire building down trapping everyone in the cellar and how would the patrol carry out their mission without the ordinance. The knot in my stomach, moved up into my throat. The grenade went off. Nothing happened. I could not believe it. I spoke to God first. Then I told Stern what we had done and not to throw any more grenades. Since the grenade incident had thoroughly rendered me sleepless, probably for a couple of days, I moved back behind the machine gun and tried to collect my thoughts. It was quiet inside and around the Bridgehead but the distant rumbling and flashing of light tell you that the war is still going on.

Those Maxims, "calm before the storm" and "too quiet" kept going through my mind. Shortly after 0300 Sgt. Cunningham come up the cellar stairs and told stern and me that the patrol had just crossed Burp-Gun Alley and would be here shortly. Meanwhile, we would retrieve the ordinance and have it ready when they arrived.

I told Sgt. Cunningham about the grenade we had tossed into the room, I got a sharp, "what!!" reaction from him, but could not see the reaction on his face, that I knew was there. The artificial moonlight was not too bright inside the room. When the patrol arrived we had the ordinance out of the room and waiting for them to pick up. When the men arrived I recognized them as being our 3rd Battalion Patrol, a group of hand picked men from the 3rd Battalion 260th Reg. that were used on special assignments. Rumors of their exploits had already began to surface in the short time we had been in Saarlautern. After observing their actions later I believe all the rumors to be true. This group was led by a 1st. Lt. whose name I cannot recall. We reminded the Lt. of the dead German in the doorway across the street and we thought he might be Booby-trapped. He replied that they had already been briefed about it. Then he led his eighteen men, three at a time across the short no-mans land into the buildings held by the enemy. Around 0500 the outgoing mail started up from across the river, landing about one-half mile to our front, probably to soften up the Germans for the probes we were sending out. It did not soften up the German artillery, they answered back with a vengeance. Since the enemy seemed to have pulled out from across the street the heavy stuff was coming into the Bridgehead hot and heavy. After about fifteen minutes the outgoing mail stopped but the German shelling went on for another fifteen minutes. When all the shelling stopped we could hear the small arms fire coming from our front. We theorized that our probes had made contact with the enemy. After daylight Sgt. Cunningham and one of the squad leaders came up the cellar stairs and told Stern and I that most of the phone lines had been knocked out and they were on their way to check if everything was alright on our outpost and that they were going by the second platoons cellar to see if they still had communications. He also told us that Sgt. Hilton was asleep and to try not to awaken him. We knew how crazy he becomes when the phones go out. Things were quiet so Stern and I broke out the sterno to heat water for coffee. While the water heated we went into the room to check the 10 and 1 rations to see if we could find something for breakfast, then we spotted it, the casualty from Stern's grenade. It had ripped a large hole in the side of one of the ration boxes. We checked the wound and found it not serious. The damage was confined to the crackers and to a couple of those weird chocolate bars. After that incident my respect for 10 and 1 rations increased immensely, it was possible that they had saved some lives, by absorbing the grenade blast. Stern and I finished our coffee and had breakfast which consisted of crackers and something from a can that was a distant cousin to Spam.

Sgt. Cunningham showed up shortly after breakfast with a couple of men from the second platoon. He told Stern and me that men were working to restore telephone service and that everything was okay at our outpost except they were running low on supplies. He told Stern and me that he was relieving us, but before we took a nap he wanted us to go with the two men from second platoon to Company Headquarters to pick up some supplies for the men on the outpost. He wanted us to bring back cigarettes, matches, a box of 10 and 1's, and a can of water. I did not relish the idea of crossing Burp-Gun Alley in the daytime, but it was much better than being on one of those patrols out in no-man's land probing out enemy positions. On the way to the alley crossing, the four of us discussed our strategy for crossing Burp-Gun Alley.

First was in what order? We all knew that going was much more dangerous than the return when crossing due to the bend in the street. Stern argued that since he was a slow Jewish kid from Brooklyn he should go first. I knew better than that for I had played basketball with him but I went along with him anyway because he was my friend. So we agreed that he would go first. No sooner had we agreed to let Stern go first, he double-crossed me, saying that since I was platoon runner that I must be faster and that I should go last. When I accused him of wanting my job he told me he knew I was fast and besides with my skinny ass I would be impossible to hit. It would be like trying to hit a bean pole. I told him not to try and make up that I still thought he wanted my job. We reached the alley. Stern ran across, no problem, made it through the door looked back, waved, then moved on to get away from the ricochets that were bound to come. The two men from the second platoon flipped a coin, number two man took off, nothing happened. We figured maybe he is not there or asleep. The third man takes off. He and the bullets reached the door across the street at about the same time but he was not hit.

My time! I waited until the gunner stopped playing, "Yankee Doodle" on the door facing across the street. Then I prepared to make my break. In my mind's eye I could see the Gunner looking down the gun barrel at the door waiting for me to come into sight. It was going to be a race between the bullets and me. Shouldn't I wait? Maybe he will give up. I saw stern walking back toward me, I motioned for him to go on that I was coming. I backed up a couple of steps to get a good start. I won that race! I was well inside the door before the first round struck. Boy did I feel good. Stern was right, I am a speedy devil! While we were at headquarters Battalion Patrol returned from their mission. Battalion Patrol was to draw enemy fire and try to pin-point the enemy's location and strong points, because the attack on the Seigfried Line was close at hand. We picked up our supplies and headed back. I was carrying a case of ten and one rations on my right shoulder and a case of matches under my left arm. Stern had a can of water and a case of cigarettes. The two men from second carried the same.

On the way back we met the Communications Sgt. with a couple of men. He informed us that they had repaired the telephone lines and that we had communications again. Crossing Burp-Gun-Alley on the return trip did not concern us too much, if you ran! One could be out of the shooters field of vision before he could react. It was agreed that I could be first to cross on the return trip. We came up to the door of the building, which opened into the alley. I got my load balanced and sprinted out into the street. I had only taken a couple of steps when something wrapped around my shoulder and beneath my right arm pit then jerked me backwards. While this was going on the machine gun opened up. That cracking sound was pretty close. I dropped the case of matches, I grabbed the case of rations with both hands and took off dragging whatever it was wrapped around me. I looked back across the alley, Stern and the two men were starring at me with open mouths. Stern asked me what had happened. By that time, I had discovered a piece of telephone line wrapped around my shoulder. I told them to watch out for the loose telephone wires as they came across. They made it across without any problems. Our summation of the situation was that the telephone repair crew had left some of the old wires hanging too low over the door. Whenever the lines were cut the repair crew usually found it was easier to run new lines. That left lots of wire pieces laying around. Stern asked me if I was going to retrieve the matches. I told him that maybe after dark, but until then, they would have to chew their tobacco if they did not have a match. When we returned Sgt. Cunningham was waiting for us. We told him what had happened and he said that it was okay. We had more to worry about than a box of matches. He thought that something big was about to happen.

The platoon leaders had to be at Company Headquarters at 1500 for an important briefing. The rumor was that we would go on the attack soon. I asked him if he thought Sgt. Hilton would be able to leave the cellar since he had not been acclimatized to the outside climate here. Cunningham replied that if Sgt. Hilton could not make it, that he, being next in command would have to go. Sgt. Cunningham told Stern and me to get some sleep that we would probably have to start our guard shift early this evening, that he was short-handed. He said that two men had become ill with flu-like symptoms and one man who was in one of our outpost cellars had pulled the safety pin from a hand-grenade and had tried to replace it. He was shaking so bad that he could not and started screaming. The three men in the cellar with him, saw what was happening and took off out of the cellar. Sgt. Hasemeir, one of our platoon squad leaders was nearby, heard the commotion and came over. The three told him what happened. Hasemeir went into the cellar where the man was still hollaring, pried the grenade from his hand, replaced the pin brought from the cellar, and sent him to the aid station. He returned to the Platoon at Regensburg.

Stern and I were awakened by Sgt. Cunningham around 1800. We were told to round up a bite to eat then relieve the men on the outpost by the cellar door. He said that we probably would be there all night. He told us that he and Sgt. Hilton had attended the briefing and that we would be going on the attack within two days, depending on the progress of the 26th Division on our left which was south east, and the 70th division on our right that was attacking to the north east. The 65th Division was to attack through the middle of the wedge formed by these two divisions. The time of our attack should come sometime on the 18th, depending on the 26th and 70th meeting there objectives, which they had done so far.

Shortly after 1900, Stern and I took up our usual guard position near the cellar door. Things were rather quiet, with the exception of an occasional machine gun burst down Burp-Gun Alley. I guess the gunner wanted us to know that he was still there. Shortly after 1000 our artillery opened up from our rear across the Saar. It was a massive shelling covering the entire area in front of the 65th

Division. The Germans were still there and they answered back shelling the Bridgehead and also there was some heavy stuff going across the river toward our artillery positions.

The shelling from each side would last about ten or fifteen minutes. Then there would be a lull of some thirty minutes to an hour. During the lull the men in the cellar who was trying to get some sleep, would come upstairs to where Stern and I were pulling guard to see and ask what was going on. They cursed the Germans for awhile then they would curse everyone who had anything to do with them being in this God-forbidden place. Everyone had an opinion on what was going on. Some saying we were softening them up to attack, others saying they were softening us up to counter-attack. There were those that said they were using up their shells so that they would not have to carry a big load when they started their retreat. Then there were the ones who said that they were just trying to keep us from getting any sleep. The shelling would start up again. The men would quickly go back into the cellar, leaving me to my prayers and Stern to whatever the Jewish do. Those long hours of guard duty that Stern and I pulled together were filled with every subject we could think of to talk about to help us keep awake. One night the conversation turned to the discussion of religion. I told Stern since I was a protestant and praying hard to survive and if he would stay close, my prayers would help him also. Because I am praying that those shells do not come too close. Stern said he thought the same went for his prayers. I asked him if he thought we were double dipping, taking advantage of our two different religions. This became a standing joke between us as long as we were together every time one of us wandered away the other would remind him not to go too far.

On the 16th, starting around 2400, the shelling from the Germans into the Bridgehead was persistent. It was as if they were at the briefing the evening before and knew what our plans were. Stern and I spent most of our time on the cellar steps, to avoid the debris and shrapnel being thrown around.

Shortly after 0200 on the 17th, Sgt. Cunningham came to the door of the cellar and told Stern and me that he had just gotten word that our six man outpost had just received a direct hit from what appeared to be an 88 shell, that it looked pretty bad. That the wounded were being taken to 2nd platoon's cellar and as soon as there was a lull in the shelling that he and Medic Coy would check out the situation and that Lt. Collins, the second platoon leader, had already called the aid station and that the litter bearers were already on their way. Sgt. Hilton, who had been awakened by Cunningham to man the phone, came to the cellar door and wanted to know what was going on. Cunningham informed him that one of our outposts had been hit and that he was going to check it out. Sgt. Hilton seemed unconcerned and asked if there was any coffee made. Cunningham answered that the electricity had been knocked out and that we were unable to make any. Sgt. Hilton left muttering something about smart asses.

The shelling let up, Cunningham and Coy left to make their way to the second Platoon. Shortly after their leaving the shelling started again. This time they were throwing everything they had including their Screaming-mimis. The shelling was relentless. The big stuff would let up, then they would start in with their mortar fire. There was very little let up. Shortly after 0400 we got word that the litter bearers had crossed Burp-Gun Alley and had taken refuge from the shelling in the cellar near the crossing and would be coming our way as soon as there was a break in the shelling. They would let us know when they left there.

Around 0500 there was a break in the bombardment. The call came saying the litter-bearers were on their way. A couple of minutes later, Stern and I heard them approach. The password was exchanged and they passed through. They were led by a man who said he knew the area. After the men passed, Stern and I started discussing the outpost that was hit and the men that were maintaining it.

We knew that Sgt. Rice was in charge and there was, Avizo, Lavine, Laughlin, Lyman and Simmons, all from our Platoon. Around 0530 the shelling started up again, Stern and I took up our position on the cellar steps. This shelling was the worst, not only were they coming into the Bridgehead, the shells were falling across the street. This is where only a couple of days ago the Germans were holding. It was at times like this, under heavy bombardment, bad communication and everyone trying to bury into the earth that a man can let his imagination run wild. Were the shells that were falling in no-man's land coming from the Germans because they feared we were about to attack, or was the shelling coming from us because the Germans were counterattacking? Regardless of what my imagination was doing, one stark reality stood out! The waiting game in Saarlautern was about to end.

There was no let up of the shelling, the Germans seemed to be concentrating on the Bridgehead. Everyone was hunkered down in low places. I know a lot of prayers were going up. I know mine were. I heard my good friend Stern, who was Jewish, utter things that I had not heard from him before. Stern and I were hanging onto our "Kilroy" positions, standing on the cellar steps with only our eyes above the floor. Due to the relative good condition of the buildings along Burp-Gun Alley, we were pretty well protected from the flat trajectory of the 88's. They were slamming into the buildings across the street, which the Germans had occupied up until three days go. We were getting alot of pieces of brick and shell fragments coming through the opening in our building. I had a piece of brick glance off of my helmet, which was evident by the red brick dust left on the helmet.

While the 88's were hitting the buildings across the street, the mortar shells were making it over onto the street and into our position. While standing on the cellar steps there was a loud plunk on the floor above us. A bright bluish light lit up the area around us and there was a spewing sound emanating from it. I heard Stern whisper "dud!" No sooner had the word cleared his lips that there came a big explosion from the floor above us. It seemed like all the bricks in Saarlautern came falling down around us. I was knocked down the cellar steps, through the blanket covering the door into the cellar. Through the dim light and dust I could see Stern coming behind me. When I hit the cellar floor, I looked around and all I could see of the men gathered inside were the whites of their eyes peering from beneath steel helmets. Stern and I were saved by the stairs that led to the second floor. They were above our heads and caught all the brick that would have fallen on us. The bricks fell everywhere except into the cellar door. We never figured out if the shell was a dud, had a delay fuse or if another shell came in close behind the first. After clearing a few bricks away from the cellar opening, Stern and I took up our positions again.

Sgt. Hilton came to the door and asked if we were alright. I answered in the affirmative, and asked him if he had heard anything from the outpost that had been hit. He said he had, that the casualties had been taken to the second platoon cellar. That so far there was one fatality, four seriously wounded and one with minor injuries. He said he was not given any names and that the litter-bearers were still holed up in the cellar due to the shelling, and as soon as it slacks they are going to evacuate them to the aid station.

Around daylight the shelling stopped. This seemed to be the cue for the man on the machine gun to start his harassing fire down Burp-Gun Alley. Shortly after daylight Sgt. Cunningham showed up with Sgt. Rakosi, Bobby Spicer and two men from the second platoon. Cunningham said they were going down to the Burp-Gun Alley crossing to help the Medics get the wounded men across the street

The litter bearers had taken a shortcut through the rail yard, since they felt safe from the snipers because of their red cross flag and marked helmets. We started to question Sgt. Cunningham about the casualties, he told us that he did not have time to discuss it, that he had to help get the wounded across Burp-Gun Alley as soon as possible. He would fully inform us when he returned, which should not take but a few minutes. Then he noticed the brick piled up around the cellar door and asked what the brick was for, that we must be expecting to run out of ammo.

The gunner, firing down Burp-Gun Alley was especially busy this morning. It made us wonder what was going on at the crossing. Sure enough when Cunningham and the men with him, returned about forty minutes later, they said that they had hell getting the wounded across Burp-Gun Alley. They said that despite the large Red Cross flag, the white arm bands with red crosses, and the helmets with red crosses, the machine gunner opened fire on them as soon as they started across the alley. Sgt. Rice, who was first to cross, managed to make it safely across with him. The next litter bearers, carrying Avizo, thinking that maybe the firing was a reaction before recognition, unfolded the thin red cross flag and started across the street. When they reached the center of the street the gunner opened up, hitting Avizo.

The bearers dropped Avizo in the street and ran for cover across the street. Cunningham ordered them to come back and retrieve the litter, they refused. Sgt. Rakosi and Bobby Spicer, who was with Sgt. Cunningham, saw what was going on. They took the red cross helmets from the bearers waiting to take Lyman across, put them on, took the red cross flag, and went out into the street picked up the litter that Avizo was on and took him across the street. They brought the helmets and flag back gave them to the litter bearers, Sgt. Cunningham ordered them to take Lyman across, which they did. Not another shot was fired after Avizo was hit. Later on when Sgt. Cunningham reported to Capt. Batts the refusal of the litter bears to obey orders. His only comment was that he should have shot the sons of bitches.

After telling us what had taken place at the crossing, Cunningham told Stern and me that he was going to try and round up someone to relieve us so we could get a little sleep. He said that we were getting short handed, especially after the platoon had lost seven men with one whack. Cunningham went on to tell us he wanted everyone to get as much rest as possible this afternoon and evening, because after today, we did not know when we would be able to rest again. He managed to get a couple of squad leaders to relieve Stern and me. We were told to try and get about four hours sleep and that he was also going to get a short nap. Around 1500 he had to be at Company Headquarters to receive the battle plans for the next day. Before we could lie down, word came down that the 261st on our left had managed to get a couple of battalions across the Saar River and established a small bridgehead. We were going to try and hold it until the main attack started the next morning. Stern and I prepared to get some rest. Cunningham was on the phone to Company Headquarters. After getting off the phone, Cunningham informed us that he had to go to a Battalion briefing that the battle plans for the next day may have to be altered, due to what had happened with the crossing of the Saar by the 261st.

Before lying down, it came to me that I had not asked Cunningham about the three other men that were on the outpost when it was hit, Simmons, Laughlin, and Lavine. Cunningham said that Simmons and Laughlin did not make it, Simmons was killed on the spot, Laughlin was evacuated to the second platoon cellar, where Medic Coy tried desperately to save him, all in vain. He died in Cunningham's arms. Laughlin was one of best liked men in the Company. If he had been one inch shorter he would not have passed the entrance exam to be an infantry soldier. In close order drill he was always placed at the rear of the column because he had to take two steps to everyone else's one and he always wore a smile. Simmons, my good friend, whom I had first met on the train when we were going to Camp Shelby from Ft. Meade, Md. We were comparing our assignment papers, when we discovered that we both were being assigned to the same company of the 65th. Division. We were also assigned to the same squad in the third platoon.

I was ammo bearer on the B.A.R team until I was picked as the platoon runner, Simmons was then put in my old position. My first thought, when I heard about Simmons was, "there but for the grace of God" but somehow this did not fit. I admit that "why him" has gone through my mind many times in the last fifty-seven years, but I accepted long ago that there is a reason for everything. Lavine was only slightly wounded, he was treated and returned to the platoon that evening. Sleep did not come quick after I lay down the anxiety of tomorrow's attack combined with the thought of my friends death kept me awake for a long time, but exhaustion finally overcame me.

Around 1100 I was awakened because the whole world seemed to be shaking. The Germans were throwing everything they had at us. They especially seemed to try and intimidate us with those nasty sounds the "screaming mimis" make. They certainly were successful in getting my attention. Not only was the shelling heavy in the Bridgehead, it was also the same along, and across the Saar River. I suppose after the crossing of the Saar River by units of the 261st, the Germans knew as much about what our plans were, as we did. I could hear Cunningham on the phone. He sounded excited, but due to the noise I did not know what was being said,. After hanging up, he came over to us and told us that we had more casualties up near the second platoon, and that the litter bearers were on their way and would be coming by us shortly. He wanted Coy, our Platoon Medic to go with them, that they probably needed more medical help. Lt. Collins had told him that the injuries were severe.

A few minutes later the litter bearers showed up. Cunningham told them he was sending Coy with them to help with the wounded and that they were to return back by us with the wounded and he would assist them in crossing back across Burp Gun Alley. A short time later Coy and the litter bearers returned with three men on litters. The first man was lying on his stomach and did not appear too severely wounded. They said he was from K Company and had shell fragments in his upper back. The next man was also from K Company. He was lying on his side facing me, with his eyes closed. I recognized him. He was Sgt. Lutz. He was on K company's baseball team with whom we at "I" Company had competed with back at Camp Shelby. I placed my hand on his forehead and called out to him. There was no response. Coy told me later that his left arm had been severed at the shoulder by brick that had been blown from a wall when an 88 shell came through. The next man was from our second platoon. He was Sgt. Robiski, he was conscious and I heard him telling Sgt. Cunningham that he thought he was going to loose his leg. Cunningham was assuring him that he wasn't. Robiski's wound was caused by a mortar shell landing behind him and spraying shell fragments into his upper legs and buttock. Neither Lutz or Robiski lived to make it back to the aid station.

It was almost 1300 when Cunningham and Coy returned from helping to get the wounded across Burp Gun Alley they said they had no trouble, not a shot was fired at the medics when they crossed. Stern and I took over our old positions by the cellar door, relieving the two squad leaders so they could get a little sleep. If tomorrow turned out as planned, they were going to need it. Cunningham told Stern and me to wake him at 1400, that he had to be at Company Headquarters at 1500 for a briefing.

The shelling had stopped except for an occasional mortar burst. Stern and I moved up behind the machine gun to check it and see if it was ready, everything seemed in order. To get tomorrow's event off my mind I decided to pick Sterns brain a little. I asked him if he thought the machine gun was in working order. He said he was sure it was. I asked him if it had been fired since we had been here? He told me that he didn't think it had. Then I wondered out loud how long this thing had been sitting here, and if it had ever been fired. Stern looked at me and said that he thought that we should test it by firing into the building across the street. I told Stern, why not, that Kraut up the street fired his all day long. Then it dawned on me that we had heard one burst from the Kraut's burp-gun since mid-morning. This was very unusual. I asked Stern if he remembered and he replied that he didn't think that he had fired any. It was almost time to wake Cunningham. When we did we would report this a cynical laugh from Stern. Just when he started theorizing about some idiot asking for the password the Germans drowned out his words with the beginning of one of their most severe artillery bombardments yet. Stern and I retreated quickly to the cellar steps. They threw everything they had at us for a few minutes until our artillery opened up and sent their mail slamming into the Germans defenses. Our artillery must have brought up support because the whole world, out in front of us seemed to be exploding. This must have sent the enemy into their bunkers because there was very little coming back. Every time they tried, our boys would put the big hurt on them again.

Around 0200, Cunningham came up and told Stern and I that our ground troops were starting to move into position for the 0430 attack. They would be positioning themselves along our position on Burp-Gun Alley. They would attack across the alley and swing left behind the heavily mined area to our left., which we think the Germans have vacated.

Shortly after 0300 our boys started arriving and taking up positions around us along Burp-Gun Alley. They were relatively quiet as they moved into position. Shining against the overcast sky, the artificial moon was casting out good light. Reflections on the faces of the men coming from the bursting shells, showed them grim and wide eyed, most of them seemed to be too young for the task at hand. There were a few men moving about whispering and using hand signals. I took them to be officers and noncoms. Up here where the dirty work is, no one wears their rank insignia, everyone wants to be inconspicuous as possible. Up here you must get to know your leaders personally.

Finally 0430 arrived, our boys started moving across Burp-Gun Alley into no-man's land. The Germans knew we were coming and we knew that they were expecting us. Not too many battles are won by surprising the enemy. Most are won by overwhelming forces, maneuvering and sometimes luck. Today we were praying for all three.

It was almost 0600 when the sounds of small arms fire out front told us that our men had made contact with the enemy shock troops that were waiting for them in the dead zone. The action seemed to be happening less than five hundred yards in front. The sounds of fighting grew more intense as the small millimeter mortars joined the fray. The German artillery started dropping a few rounds into the Bridgehead but they were quickly overwhelmed by the superior fire power of our artillery and chose to sit it out. At 0630 we got word that the 261st had put more troops across the Saar River and was meeting very little resistance. The strong resistance was coming from the 259th, and the 260th zone. The Germans knew where the main attack was coming from and were waiting. The progress of the 259th and the 260th was very slow due to the heavy resistance the enemy was putting up.

Around daylight we heard that ominous sound that tanks make coming from our right, up Burp-Gun Alley. A wave of relief rolled over me when I saw it was two of our Sherman's, followed by some of our boys on foot. The tanks stopped in front of us, abreast the one on the right began firing into the pillbox that was about four hundred yards down Burp-Gun Alley, sitting on the right side. The tank on the left began firing into the buildings across the street from the pillbox. There was no return fire. After sitting for a few minutes, the turrent on one of the tanks opened, a man appeared and motioned to the rear to come forward. A tank Destroyer appeared, loaded with men and equipment and pulled past the tanks a short distance and stopped. Some of the men following the tanks proceeded on to the tank Destroyer. We motioned for the men still behind to come over to where Stern and I were, behind the machine gun. They came over, so we asked what was going on and they told us that the men on the tank Destroyer were engineers and they were preparing to clear the streets of mines. Looking up the street at all the shu-mines they had one hell of a job ahead of them. We asked the men what outfit they were from and they told us the were from the 1st Battalion 259th and their orders were to protect the engineers for a while and if they were not attacked they were to move out in support of the attacking forces in front.

We watched in awe as the engineers went about their job of clearing the streets. They would slowly pick their way though the shu-mines tying to primer cord at three feet intervals a quarter pound of TNT, criss-crossing the street for about fifty yards so that there would be a quarter pound of TNT covering every square yard. They then would set off the explosives, clearing fifty yards at a time, then repeating the process until the area was cleared. The German shelling into our area had stopped shortly after daylight and all of our men from the third battalion came out of their cellars and holes to watch the action of the engineers as they went about their work. After about an hour, the tank commander, a 1st Lt. came across the street to where we were watching the action and the first thing he asked was about how long that kraut had been lying in the street. We told him that he was here when we arrived ten days ago. The Lt. wanted to know where the officer was that was in charge here. We told him that there was no officer here that we were in touch with our C.O. by telephone and he could talk to him if he wanted to. He then wanted to know what non-commissioned officer was in charge. We called Sgt. Cunningham from the cellar where he was on the phone to Capt. Batts. Cunningham reported to the tank commander, who seemed surprised that a Staff Sgt. would be in charge. He informed Cunningham that he and his men had to move out and that he would like for us to keep an eye on the engineers and if they ran into any trouble, to report it to our superiors, and help them out. Cunningham promised he would.

Around noon Capt. Batts showed up with his staff. It was the first time he had been to our area, that I was aware of. First Sgt. Harrell was with them, it was the first time I had seen him since France. Capt. Batts and his staff walked out into Burp-Gun Alley, took out some maps, placed them on the ground, placed a compass on top of them, kept turning the papers and pointing in all directions, mostly toward the direction of where the sounds of fighting were coming from. They picked up their maps and started walking towards the area of the alley that the engineers had cleared. They beckoned to Sgt. Cunningham and Lt. Collins, the second platoon leader, to follow them. They picked their way slowly through some of the cleared area, checking it closely, until they came to the next street corner, where they placed their maps on the ground again and took more readings. They then returned to where we were. Capt. Batts told us to listen up that he wanted to bring us up to date on what was happening and what our plans were. He told us the 259th and the 260th were meeting strong resistance from the Germans and their gains had been minimal, but on the other hand the 261st had done better than expected. They had met all their objectives and were still advancing rapidly. He went on to tell us that the 26th Division of the 3rd Army had met all of their objectives as had the 70th Division of the 7th Army. Their main objective was to come together and trap the Germans in the Saar pocket. He also told us to get all our gear together that we were moving up closer to where the fighting is taking place and we may have to relieve the 1st battalion of the 261st that had been attached to the 260th. When the attack started, they would revert back to the 261st which was making the most progress. The 260th objective was to take the town of Saarwellingen. He told us that we of the 3rd Battalion were lucky that we were not in on the initial attack this morning, that we were originally scheduled to be, but it was changed at the last minute due to the fact that we were the Battalion farthest out front. It was easier to move a Battalion through than to have to move two Battalions. He said that he would be leading the way, not to worry, that he had spent hours studying maps of the area. He knew more about Saarlautern than he knew about his home town back in Kentucky. He told us to have all our gear ready to go at 1600, we will be moving out at dusk. He told us the company would be moving out in numerical order, except the weapons platoon will go third, placing the third platoon in reserve at the rear. Capt. batts said that he would be in the lead and that he wanted all platoon runners up with him. I'm thinking there goes my chance to be in the rear echelon shot to hell. He informed us that he had to go and brief the rest of the company, that he would be returning in a couple of hours and for us to be ready to go. We spent those two hours cleaning our rifles, checking our ammo, hanging grenades in button holes, rolling up shelter with blanket, clean socks and underwear inside, still the same ones I left France with. Not bad, it had not been but three weeks since I had changed. I had to smile when I remembered what my mother would tell me when I would leave the house, to be sure and change underwear in case I had an accident and ended up in the hospital. I wondered what instruction she would give me today. My mind seemed to be working overtime, my thoughts ran from cursing my luck for being here to praying for my safety. "Attack the Siegfried Line," that had an ominous sound to it.

Capt. Batts returned around 1700, he had with him Lt. Montgomery, leader of the 1st platoon and Lt. Collins of the 2nd platoon. He asked where Sgt. Hilton was. We told him that he was still in the cellar. Capt. Batts told Cunningham to tell Hilton to report to him, which he did. Capt. Batts asked Sgt. Hilton if he was going to be able to lead the 3rd platoon. Hilton answered in the affirmative. Capt. told him that if he was not sure, now is the time to speak out and I will put Cunningham in control with no questions asked. Sgt. Hilton insisted that he was alright. Capt. Batts then pulled out a roll of maps and he and the Platoon leaders plus Cunningham, studied them for a few minutes. Then passed out smaller maps to each squad leader within the platoons. He then informed us that pretty soon K and L companies would come by us heading north (to our left) down Burp-Gun Alley, at the first street past our position they will turn right (heading east) toward where the sounds of fighting was coming from.

Shortly after the Captain's briefing the first men of K Company appeared coming down Burp-Gun Alley. There were about a half dozen scouts about one hundred yards out front, behind them was the company Commander and his group which consists of two radio men, who alternated at carrying the 300 radio and the walkie-talkie. Usually a runner from each platoon, sometimes the First Sgt. and sometimes the Company Executive Officer and various other men that were there as decoys. You could not tell one from another. They all dressed alike, carried the same type weapons, and no insignia visible. At this stage of the war Junior Officers were a premium. The enemy sniper's main objective was a Junior Officer, and every precaution was taken to conceal their identity.

The two columns of men, one on each side of the street moved along slowly. It took about two hours before the last of L Company moved past our position. We of "I" Company fell in behind them, with Captain Batts leading. We slowly moved toward the sounds of the fighting. Slow was alright with me. I was in no hurry. While moving along, Captain Batts was in constant communication with Battalion headquarters group and the leaders of K and L Company's. The one good thing about being a runner was that usually you could tell what was going on by listening to the conversing of the Company Commander while most everyone else is wondering what the hell is the hold up. You are afraid to sit down, when the column stops you might go to sleep and wake up being all alone. You wonder which is worse being behind all alone or being up front with more company than you want.

Communication was the big problem when at or near the front line, the best you could ask for was some sort of organized chaos. This is where your training and experience combined with your instinct paid off. Concentrate on your war which usually covered only a small area, listen to the sounds around you they will tell you a lot. Try to determine where both the incoming and outgoing artillery is falling, that will give you some clue to where the troops on both sides are. To do these things one had to keep his cool. This was very hard to do under fire. The men who seemed to handle it best were the men that had a resignation quality about them. The ones that knew they were going to "make it" and the ones that were resigned to not making it. For the rest, it was a reaction derived from training, like any other team training, you repeated the process until it be comes automatic.

The noise, in a fire fight a casual observer would wonder what is all this shooting about when I can't see one person to shoot at. Intimidation, that is what it's all about. You knew when you checked your ammo before the fight and counted one hundred and fifty rounds that you would not see that many Germans. But if they were out there you were going to keep them guessing. One of our biggest problems was men not firing their weapons even after intense firefights. When weapons were checked it was found that almost half the men involved did not fire a single round. The statistics of WWII say for every 25,000 rounds of small arm rounds fired only one produced a casualty. Today with the increase of rapid-firing weapons the ratio is one in 200,000. The defending forces are usually defending from a prepared position, their main objective is to pin the attacking force down. To do this they used the sounds of battle to produce a psychological affect on the attackers. The Germans were good at this. First they had the self- propelled 88, its reputation was legendary especially among our armored forces. The sight of one would automatically throw a Sherman tank in reverse. They had the screaming-mimis with that weird sound that you heard from the time they left their tubes until they exploded. Then there was the Grunts worse nightmare, the MG-42, the machine gun that fired 1,200 to 1,500 rounds a minute. There was no other sound on the battlefield like it. I have heard many descriptions of the sound, the one I agreed with most was that it sounded like a sheet being ripped, magnified a thousand times. The intended purpose of all these sounds were to pin down the attacking force. When the first sounds of battle came everyone's first instinct was to hit the ground. This is where your training takes over. You know that you must move forward, although it probably means death, but to get pinned down means certain death. Because then they can bring all the forces they have down on you.

As we moved slowly towards the sounds of the fighting, the rules of engagement kept going through my mind. Then I wonder if I will panic. Does one forget everything when he panics? I pushed these thoughts out of my mind and tried to concentrate on the conversation that Capt. Batts was having over the radio. Our movement toward the front had slowed to a snail's pace. Around midnight it stopped altogether. Capt. Batts switched from talking over the 300 radio to the walkie-talkie. I could hear him informing our platoon leaders to tell all the men to relax, that he was waiting for further orders and that the battle plan seems to be changing. He turned to us and said that we could sit down if we wanted to. The sounds of the fighting up front was becoming sporadic and after a while it stopped altogether.

The artificial moon was doing a good job tonight shining against the cloudy sky. Our field of vision was excellent. Looking around, we seemed to have moved to the edge of the city. To our left front there was an open field and through the dim light you could see those concrete dragon teeth that were so prevalent throughout the Siegfried Line. We seemed to be on higher ground than we were in the Bridgehead. As I sat and felt the soil it was dry and sandy, unlike the mud we had been in for eleven days. We sat and waited for a long while, the longer we sat the quieter it got. After a while the only sounds were the shuffling of the men around you. After a while we begin to hear these bird like whistling coming from our front. Under our present condition and your mind going a hundred miles an hour it did not take much imagination to think that this was the Germans signals to each other to start dropping those mortar shells. I looked around and I could see neck stretching going on around me but nothing happened. I guess it was birds, glad to be able to communicate for a change. What a dichotomy of expectation. Here I am sitting in the middle of the Siegfried Line and it is more peaceable than it has been in days, even to the point of hearing birds sing. I began thinking that I must be hallucinating, when my thoughts were interrupted by the sound of Capt. Batts speaking on the phone. When he finished, he spoke to us around him and told us everything was going great, that we had been pinched out of the action and were to return to our old positions inside the Bridgehead. He then got on the walkie-talkie and gave the platoon leaders the same information. The signs of relief coming from around me almost blew me away. Capt. Batts was still on the phone, speaking to the platoon, assuring them that we were not retreating but going into Division reserve and for them to stay in place that he was coming back to the rear of the company and lead them back. As we moved back through the ranks, there was a small amount of grumbling coming from the men, but the vast majority of the troops were like me, happy. I thanked God that with all the changes made in the battle plans lately, they seemed to work toward my good luck.. We arrived back at our cellar on Burp-Gun Alley around 0300, it looked so good. Stern and I decided to change the name of the street to Burp-Gun Place. We were told to try and get a little sleep that we were going to be up at daylight clearing out the city of Saarlautern. I thanked God and just as I started to unroll my bed roll Cunningham came by and informed Stern and me that the outpost still had to maintained and for us to get on the job. I'm thinking well at least I will not have to worry with rolling and unrolling my bedroll.

Stern and I took up our old position by the cellar door. We were not too sleepy anyway still riding that high we received when we were told we were in reserve instead of to the front. A short time later Cunningham came up. He said that he had been on the phone with the brains and it seems as if the Germans are pulling out of the Saar Basin before being trapped by the 3rd and 7th Army's closing in around the Basin. He told us that about daylight we were going to start clearing out this part of Saarlautern to see if there were any stragglers left to be served their eviction notices. Cunningham went on to say that he was taking half the platoon and Sgt. Hilton was taking the other half and that we had already been assigned our sector to be cleared out. He told us that he had lobbied hard for and got the sector that he wanted most and that was Burp-Gun Alley. Starting from the crossing, which we had controlled since our arrival in this fair city, going to our left for some five hundred yards toward where that S.O.B. had been firing that machine gun since last November and no one was able to stop him. Cunningham said that he felt like he owed the Gunner something and that he hoped he was still there. I told Sarge not to get "carried away" that I hoped he had left with the crowd. I was told to "watch my mouth" or I would be going with Sgt. Hilton's half of the platoon. I told him that I would watch it and even wash it out with soap, if he so desired. Stern asked him if the two of us were going with him and he answered "you bet." Then he rose and moved toward the cellar door, telling us he would see us at daylight. Stern and I checked the time 0530, a couple of hours until daylight. We tried to remember the last time we had slept. It had been a long twenty five hours since the attack on the Siegfried Line at 0430 yesterday seems like a week ago. Stern and I decided that since we had a couple of hours until daylight, that each of us would sleep an hour while the other stood watch. Stern went first, he sat down on the cellar steps leaned his head against the wall and within two minutes he was breathing deeply. I had to stand and move around to keep from joining him. The next hour was a long one for me. When it finally passed I shook Stern awake and he said that he had not gone to sleep yet. I replied that I knew that was a lie because I did not remember him keeping his mouth shut for an hour, since I had known him. He stood up and said "go to sleep and shut the hell up" and I did.

I was awakened a short time later from the sounds of Stern's and Cunningham's voices discussing making coffee and opening X rations. They were using the K ration boxes to start a fire to heat water in their canteen cups in order to make coffee from the powder that was in the K rations. I asked them what the hell was going on, that I had not seen that big of a fire or heard that much loud talking in days. Stern said that he was sorry, that they had not intended to wake me. Their plans were to serve me breakfast in bed this morning and would I prefer the gourmet eggs and crackers over the cheese and crackers. I informed him that my preference this morning would be the eggs, since things seemed to tighten up in the last couple of days, and when it is ready just sit it here by the cellar door so that all I will have to do is turn over and eat. Cunningham told me to get my lazy ass up off the cellar steps that he was calling the men up to get ready to move out and if I didn't I would have tracks on my ass.

After breakfast the platoon formed up in the middle of Burp-Gun Alley. It seemed strange standing there after days of not being able to stick your head above the window sills. It looked as if it was going to be a great day weather wise. The sun was up and starting to burn the haze from the river away. Sgt. Cunningham had made out a roster. He called out thirty-two names, eight less than when we arrived in Saarlautern. There was no mention of their names, we all knew. I missed them all, but I really missed my good friend Dayne Simmons. Cunningham called out the names that were to go with him and the rest were to go with Sgt. Hilton. Of course Stern and I were on Cunningham's list. Our platoon had been assigned a thousand yards of Burp-Gun Alley to clear. Hilton was to clear out half to the south and Cunningham the northern half. Our objective was to clear out every house on both sides of the street. Cunningham and two men searched the houses on the left side and Sgt. Smith and two others searched the houses on the right. The rest of the men stayed in the street to cover. Everything was going great. There seemed to be no one around but us and our Fly-boys above. Someone remarked that they bet those Jabos were having a field day with those retreating Germans. How true this turned out to be.

The search was slow as we were careful not to come in contact with booby traps and the land mines that the engineers might have missed. The search of the houses was conducted in various ways, sometimes going through the entire house, other times just looking through windows and throwing hand grenades in through cellar windows that protruded above ground level. Some of the houses, there was not much left to search. We were about half way through our search when I was a witness to my first miracle. We came upon a small building on the left side of the street. The front yard was fenced in with a fence made of iron bars about four feet high. There was a gate in the center of it and there was a cement walkway leading from the street, through the gate, to the door of the building. Most of the houses had been blown away leaving only the front wall with the door and two blown out windows one on each side of the door. Beneath the window on the right at ground level was a small barred window leading into the building's cellar. Cunningham, noticing the window, told everyone to stay down that he was going to put a hand grenade through the cellar window. Everyone was kneeling and watching from the street as Cunningham stepped to the right of the window with the grenade in his left hand. He pulled the safety pin, bent over the window, while holding his carbine in his right hand and attempted to toss the grenade between the bars. As he tossed the arming device, it popped up hitting the bars and causing the grenade to fall outside the window. Seeing this Cunningham tried to place the grenade back between the bars but failed again. With no time left Cunningham, forgetting about the fence, turned to run around the corner of the building. When reaching the fence he attempted to go over it. Then getting hung up with his feet and legs and his rear-end dangling at about a forty-five degree angle no more than five feet from the grenade, this is the prime killing zone for the grenade. I was the closest one to him, lying in the street at the end of the walkway. Observing what was happening, my heart stopped. I uttered a short prayer, stretched out below the curb and heard that awful sound. I could not look up until I heard someone mumbling. I lifted my head slightly, glanced toward the building, my heart started beating again. There was Sgt. Cunningham walking down the walkway toward the gate rubbing his ass. I thought that I was dreaming. We jumped up met him at the gate, asking him if he was alright. He said that he was not sure, that he felt a slight burning on his ass. We turned him around and there was no sign of damage. We then pulled down his pants and there was only one small red spot on one cheek. Impossible! The men working the other side of the street came running over with firearms in the ready position and surrounded the building. They thought that someone had thrown the grenade back out of the cellar. We tried to explain but everyone was excited, no one was listening, and to this day some believe that the grenade was thrown back. I know what happened, I was watching! It was a Miracle!

After the excitement of the hand grenade died down we went on with the job at hand. Burp-Gun Alley appeared to run along the Western edge of the Siegfried Line. On our right was an assortment of bunkers and pillboxes with a scattering of dragons teeth through out the area. There were recent cut trenches crossing Burp-Gun Alley that lead from the bunkers on the east of the street to the buildings on the west side. There were tunnels leading from the bunkers to the trenches and tunnels leading from the trenches to the cellars of the buildings on the west side. It was obvious that the Germans had been busy the last few months concealing their movements in getting snipers in position and also to change positions of their mortars and other light ordinance.

Our progress was slowed when the process of checking tunnels and bunkers started. When we reached the point where we thought the machine gunner had been harassing us from, Cunningham brought up the point again that he wanted to find the spot where the machine-gun was firing from. I asked him why? Was it because he wanted to toss another hand grenade. This brought out the explicitness from him and he pointed toward the other end of Burp-Gun Alley and told me to go join Sgt. Hilton's part of the platoon. Since I was the platoon runner, he wanted me to run all the way there and to tell Sgt. Hilton the messenger was arriving and that he could kill him. I promised Sgt. Cunningham that I would be good and carry all of his hand grenades for him, if he would let me stay with him. He told me to keep on that I was digging my grave. Cunningham called Stern, me and the platoon sniper, Jasperson over to where he was and asked us if we thought the machine-gunner had been firing from the bunker that was now about one hundred yards across the street from us. We told him that we thought that he was, and from the condition of the front of the bunker, the artillery observers thought so to. We decided to go and check out the bunker. When we reached the right side of the street we noticed an iron ladder leading from a hole in the ground, up to the street fastened to a cement footing. We crawled down the ladder to check it out. It led into a concreted tunnel that angled off toward the bunker. It was obviously part of the Siegfried Fortification. We moved on to the bunker and entered a door at the rear, which had been left open. Being very cautious, Cunningham produced a flashlight, telling Stern and Smith to stay outside, he and I moved slowly inside carefully checking for mines and booby-traps. The room appeared to be about fifteen feet with a dome shaped front and top. The dome front had three slit openings to fire through, these were the only openings besides the door. There were no light fixtures inside the room but there were electric outlets along the wall next to the floor. The concrete walls in front appeared to be about eight feet thick, and the rear where the door was they were about three feet thick. The inside was painted white. To the right of the entrance was a hand rail that ran along an opening in the floor where steps led down to another level. There was nothing else in the room, it was perfectly clean. We moved slowly down the stairs to the next level, the room was square. One side contained three bunk beds with mattresses. There was a concrete table built onto the rest of the walls with the exception of a single door on the side facing Burp-Gun Alley. The tables contained what appeared to be busted up communication equipment and papers scattered about. We turned our attention to the door which was open. It led into a tunnel, we looked through it, sure enough we could see light about a hundred yards away. We made our way slowly toward the light and climbed the latter onto Burp-Gun Alley. We looked over toward the bunker and there sat Stern and Smith patiently waiting. We whistled and waved for them to come over. They arrived with a questionable look on their faces. We explained the situation to them and that we thought the machine gun had not been firing from the bunker. The field of fire did not cover as much of the street as the gunner had covered. As we stood there looking back down the alley toward where our crossing was, we could see the doorway where we were fired on when bringing up supplies. Cunningham noticed something. He told Jasperson to bring the sniper's rifle over, which Cunningham took and scoped out the door and the street. This was approximately five hundred yards away. After a couple of minutes he took the rifle down saying "I'll be damned." We asked him what the problem was. He handed Sgt. Smith the rifle and told him to scope out the door and street at the crossing. He asked Smith if he could see the entire street at the crossing. Smith took another look and told him he could. Cunningham kept saying, that was it! We asked him what was it? He pointed down the street toward the crossing and asked us if we saw the gradual turn to the right that the street made as it moved away from us, we said that we did. Then he asked us if we remembered that the sniper could only cover half of the street with his firing. We answered in the affirmative. Cunningham went on to say that the machine gun must have been set up on the other side of the street which limited the gunners field of fire to the left side of the street due to the slight turn to the right.

By then I am thinking, "what difference does it make, they are gone!" I did not speak out because I had already said too much and I knew that once Cunningham set his mind to something there was no changing it.

Cunningham started walking across the street, motioning for us to follow him. The buildings were all close together and sat an equal distance from the street, except the last building in the block which sat about four or five feet closer to the street, exposing about that many feet of brick wall. Cunningham, like a bird dog going on point, walked straight to the wall, bent over and pushed in several bricks from the wall at ground level. We walked up and peered into the cellar. We went into the building which was partly destroyed and found the stairs leading to the cellar. Then we went down them. The light from the flashlight and the small amount of light coming through the little windows that were at the top of the walls, we could see a platform in the corner where the loose bricks were. The platform was just high enough and large enough to accommodate a man and his M-G 42 firing through a slit where bricks had been removed. After firing, the bricks could be replaced, making the wall inconspicuous from the outside. The rest of the cellar was undamaged. It was clean and contained two small beds, two chairs and a table. Cunningham kept saying over and over that he knew that he could find the spot and he wished that rascal was still here. I told Cunningham that he probably was until he observed how infallible you were dancing over that hand grenade. I then ran from the cellar.

We returned to the street and the rest of the men sitting on the curb building little fires, using K ration boxes for fuel. They were heating water to make coffee so that they would have something to wash those crackers and that "stuff" in those cans down. As we walked up, Cunningham was saying that he did not remember calling out chow time. Not one man looked up. Cunningham looked around, and said okay I am saying it now, "chow time." After can trading, to try and get something you liked, we sat down on the curb to eat. Most used their hands and crackers to dig the "stuff" out of the cans, saying the did not want to dirty their spoon because they had no place to wash them. From the looks of most of the hands I believe I would rather eat with a dirty spoon.

It was a perfect day,. The sun was warm reflecting off the street. We sat there for a while, some laid back and dozed. The only signs of war, if you ignored the bombed out buildings, were the many planes overhead. Bombers up high, coming and going and the Jabos doing their thing at lower altitudes. Someone suggested that we should put our colored markers out so they would be able to recognize us as friendly forces. Someone else said that it didn't make any difference, if we put it out it would make a good target for some crazy German flying by.

Cunningham stood up and told us to get ready, that we had work to do. Everyone sat up and lit up. There was no wind so the smoke just hung in the air above our heads. Everyone smoked, bad health from smoking was not an issue here. The only issue debated was why did they send us those little packs of Chelsa and Raleighs in our K rations when no one in the States smoked them. Even in France when they asked for a cigarette and you produced that little pack of Chelsa, they would look at you with that little grin that said "you are shitting with me yes". As I sit and listen to the griping about the cigarettes, I look down at my "combat" boots that I had been wearing since Camp Shelby. I am wondering how many hours have I stood in snow, wearing these little "jobs" with two pairs of socks on, stomping through to mother earth trying to find some warmth. These leather boots had enough "dub bing" rubbed on them in the last two months to grease a battle ship. It was odd how the "grunt" would only occasionally mention the large problems and continuously griped about food, cigarettes and "these damn wet matches." I believe he would have fought naked if you fed him what he wanted, furnished him smokes and occasionally a beer. As I looked around at the men in my platoon the metamorphosis taking place was astounding. The roll of son, husband and father was disappearing. There was very little conversation about home or family anymore. The "grunts" every thought and action has to do with his survival. He has become like the pack animals, each ones survival depends on the other members. All vestige of humanity is slowly slipping away. You remember when you bathed and changed clothes, washed your hands, combed your hair, shaved, slept more than two hours, no sleep at all without your buddy lying next to you keeping each other warm. There was no such thing as privacy or dignity. Body functions were almost never done in private. Sanitation was not a priority. Very few "grunts" died from a disease. Stench didn't matter any more. Everyone and everything stunk. The Infantry man could not escape it, if he advanced he moved into the enemy stench, if he retreated he ended up in rear echelons smell. After a while the C and K rations wasn't so bad. They became compatible with the environment.

While I was pondering our fate, Cunningham had been on the walkie talkie speaking to someone at Company Headquarters. When he was finished he called us around him and told us that things were looking up for us. He said that after we cleared out a couple of more blocks, we were to return to our old haunts for one more night. The good news was that the 259th and the 261st had already broken through the Siegfried Line and they, with a little help from their friends, had the German army headed for the Rhine. This bit of good news put a little pep into the men and it did not take long to clear the rest of the area.

When we reached the cellar Sgt. Hilton and the rest of the platoon had already returned. He informed the squad leaders that he wanted the men to fallout into Burp-Gun Alley. He wanted to fill them in on what was going on. He repeated what Cunningham had told, us and went on to say that for this evening meal, we were to finish the 10 in 1 rations we had on hand and that sometime before midnight we will receive a days supply of K rations along with the days ordinance. At the crack of dawn tomorrow morning, we will leave this city on foot, walking east. The 3rd Battalion of the 260th Infantry will be bringing up the rear of the 65th Division, as it chases the enemy toward the Rhine River. Some more good news, that if things worked out as planned, maybe by tomorrow night and no later than the 22nd we would be getting a hot meal, shower, clean clothes along with a few days rest. That brought on some cheers. Sgt. Hilton finished up by telling us that all the outpost and guard positions will be maintained as before. That we didn't want any surprises, this brought out the groans.

It was apparent that Sgt. Hilton was trying to re-establish his position as platoon leader. I was wondering, along with others what would happen if a rifle accidentally went off. I know there were plenty of skeptics in the platoon.

By the time we finished our 10 in 1's it was around 1800 and getting dark. Cunningham and Rakosi came by where Stern and I were sitting and Cunningham told us that they were on their way to post the guards as instructed. Stern and I were to cover the cellar door four hours, that he had enough men so that would be all that we would have to do, that we could sleep until time to leave in the morning. That was music to our ears. Stern and I started our four hour tour of duty, being the first time we had relaxed in several days. We found it almost impossible to stay awake, even the cats licking out the ration cans couldn't raise your hackle anymore. Best of all, that knot in the pit of my stomach had gotten smaller, helping me to take a full breath through my nose, which was great, although the stench was getting worse. Finally 2200 rolled around and right on the money was Cunningham with our relief. Stern told Cunningham, that he had arrived just in time, that in another couple of minutes, he would have caught us asleep and would have to send us back to the "Guard House." Cunningham told him that he must be asleep "dreaming about such nice things". With that little dig, the three of us went down into the cellar. Cunningham told Sgt. Smith, who was C.Q. to handle the next shift change and to awake him at 0400. We then went to the rear of the cellar, each rolled up in his bedroll of shelter half and blanket, pushed up against each other for warmth, and slept sound for the first time since Camp Shankes.

I awoke to the sound of Sgt. Hilton's voice, telling Cunningham to wake up. Then I heard Cunningham saying that it was after 0600 and what happened. Hilton was telling him that things had changed while he was asleep, that it had something to do with, "road priority" and that it probably would be after 0800 before we moved out. Hilton went on to say that another thing had changed. They were not bringing our rations and supplies to us, that they were setting up a supply depot outside of town and we were going by and pick them up as we left town. We would have to deal with breakfast the best we could. He said to tell everyone to search their pockets for coffee and crackers, that he knew that everyone carried at least one spare pack of these. He said that they could start that coffee thing now but be careful and not set the place on fire. The way things were going we may be here another week.

I took inventory of my fatigue pants pockets. I found plenty of coffee, one pack of hot chocolate mix, two packs of crackers and one pack of grape jelly. A hard decision to make. Would it be chocolate or coffee? Being breakfast I chose coffee. I brewed it up, pulled out my two packs of crackers and started to break open my pack of jelly. I thought about it for a minute, knowing that the most I would get out of it would be another layer of dirt on my hands, so I returned it to the pocket.

After the gourmet breakfast, we all sat around and smoked our Raleigh and Chelsas. That old bug-a-boo "hurry up and wait" had come to the forefront again. For me the definition of that term had changed. Give me one good buddy and furnish me with K ration and I will spend the duration right here. I was not seeking to be a hero. My motto "you First".

Finally, someone said, "let's go" everyone grabbed their gear and moved out into Burp-Gun Alley. Up to the crossing, we had sprinted across so many times in the last two weeks, onto the trail leading to the supply depot. As we approached it today, there were lots more men around it. They were passing out supplies as the men walked by. Some were placing bandoleers of ammunition around your shoulders, others were placing hand grenades in pocket flap buttonholes, and still others were handing out K rations. After about an hour of walking, we began leaving the city and moving out into the countryside. Everyone seemed glad to be leaving Saarlautern behind. A wave of apprehension rolled over me as we left Saarlautern. I am thinking "good riddance" realizing at the time that I would never be rid of Saarlautern. The rude baptizing, the sounds, the smells and the loss would be with me as long as I drew breath.

The terrain we walked through after leaving Saarlautern, was rolling hills with little forest. There were no homes scattered along the roadway, like back home. Everyone lived in small villages scattered around the landscape. We began to see the first civilians, since leaving France. They stood and watched quietly, most with arms folded across their chest. I wondered what their thoughts and feelings were as they watched the invaders move through, and what was their reaction was a few hours earlier, when they were being abandoned by their defenders. As I looked around at my buddies I could see the change taking place as we moved from Liberators to Invaders.

After about three hours of walking, the weight of the ammo, light breakfast, and the lack of physical exercise the last few weeks began to take its toll on us. I suppose the brass noticed this, they called us to a halt, at 1300 and told us to break out our lunch K ration. That we were having an hour lunch break. The little fires, started from setting K rations boxes on fire in order to heat water for coffee, began to appear up and down the road. Coffee was the obvious choice of drinks for the "grunts." All the other choices were unidentifiable by taste only by reading the label. Today, marked the first of these little fires that we would start, in our march across Germany.

After about an hour's lunch break, we started again on our trudge eastwards. At first the only signs of war was the coming and going of the Jabos. About mid afternoon we began to see the results of the Jabos work. I was amazed at the amount of horse drawn equipment the Germans were using. With the weather improving the Jabos had wrecked havoc among the Germans trying to escape being cut off and trapped in the Saar pocket. There were miles of intermittent destruction of horse drawn equipment and dead horses with some coke burning vehicles. All destroyed in and along the roadside. The scene was reminiscent of World War 1. I was shocked at seeing the German Army, with their blitz-krieg reputation, using horse drawn equipment. Maybe they were running out of fuel. No such luck! Maybe short but not out. We found out later their petroleum burning vehicles had gotten out earlier and most of them had made it safely across the Rhine River. The destruction that we were witness to, seemed to have happened no more than twenty-four hours ago. Some of the vehicles were still smoldering and the horses rear legs where large chunks of meat had been cut from them, still looked fresh. Either the nearby civilians had gathered fresh meat or the German soldiers were running low on rations. In all this carnage I did not see one dead German, I don't know if the enemy took their dead with them or some Grave Registration outfit took care of the dead. I am sure some must have died.

The news coming to us was that the 259th and the 261st was about a half a day ahead of us. They were still chasing the enemy but they would be halted at Neunkirchen for a few days rest and get replacements. We of the 260th would not reach Neunkirchen until sometimes tomorrow, the 22nd.

It was late in the afternoon, on the 21st when we of the 3rd Battalion 260th reached the small town of Sulzbach, where we were to spend the night. This was the first night, of many to come, that we would route the enemy from their homes and take over their beds. At first the griping and pleading of mothers, the crying of babies, the grumbling of the elderly and the barking of dogs would give me a pang of distress. After thinking of the places I had slept getting to this point, and not wanting to come, I not only shrugged it off, I laughed it off. That night I slept on a mattress for the first time since January 8th at Camp Shankes, New York.

I suppose every building in Germany had black out curtains installed in the windows so that not one speck of light could be seen from the outside. We were always warned to make sure the black out curtains were in place whenever we confiscated private homes to be used as billets. Whenever you were outside at night, in Germany the darkness was total, except for the flashes of light coming from wherever the battles were being fought. When standing outside on a clear night in total darkness it was amazing how the stars command your attention when there is nothing else to look at.

The electricity was off in Sulzbach but the plumbing was alright and with the help of a few candles we found in the homes we made it through the first night on the road to wherever.

Getting enough sleep is not a simple thing in a war zone. Beside the high anxiety, there is always the changing of the guards or men on outpost and every movement calls for the password. Your training, combined with the instinct for survival has made an animal out of you.

About daylight the guards and noncoms came around shouting for everyone to get up, that we were moving out towards Neunkirchen in about thirty minutes, using a full thirty-inch step, which should bring us to that fair city in about eight hours. This brought a groan from the men, but when the message that we would be there about five days for a rest, the cheers went up and everyone seemed to pep up. Bathroom facilities was limited. So straddle trenches were dug in the back yards to speed up the process. In about thirty minutes everyone was out in the street for a nose count. We were then told to go by the company kitchen truck, which was parked down the street, and pick up two boxes of K ration each and that we will have a hot meal waiting for us at the end of the day. That brought on another cheer. As we moved out, I noticed the men had a little extra spring in their step. I couldn't help but wonder if it was because of the good news or was it because of the lighting of the load when some of the excess ordinance accidently fell into some of the straddle trenches.

The march toward Neunkirchen was about the same as it was the day before, except there was less evidence along the road of the Jabo's work. The people in the small villages along the way, mostly stood and watched us pass in silence. The few exceptions were from the older ones, probably veterans of WWI. When we asked Grant Weik, our interpreter, what they were saying? He told us they wanted to know why the Americans were invading their country. Made me wonder where they had been since 1933. We arrived in Neunkirchen around 1500. The 259th and the 261st had cleared out the city the day before and moved on to nearby villages to have a few days rest and regroup for the push to the Rhine River.

Arriving in Neunkirchen, we marched right to the heart of the city and the entire 3rd Battalion assembled on the city square. The advance party had done a superb job preparing for our arrival. All the buildings around the city square had been cleared German Civilians and prepared for our use. It took about an hour to make the billets assignment around the Square. The buildings were mostly two and three stories. Most of the stories except the ground floor, were apartments. Everything was at our disposal. We were the conquerors. We used their beds and bed clothes and drank their wine. These are the two most popular items that was available to an Infantry soldier. There was some looting going on but what could a foot soldier carry without throwing something away. He could barely carry his essentials. The most amazing thing about an Infantry platoon is their unselfishness. Everyone understood that their very survival depended on their buddy or buddies. Being unselfish made things run smoother. The leaders understood this and when they pointed out a place that a platoon would be billeted, that the men would work it out among themselves so everyone would be happy or everyone would be unhappy. We all shared. An example would be, if half a squad of men walked into a room with one bed no one would grab the bed and say he was sleeping there tonight. We would take the average bed consisting of cover, mattress and inner springs, break it down and scatter it over the floor and have six men sleeping comfortably within thirty minutes.

Sgt. Hilton, Sgt. Cunningham, Sgt. Rakosi, Weik, a Pennsylvania Dutchman who was our interpreter, Stern and I all shared a room on the second floor overlooking the square. Sgt. Hilton trying to look busy shuffling through some papers, asked Sgt. Cunningham to go and find out where the kitchen truck was located, what time the evening meal would be served and notify all the men in the platoon. The four of us started following Cunningham out the door. Sgt. Hilton noticing that we were all leaving and told Weik to stay with him, he might need him before we returned. He also told Cunningham to inform the squad leaders that no one was to leave the building until time to go to chow. Then after we ate we were to form up in front of our building for further instructions on what to expect while we were in Neunkirchen. We left the building and went straight to Company Headquarters. There we met and talked with 1st/Sgt. Harrell. He told us that we would have a company formation at 1700, before we ate, to get instructions on how we were to conduct ourselves while we were in Neunkirchen. He then pointed out where the kitchen truck was set up. It is about a half block off the city square. He said to make sure that everyone must bring their mess gear. By the time everyone was informed of the procedure we were to take, it was time for the company formation. The first thing that Capt. Batts said is, that he wanted us to know how proud he was of our performance in our initial combat. That we had made him and all the junior officers look good. Then he began talking about the heart breaking loss of our buddies and read off the casualty list, then had one minute of silence for them. He went on to say that we probably would be getting replacements in while we were here and for us to help them all we could. Capt. Batts informed us that we probably would be here for about five days and that there were rules that we must follow while we are here.

First, remember we are at war and we are in the war zone. Anything can happen, remember the Battle of the Bulge, it happened less than ninety days ago. You will be free to move about the area and look things over but do it in groups of no less than four men. Let me remind you of the 'no fraternization rule'. You are not to speak to any civilian, Male or female. Always carry your designated arm with you. That means, the one your M.O.S. calls for, not the one you took off some dead German or your buddies side-arm. The Capt. finished up his speech by warning us that there were lots of bypassed pockets of enemy soldiers out there. Some were trying to get home, some were trying to make it back through the battle line to rejoin their outfits, and there are the fanatics. They're just waiting to make a statistic out of you. Capt. Batts, turning into a mellow mood, told us that he knew that we had heard of a 'last meal' but tonight we were going to have a "first meal." Our first hot meal since entering the fight. He told us that the 65th Division, to show their appreciation for our fine effort in the Saar and Siegfried line battles, has made every effort to make our first hot meal something special, and tomorrow morning for breakfast we are going to have real eggs and real ham, obtained by scrounging every farm in France. This brought a loud cheer from the men.

There is something about the relationship between G.I.'s and fresh eggs that is baffling, even to the army psychologist Coy, especially in a combat zone. Nothing awakes him as quick as the words "fresh eggs for breakfast". The first words that he learns of the country he is in are, "do you have eggs". He will trade anything he has for an egg. My theory on this is, there is so much "stuff" coming down from the top that a Grunt must accept without question, even to the point of their pissing on your leg and telling you it's raining. The one thing he can rebel against, without consequences, is that every tin can that contains some yellow goo and has "eggs" written across the can, does not contain eggs. And he will prove his point by swapping the farmers daughter, the can of goo, a chocolate bar, a pack of Raleighs and throw in a pack of Chelsas for one egg.

We were informed that we would have a company formation at 0700 tomorrow morning at this same spot. We were then dismissed and told to enjoy. As we moved closer to the mess tent, the smell got better. The rumor was that we were having steak. There were two serving lines moving through the mess tent. As I moved inside the tent I could see the steaks stacked in large pans at the far end of the tent. It reminded me of the last time I had witnessed this scene back at Camp Lucky Strike in the transit mess. As we moved through the chow line, we first came to the red beets, then the green beans, followed by mashed white potatoes with brown gravy, an eight ounce New York cut placed on the potatoes and gravy and topped off with a hunk of french bread. All this balanced on your mess kit in one hand, a cup of hot coffee in the other hand, a M1 rifle slung over your shoulder and a cartridge belt containing five pounds of lead around your waist. With it threatening to slide over your ever thinning hips and trip you face down into the gravy. Either that or your buddy recognizing your peril and comes to the rescue. You find the nearest curbside to sit down, place your coffee in the street, replace etiquette with expediency. Then grasp your steak with one hand, the spoon in the other and get after it. It was a memorable meal. After dipping our mess gear in garbage cans filled with cleaning and disinfectant liquids, we returned to our Quarters in the gathering of darkness. We managed to find some candles, which was not a difficult task because they were a necessity for the German people due to the constant blackouts they had to endure. Sgt. Hilton told Cunningham to bring the platoon's squad leaders in. He had some instructions to pass on to the men before they retired for the night. When they arrived Hilton instructed them that there would be a company forma tion at 0700 tomorrow morning and that the powers that be are working on arrangements for everyone to get a bath and clean clothes tomorrow. They will know and will be able to give instructions on how to proceed at the 0700 formation. I tried to remember when I had taken my last bath. I couldn't remember, but when I unrolled my bed roll to get ready to sleep, I could tell by the smell of the dirty socks, it had been too long.

With the excitement of the day's happenings we did not realize how tired we were, until we got still and started discussing the day's events and the probabilities of tomorrow's. It did not take long for us to incorporate our bedrolls with the German bedding and fall asleep.

I was awakened shortly after daylight from the sounds of a bell and someone shouting. It was coming from toward the town square. I pulled back the blackout curtain and there standing in the town square was a man dressed like a Plymouth colony pilgrim with a school bell in one hand and a paper in the other. He was ringing the bell and shouting to the top of his voice. By now everyone in the room was awake and over by the windows pulling back blinds and opening them. I asked what the hell was going on with the man? Grant Weik, our interpreter, listened for a few seconds and told us the man was the town Crier and was reporting the latest news. He told us the Crier said that Patton's third army had crossed the Rhine River last evening, at about 2900 hrs. in the vicinity of Oppenheim. Parts of two Divisions were already across, but they were under heavy counter-attack by the troops of the Fatherland. The Town Crier, I had read about them but this was my first time to receive the news via crier. We did not have too many of them in Mississippi.

The news that the Third Army had crossed the Rhine, caused a little excitement among the men. If the news was correct, that meant the front line was some seventy five miles in front of us. This sure made me feel better. I was hoping the war would be over before we caught up to the front lines again.

At company formation everyone was upbeat. Word had gotten around about the Rhine crossing and when Capt. Batts told us he had some good news for us this morning, there was a lusty cheer from the men. He informed us that the Third Army had crossed the Rhine River at 2200 last evening and that the majority of the 5th and 90th Divisions are on the east bank of the Rhine this morning. After the cheering, Capt. Batts told us not to read too much into this good news, that knowing Patton, he probably has half the German Army cut off, left on the west bank for us to clean up. More good news, we were all getting a bath and clean clothes today. It seems the Regiment had found showers in an abandoned factory still in working order and that they would be able to shower about a platoon at a time. "I" Company was scheduled to shower around 1400. Capt. Batts told us that after lunch, which was to be at 1200, that we would have a company formation at 1300 and that everyone was to report with all their equipment and clothing. The truck with our duffel bags, that we had not seen since France, would meet us at the shower site with a change of clothes. This brought a cheer from the men. He went on to tell us he had some bad news for us this morning, that they could not come up with enough fresh eggs for breakfast this morning and they had to mix some powdered eggs with them and scramble them together. He thought we would not be able to tell there was a little powder mixed in. This brought out the Bronx cheer. We were told that after breakfast we could look the town over and to remember our previous instructions concerning our movements. We were then dismissed for breakfast. The eggs were great along with the steak, bacon and hashbrowns.

After breakfast we decided to look the town over, except for the architecture, it looked like an army base in the states. There were G.I.s and equipment of all descriptions everywhere, waiting on road priority to move toward the Rhine River. There were a few German civilians standing around seemingly awestruck by the vast amount of equipment that had moved up so quickly With mostly G.I.s and army gear to look at. We became bored quickly and the five of us, Stern, Weik, Cunningham, Rakosi, and I decided to go back to our Quarters and clean equipment, maybe write letters home or take a nap. When we arrived back at our room Sgt. Hilton was still fooling around with papers and writing. We asked him what was going on, he answered that he was changing his will. His tone of voice suggested that we should have known what he was doing. The five of us began giving each other those sideways looks, but said nothing.

I laid down to get a short nap before lunch but couldn't go to sleep. I kept thinking about Sgt. Hilton's strange behavior and what effect it might have on the platoon. Especially me, since I was the platoon runner and most of the duties would come from his direct orders. As we started gathering up our dirty clothes and rolling them into our bedroll, to have them ready to go after lunch. I spoke to Cunningham about my concerns. He told me not to worry, that he was being monitored and that his days were numbered.

After lunch everyone retrieved their bedrolls and returned to the town square for company formation. We were told that we would march to the shower location which was less than a mile away and that when we arrived there the trucks with our duffel bags, which we had not seen since France, would be there. When we arrive at the location everyone is to remain in formation, the duffel bags will be unloaded from the trucks and your name will be read aloud from each bag, when your name is read out secure your duffel bag and return to formation. You will then be given further instructions. We were then asked that questionable question, "is everybody happy?" The yea's and nay's were evenly split. On the way to the factory we met M Company returning they all looked "spick and span" with their clean shaven faces and clean clothes. They shouted their greetings as they went by but I noticed some turning up their noses and sniffing the air as we went by.

When we arrived at the factory there were three trucks from the 65th. Quartermaster Company along with six men waiting for us. As soon as we came to a halt, three men started unloading bags from the trucks and the other three began reading names aloud, from the duffel bags. Each man secured his bag as his name was called and returned to the ranks. After the unloading they asked if everyone had a bag, there was no response.

As they called out the names written on the duffle bags, I kept waiting for the names of our friends, who were no longer with us to be read off, but it never happened. In less than a week each one of these men had become a statistic to the Army. It was now up to his buddies and family to keep his memory alive.

The trucks pulled away. We began getting instructions on how we were to proceed in obtaining our showers. We were going in one platoon at a time, first, second, third, then weapons. Each platoon would be given about twenty minutes to finish the process, so we must pay close attention to the instructions we will be receiving once inside and no griping about the water temperature, it will not change. Sgt. Harrell instructed the first platoon to gather all their gear and enter the building, through the double doors, which he pointed out. The rest of us were told to relax. Sure enough, after about twenty minutes the men from the first platoon started returning. I noticed that the first men coming back were all the younger men. This puzzle was solved when all of the older men came out griping about having to shave in cold water. The second platoon took their turn, then it was time for us of the third to enter the doors. Going through the doors we entered into a large room with tables, it appeared to be a former dining room. We were told to place our duffel bag and bedroll onto the tables, take out of the duffle bag all the clean clothes, plus the barracks bag. Take all dirty clothes from your bedroll and place in the barracks bag, now take off all your dirty clothes and place them in the barracks bag. Do not place your field jacket into the barracks bag, we do not have clean jackets. Take the barracks bag and place it back into the duffel bag and close it. Now all you people that intend to shave, bring your razor, everyone follow me. We entered a large room which had a network of pipes overhead, on the right wall a shelf that ran the full length of the wall, and above the shelf there was a stainless steel mirror that also ran the full length. Beneath the shelf was a trough that had water faucets about three feet apart. On the left wall hung a series of containers filled with liquid soap. After we were inside we were told that this factory used slave labor and this was where they showered after working a twelve hour shift, seven days a week. We were then instructed to move to the right side of the room and place our shaving gear on the shelf. Then move to the center of the room where the showers will be turned on to wet us down. We were to move along the wall with the soap containers and soap ourselves down. Then move back into the showers and rinse off. Then you will proceed to where you left your shaving gear and shave. We were told there would be no time for soaking and as soon as we had shaved, move through the doors at the rear of the room into the drying room. There we would find towels, we were to dry off and leave the towels in the drying room. Then move through the doors on our right, which will take us back into the room where we had left our clothes. We were to dress as quickly as possible then take all our gear back outside, stack our duffel bag where instructed and fall back in rank. The whole process took about twenty five minutes I think the cold water was part of the plan to speed up the action. After the weapons platoon finished their showers it was around 1500. We marched back to the company quarters. We were told that chow would be served at 1700 and the next company formation would be at 6700 tomorrow morning the 24th of March. Before dismissing the company, Capt. Batts told us that Sgt. Harrell had some good news for us. Sgt. Harrell stepped up and yelled that the U.S. Mail had finally caught up with the 65th Division. This brought a big cheer from the men. He informed us that the Company Clerk was on the way over with the mail. While waiting, I tried to remember the last time we had "Mail Call." I believe it was at Lucky Strike. 1st Sgt. was still talking, telling us that we would have the rest of the day off to eat chow, read and answer our mail. Sgt. Harrell was still talking when the Company and Mail Clerks drove up in a jeep and each took a mail bag from the rear seat. The cheers drowned out the 1st Sgt.'s voice, he waved and walked away.

If one wishes to witness the full range of human emotions in a short period of time, they could do no better than to attend a mail call of an Infantry Co. in a combat zone. They go from object disappointment to the pinnacle of glee. Me, being drafted out of high school, leaving no lover behind, having only my family to correspond with and averaging about one letter a month from my Mama. I had plenty of time to observe the spectacle of "Mail Call." Up front would be the men that their wives or girlfriends wrote them everyday. They had that confused look of "what am I going to do with all these letters. I still have last months mail that I'm lugging around." You have the ones that receive pictures of their new born baby, that they have never seen. They want everyone to look at it and you feed their ego by telling him that it looks exactly like him and he smiles. There are the ones that just walk away when they start mail call. They don't write and they do not receive mail and could care less. Then there are the ones I called "neck stretchers" they stood in the crowd stretching their necks, listening for their names to be called, because someone back home promised them they would write everyday. After mail call they would walk by the mail clerk and ask them if that was all, sometimes even picking up the mail bag and looking inside to make sure their letter was not overlooked. Then there was the occasional, "Dear John" this is when I would walk away. This called for the Chaplain's expertise.

After mail call most of the men returned to their living quarters to read and answer mail. The rest cleaned and oiled equipment or just sat and waited for chow, which was at 1700. The rumor around the mess tent was that we were moving out the next day, moving toward the Rhine. Our source of information was the Company cooks, who knew that tomorrow morning would be our last hot meal for a while. They would be packing their equipment after breakfast on the 24th of March and start moving east. If you wanted to know what was going on or about to happen within the Company one would try to get information from the Company clerks or cooks. They were always the first to know. The powers that be seemed to take delight in surprising the "grunts" in what was about to take place.

I suppose they didn't want to give us too much time to analyze the conditions, everything must be automatic, you may not learn from the mistakes but others will. Keep the replacements coming.

When we awoke on the morning of the 24th and looked outside the weather had changed. It was very cold and a light rain was falling. The prediction was for sleet and snow later in the day. Just what we needed while on the move. Winter holds a firm grip on this part of Germany until about mid-April.

At the Company formation on March 24th, at 0700 Capt. Batts told us to listen up. He had a lot of information for us to digest this morning. First off General Montgomery's Ninth Army crossed the Rhine River last evening. This morning he has two divisions across heading east. The Third Army has finished building a pontoon bridge over the Rhine at Oppenheim and was flooding the east bank with men and materials. Capt. Batts went on, telling us, even as he was speaking, we were assembling the largest Airborne operation ever assembled. It is even larger than D-Day, it was to be dropped behind enemy lines east of the Rhine. In fact, at this very moment the American 17th Airborne Division and the British 6th should be falling out of the sky onto the enemy. We were told the weather was better along the Rhine. The troops were getting lots of Air Force support, also we would be moving out today heading for the Rhine River crossings near Mainz and Oppenheim. There we will join in the fight to bring an end to what the Germans had started. We were told that we would start out today being transported by trucks, the time of leaving and the progress we make will be determined by road priority. There is lots of traffic moving east at this time and we feel sure that after we get started we will be moving throughout the night and at least through tomorrow. Also we are getting six replacements coming into the company today. There will be two each for the first, second and third platoons. Welcome them and help them out as much as possible. Third platoon's assignments were both from Kentucky. One of them had the last name "Stamms, the other one's name was hard to pronounce, so we called him "Kentucky." Still can't "remember his name. We were dismissed to eat breakfast and told that after we ate, that we were to remain in our quarters until we got the word to move out.

Breakfast was like a last meal, in quantity but not in quality. We received generous portions of things that we figured the cooks were trying to get rid of because of spoilage, or they were making room on the kitchen truck for more important things. There was an abundance of powdered eggs, bacon that was bordering on rancid and a failed attempt at making hashbrown potatoes all served with stale bread and tepid coffee. Most of which ended up in the garbage cans. After cleaning our mess gear, we were given a twenty four hour supply of K-rations. After receiving the K-rations and conversing with each other, we changed our minds on why we had the bad breakfast. We came to the conclusion that it was a psychological plot to make us appreciate the K-rations more.

After returning to our quarters, everyone from the assistant squad leader on up kept repeating for the men to have everything ready and able to move out on a moment's notice. After hearing this for about four hours, I came to the conclusion that they like to hear their voices giving orders. Surely they know that it only takes a foot soldier five seconds to pick up his battle gear.

Noon came, still no word to move out. We ate our lunch K-ration, it was better than breakfast. Everyone kept going to the windows overlooking the town square and watching for any activity that might indicate our moving out. There was none. The only movement was a fine misty rain being pushed across the square by a cold north east wind. Everyone had their raincoat pushed down behind their cartridge belt, training and experience had taught us. Whether riding on an open six-by, walking, or just sitting in a foxhole with a cold rain falling, you must have that raincoat on with the collar turned up underneath the steel pot that is on your head or die a slow agonizing death. The WW2 steel helmet was not only useful for misdirecting debris and shell fragments, it could be used as a wash basin or a roof, especially for us pinheads.

It was around 1500 before the word came for the Company to form a line at the usual place on the town square. There was no griping about having to wait. It was amazing how the perception of the term, "hurry up and wait" had changed since arriving at the war zone. Most of the men would prefer sitting here until the end of the war.

After they the "present and accounted for" routine was over, Capt. Batts gave a short speech welcoming the replacements. I glanced at our two and they didn't seem to be enjoying the reception speech too much. We were then marched off to what they called a staging area, which was only about five blocks away. At the staging area, there were G.I. trucks of every description. They were mostly six-bys, some with canvas covers. There were artillery weapon carriers, some pulling guns and some pulling trailers. We were told that we were the last of the 260th to board the trucks. That the 1st and 2nd Battalions had already moved out. This bit of news didn't hurt my feelings. The more people between me and the front line the better I liked it.

"I" Company was the last of the 260th to load. We loaded by the numbers, 1st Platoon, 2nd Platoon, 3rd Platoon and then the Weapons Platoon. The Weapons Platoon due to their heavier equipment, rode on the artillery trucks. I found out later that the artillery trucks are not the best mode of transportation for a foot soldier. Those big gun boys owned those trucks and they had their territory staked out. They allowed us "hitch-hikers" only twelve square inches of space while allowing themselves six square feet. They could carry more loot on one truck, than our whole company could carry.

Sgt. Hilton, Sgt. Smith and Sgt. Cunningham finished supervising the loading of our platoon. Sgt. Cunningham motioned for me to follow him. The four of us moved to the next truck in line. I couldn't believe it! It was our own company's kitchen truck. We crawled up into the back of the truck. It contained pots, pans, two field stoves, and two cooks. Plenty of room for everyone to stretch out their legs. Which was always a problem when spending long hours riding in Army trucks. I asked Cunningham how he managed to get us this private limousine. He laughed that quick laugh of his and told me not to ask silly questions.

It was after 1700 hrs. and it was getting dark. We decided to break out the K-rations and have dinner before total darkness came. Experience had taught us that opening cans in the dark could get a man a Purple Heart medal. Worse yet, one could not tell what the hell he was eating. All the smells around you masked the smell coming from the can. The cooks had brought a can of water aboard, so we did not have to tap our canteens for water which was to mix the lemon powder into.

In the cold misty rain, darkness came quickly and with darkness comes the end of smoking and about an hour after no smoking, the griping and bellyaching started up. Everyone's ears, from "those fools at the drafting board" right through to "those sons of bitch" Nazis, had to be burning. After assigning blame for their predicament, everyone turned to the weather, God and why this had been the worst winter in the history of mankind. Why we have been sitting here in the rain and have not moved one inch since we loaded three hours ago. The last statement could be translated to "I need a cigarette". It wasn't only the smokers having problems, some of the non-smokers had other things going on inside their heads. Our own Sgt. Hilton kept asking us what time we thought we would get home and do we think everyone will be up when we arrive. Every time he repeated this, Sgt. Cunningham would elbow me in the ribs.

Finally, everyone seemed to settle down and was trying to get a little sleep. You could tell by some deep breathing and an occasional snort that we were surrounded by total darkness. With all the equipment and supplies on the kitchen truck there was not a lot of room left for the four of us to stretch out our legs. After sitting on the truck for about three hours and not moving, we decided to try and work out a system for sleeping. We decided to lie on the floor of the truck with all our heads in the same direction, so that we would not be kicking each other in the face with those combat boots. We would use our bedrolls for pillows. Although our bedrolls contained a blanket you never unrolled it under extreme conditions at night unless it was a matter of life or death. To do so you would subject yourself to the loss of dry underwear, socks, shaving gear, toothbrush and just maybe some valuable loot. The four of us sleeping on the truck floor was an example the cooperation and respect that was imperative for the men in the Infantry if they were to survive. Sleeping close together to keep warm, with a rifle butt between your knees, the muzzle sticking up by your head and when one man turns everyone turns automatically. There was no individualism among the enlisted men in the Infantry. This respect and loyalty is what brings smiles and tears to old buddies faces when they meet. Even though it may have been decades since the last meeting.

About the time we got situated in the floor of the truck, the truck engine started up. We moved slowly forward. I punched Cunningham and asked him what time it was. He had been issued one of those G.I. watches with a luminous dial. He slowly pulled his arm up and told me it was 2300. It had been over six hours since we had boarded the trucks.

The first leg of our journey was not too far, about a hundred yards. Then another hour of waiting. This stop and go went on all night. I give credit to the truck drivers for doing an outstanding job. How they managed to sit under the steering wheel, watching that small (black out light) on the back of the truck in front of them, move when he moved and stop when he stopped. All night without going to sleep or being hypnotized. Finally, someone opened the canvas at the rear of the truck and looked outside. I was half asleep, but I heard them theorize that it would be daylight in a few minutes and we would be able to make coffee and smoke. This jerked everyone awake from their hallucinatory state. Everyone started going through their pockets, looking for coffee powder and cigarettes. I looked out the back of the truck, sure enough it was almost daylight. The weather was still cold and misty. As I looked out at our men who were riding on the artillery behind us, I felt a small pain of guilt run through me. They were sitting everywhere on the open trucks, hunkered down inside their raincoats, with their heads pushed up so far into their helmets you could not see their eyes. I did notice one thing, those Artillery boys didn't have as much space as they had when we started out.

The trucks came to a halt and everyone started jumping off the trucks. They began opening K-ration boxes, pulling out the goodies from them, and using the wax coated boxes to start a fire. They wanted to warm water for making coffee and to heat that little can of eggs that was the centerpiece of the breakfast K-ration. No one seemed to know how far we had traveled during the night. The rumor was about ten miles, that sounded good to me. We had one hundred miles to the Rhine, maybe the war will be over before we get there.

Words were filtering down about the massive Airborne operation that had taken place the day before and it was reported to be a success. It had not been a Sunday "walk in the park." The Glider operation seemed to have gone rather badly and the entire drop had met strong resistance. This was not good news to us. Our hopes that the end was near were dampened. I could feel that old bug-a-boo returning to the pit of my stomach. Oh well, we are still a hundred miles from the main action and the pace is slow.

After breakfast, most everyone took their trenching tool and spread out over the countryside, answering natures call. The terrain we were moving through was rather rugged high hills and some moderately deep valleys.

Our destination today was rumored to be the city of Kaiserslautern, which was about thirty-five miles away. It was not too far away, but the retreating German Army had adopted a scorched earth policy and had destroyed all the bridges behind them. Our Engineers were a busy group, building and repairing bridges, making detours, helping trucks and equipment over soft ground. The only signs of war, was that occasionally we would come upon a stretch of road containing destroyed and burned up German Army trucks and equipment. It was evidence that the Jabos had been there. Around noon we moved onto a wide four lane highway. Voices were saying that this was the famous German Autobahn. I suppose it was but it made a great parking lot. Only two lanes were moving, one east and one west. The other two were filled with parked U.S. military vehicles of every description carrying U.S. military equipment of every description. There were guns, tanks, pontoons, and all types of boats. All of these vehicles were parked and headed east. As we moved, there were lots of banter going on between us and the men with the equipment convoy. We questioned them about what outfits they belonged to. We found out there was every organization represented there. Some that we had heard of and some that we had not. Even the Navy was there. They told us they had been sitting there for three days and that they were getting restless. We informed them that we would trade places with them but they refused. We told them to hang on a few more days, that we were going up front and get things moving again. After traveling the Autobahn for several miles, we left it and again were traveling on a two lane road.

Around 1300 the convoy stopped for a break and to open up that lunch K-ration box. As soon as the men hit the ground those little fires started popping up. They were heating water for coffee. Nothing does it like a cigarette and a hot cup of coffee. It helps a man relax and the coffee helps to keep your pipes open after eating those cheese and crackers that came in the lunch K-rations. After lunch everyone was motioned back onto the trucks. While the present and accounted for routine was going on, Sgt. Cunningham noticed Sgt. Hilton standing alone in a field about two hundred yards away. Sgt. Cunningham beckoned him to come forward, that we were ready to move. Sgt. Hilton waved and kept standing there. Finally, Cunningham went over to where he was standing. They seemed to be discussing something for a minute, then they both returned to the truck. After Sgt. Hilton got aboard Sgt. Cunningham motioned me to come around to the front of the truck. When I asked him what was going on with Sgt. Hilton, Cunningham told me that Hilton had informed him that he was tired of riding the truck and was waiting on a trolley. Cunningham told me that he was going down to report the platoon was ready to move out, and that he was going to inform Capt. Batts of the incident with Sgt. Hilton. When Cunningham returned, Sgt. Smith and I met him at the front of truck and asked him what was Capt. Batts reaction to Sgt. Hilton's odd behavior? Sgt. Cunningham informed us that Capt. Batts told him to get ready to take over the platoon. By tomorrow this time he would be the leader of the Third Platoon, Sgt. Smith would take his position as Platoon Guide, and Sgt. Rakosi would take over Sgt. Smith's squad. Cunningham told Smith and me not to tell the men what was about to take place. To do so could complicate the plan.

We arrived at the city of Kaiserlautern around 1800 on March 25th. The trucks carrying "I" Company pulled into a nice residential neighborhood with huge homes. The men of "I" Company were told to unload into the street with all their equipment and stand clear so the trucks could move out. The company was formed up in the street and to be at rest while the Officers and Non-Coms evacuated the residents from the buildings. As we stood outside we could hear the Officers and Non-Coms inside telling the residents that they had five minutes to clear out of the buildings and find another place to sleep tonight. These orders were followed by the sounds of dogs barking, baby's crying, and loud voices of women, some begging, some cursing, and some crying. The women emerged shortly, all pulling one of those small wooden wheel wagons that everyone one in Germany seemed to own. The wagons were filled with bedclothes, crying children, and most were followed by a dog on a leash. As they passed by, there was growling from our men as well as from the dogs. After spending twenty-four hours on the trucks, we were unable to straighten out our legs, and were not in any mood to show sympathy for any German, no matter what the gender or age. After a short Company meeting, it was decided that the homes were large enough that each home could accommodate a platoon. "I" Company ended up with five houses, one for each platoon and one for the men of Company Headquarters. Before dismissing the Company, Capt. Batts warned us again that although we were still quite a few miles from the front, that there was still danger from the pockets of the German Army that had been bypassed. Especially the SS and the German Youth organization, that there had been reports of suicide attacks by these groups. He told us, "Everyone was confined to their Quarters until departure time early tomorrow morning. We would be notified of the exact time later and that we had better get all the sleep that we could. He did not know when we would get a chance to rest after tonight and he did not know if we would leave here tomorrow riding or walking. Try not to mess up your host's belongings and home". He dismissed us and told all the platoon leaders that he wanted to meet with them at his Quarters after they got the men settled down. Sgt. Hilton picked out a private bedroom and after warning everyone not to enter his bedroom, he and Cunningham left for the Captain's Quarters to be briefed on what tomorrow's plans were. They returned a short time later. Hilton asked Cunningham if he remembered what Capt. Batts had told them? And Cunningham said "he had". Hilton said good night then, and went into his room. Cunningham looked at me and gave a wink. I knew then that something was going on that I did not want to know about, at this time. Shortly afterwards, a runner came over from the Company Headquarters building and informed Cunningham that Capt. Batts said that there was plenty of room over at their building. If he was strapped for room he could bring a couple of men and spend the night in the Headquarters Building. I asked Cunningham if I should inform Hilton that I was going but he said no.

On the way over to the Headquarters building, Cunningham confided in me that the plan is to relieve Sgt. Hilton of his command of the Third Platoon. Rather than an attempt at removing him for medical reasons, which was obvious, the plan was to try and remove him for "Dereliction of Duty." This was usually more simple and quicker than for medical problems. His medical condition could be addressed after his dismissal. The plan was simple, Cunningham had always accepted the transfer of Sgt. Hilton's obligations onto him without question. This action had become very prevalent since Cunningham attended all of the briefings. Sgt. Hilton lately had failed to issue any directive to anyone in the Platoon leaving everything up to Cunningham. At the briefing, the platoon leaders had been told to place guards at the doors of the sleeping quarters and to have the men in the street ready to board trucks at 0600 tomorrow morning, on March 26th. Sure enough at 0600 when Capt. Batts, Headquarters personnel, Cunningham, and I arrived at the assembly point all the Company was waiting in the street with the exception of the Third Platoon. We walked straight to the door of the Third Platoon's billet. There was no guard on the door. Capt. Batts knocked on the door, but there was no answer. Capt. Batts told Cunningham to knock and to call out to Hilton. Finally a face appeared at the door, Cunningham asked him where Sgt. Hilton was. He said he did not know. Then Cunningham instructed him to bring his squad leader to the door. Sgt. Kendoll appeared at the door and Cunningham told him to get the men up and outside, that we were late already, and to wake Sgt. Hilton and bring him to the door. A short time later Sgt. Hilton appeared at the door wanting to know what was going on. Capt. Batts ask him did he not know that we were to leave at 0600 this morning. Hilton answered in the affirmative. Capt. Batts asked him why he did not have the men ready to go. He answered that he thought Cunningham would have them ready. Capt. Batts asked him if he had instructed Cunningham to have the men ready to go at 0600 and to place guards outside the door. Hilton answered that he had not, but Cunningham was at the briefing the evening before and knew what had to be done. Capt. Batts then informed Hilton that he was the platoon leader and that it was entirely his responsibility to see that orders and instructions pertaining to his platoon would be carried out. Since this was obviously not the case last night, he was relieving him of his command of the

Third Platoon because of his dereliction of his duties. He then instructed Sgt. Cunningham to take charge of the platoon, get them outside and onto the trucks as quick as possible. He then got on the radio and called the M.P.'s and informed them of the situation. They arrived shortly and took charge of Sgt. Hilton. They escorted him back into the house to take charge of his weapon, equipment, and then headed for the Provost Marshal, who would review the situation and take the necessary action. As the jeep pulled away from the curb, carrying Sgt. Hilton and the two M.P.'s, Sgt. Hilton turned, smiled, and waved. That was the last time I saw or heard from him. I often wondered who outsmarted who that day.

The loading procedure was the same as the day before, with the exception of the artillery trucks. They were no longer with us. Taking their place were three six-bys. This improved the morale of the men that had been riding with the artillery.

Cunningham, Smith and I returned to our places on the kitchen truck. There were just the three of us now. A wave of nostalgia swept over me. It's hard watching a buddy go, regardless of the circumstances. I was sure Cunningham and Smith were sharing my feelings. When I glanced at them, they were staring at their feet. Finally, Smith broke the silence and said that he thought Hilton was better off now and probably would end up in the hospital for a short time and be home ahead of us. I agreed with Smith and went on to say that I thought all of us were better off. Then I asked Cunningham if he realized that he was the man now? He answered in the affirmative and said that he thought that he had already proven he could do the job. Smith and I agreed with him and that we knew that the rest of the men in the platoon felt the same way we did.

After the discussion we felt better about the situation and began observing the countryside as we passed by. We were traveling along a two lane road that traversed small villages every few miles. The people in the villages all looked the same, most of the elderly stood with arms folded across their chest and with a solemn look on their faces. The young children stood in front, some making half hearted waves to our troops, then looking back at their elders as if they had done something wrong. At first we moved along at a pretty fast pace, heading right into a strong east wind that seemed to be blowing out of Siberia. The three of us on the kitchen truck were lucky, we were on one of the few trucks that had a canvas cover. As I looked out over the troops in the open trucks, I could see them all hunkered down with their steel helmets pointing into the wind and I felt a little guilty. Then I remembered that line about "there, but for the grace of God" and I felt much better.

I glanced at the two cooks that were riding with us. They had all kinds of blankets that they had confiscated. They wrapped themselves in them and were snoring away. Why in the hell did I not go to cook and bakery school? I laid down on the floor of the truck and tried to sleep, but all I managed to do was hallucinate.

Around noon the trucks slowed down to a crawl. We had caught up with all the traffic heading for the Rhine River crossings. Our trucks pulled over and stopped. Word came down that all of "I" Company would unload with all their gear and move to the right side of the road. Capt. Batts came back and called the company into formation. He informed us that we were going to walk for a while. There was not to much opposition to this. I think all the men were ready to walk and maybe warm up some. He told us that the trucks were doing shuttle work and were returning to bring up more of the 260th. He said that we would take a break, have lunch, then we would start walking east, a column on each side of the road. He went on to say that he did not know, as of now, where we would be spending the night. Capt. Batts informed us that while we had lunch he would be meeting with the Battalion Executive officer and find out more about what our orders were. It was around 1330 before Capt. Batts returned and gathered the company together. First, he informed the men of the change made in leadership of the Third Platoon. Due to a medical problem Sgt. Hilton would no longer be with us and that Sgt. Ellsworth L. Cunningham would be the platoon leader of the Third Platoon. Capt. Batts went on to say that due to terrific traffic jams caused by movement of men and equipment toward the Rhine River crossings, that our movement would be by foot on secondary roads. These roads will only be able to accommodate men and light vehicles. He told us we were going to form up and walk, a column on each side of the road that we are now on. About a half of a mile down we will turn northeast onto a secondary road. About five miles down this road will be a village where we will spend the night: The village has already been cleared of civilians. Troops spent the night there last night. Tomorrow morning around 1700 we will leave this village on foot and head for Mabach. A town we will remain in until it is our turn to cross the Rhine River. Remember you are in the enemies homeland and there have been lots of enemy troops bypassed. So always be on the "alert." As we moved along the jammed up highway, we asked the men how long they had been sitting and waiting? They said they had not moved in five hours. They told us that they were some Tank Destroyer outfit and had been attached to the 70th Division. We figured then that we must be on the southern flank of the 3rd Army.

The road we turned on was not much more than six feet wide. It could barely accommodate a jeep. It was cut into the earth and in some places the banks were ten feet high. With trees growing along the banks, it sometimes appeared that you were traveling through a tunnel. This road had to date back to the middle ages. It was cut into the earth by millions of horse drawn vehicles and men on horseback. The Gothic Architecture of the churches in the few villages, one could imagine knights traveling here and wonder about the legions of soldiers that had passed this way and would we be the last.

We arrived at a small town late in the afternoon. There was some signs that there had been some fighting inside the town. There was considerable damage to the western part of it. There were no civilians visible. The town seemed deserted, except for a small group of the Third Battalion's advanced party, who met us and pointed out where our sleeping quarters would be. The best that could be said about our assigned billets, was that they kept you out of the wind and dry. The town was completely void of any utilities, plus the troops that had spent the night before there, were sloppy housekeepers. There were K and C ration cans scattered everywhere and they had forgotten to shovel earth back into their straddle trenches they had made in the backyards. This made it dangerous for the night people, so we had to dig our trenches in the front yard. Due to the approaching darkness, the guards and outpost assignments had to be made ahead of anything else. It was always better to get your orientation while daylight. We were warned to go easy on our meal rations tonight, that the supply and kitchen trucks were caught up in the traffic jam and we may have to walk some distance tomorrow before making contact with our supplies. This bit of good news started everyone to taking inventory.

As I was staking out my claim to a spot on the floor of our new found home, Cunningham came into the building calling out Stern and my names. He informed us that he had one more outpost assignment to make and that he wanted Stern and me to have it since it had been several days since we had worked together and felt that he should give us a chance to become acquainted again. Cunningham took Stern and me to a rather small out building that appeared to have been some sort of arms and ammo. storage facility for the Germans. There were broken up rifles and rifle ammunition scattered about. Lots of the ammunition had wooden projectiles. Stern picked up one of the wood bullets and wondered aloud, how it would feel to have this splinter stuck in your ass. Stern and I did not agree with Cunningham's assessment of the situation, but said nothing until he was finished with his instructions and was out of ear shot. Cunningham had told us that our outpost was a "listening post" that we would have a phone set up for us shortly. One of us was to be awake at all times and were to report any unusual sounds and activity to Company Headquarters where someone will take your call. I am thinking what sounds emanating from the heart of the Rhineland would seem unusual to a kid from Brooklyn and a farm boy from Mississippi? He told us we should go outside, eat our K's, make some coffee and smoke before total darkness sets in. And another thing, check your water supply in your canteen, there is no water in this town and we don't know where the next water will come from. So you may want to save a little for tomorrow's coffee. Remember no smoking or you just might have some of those splinters that you were speaking of in both your asses. The gun powder that is strewn around inside the building has the same properties as gasoline.

While Stern and I were smoking and drinking coffee, the communications people ran a line and placed a phone inside the building. This made us feel better. At least we did not feel isolated. After the telephone was installed, Stern and I moved inside the building and unrolled our bedrolls. Night was coming fast so we moved outside for one last cigarette. It was cold and the sky was overcast. We moved back inside the building and closed the door. The darkness was total, even though there were two small windows, the darkness was so total inside and out, so that you could not tell where the windows were when looking around. We fumbled around and finally found the phone and placed it so that we could find it if we needed to.

It was cold and getting colder. The room was bare, you sat on the cement floor or you stood. There is nothing colder than a cement floor. No amount of sitting or lying will warm a spot. Stern and I discussed how we could best handle our duties under the conditions we faced. Our decision was to take both our bedrolls and combine them, so that one man could sleep while the other stood guard. Our theory was that the man standing guard would be too cold to fall asleep and the man resting would be warm enough to sleep. Our only decision now was, how long the tour of duty would be. We decided on four hours, but if the cold became unbearable, the man standing guard would wake the other and exchange places.

Stern and I picked up our conversation where we had left off at Saarlautern. We were cursing our luck for ending up in the Infantry. Why were we drafted right out of high school and before we developed some special skill like shooting really big guns while someone up front told you where to shoot. It doesn't matter about short rounds, there are plenty more where they came from.

Around 2100 Stern and I decided we had better get started with our plan if we were to get any sleep. I would stand guard first and try to make it until 0100. I started my watch off by sitting on the floor with my back against the wall. It was not long before Stern was breathing deeply. A short time later the sound of the gongs from the many clocks in the villages around us marked the half hour. Within one minute at least a dozen clocks had told me it was 2130 hrs. The clocks were the only positive thing we had going for us. We P.F.C.'s were not issued watches with illuminating dials and the conditions we were operating under in this building, I didn't dare crawl under a blanket and strike a match to check the time. As I sat against the wall, I began to lose the feelings in my buttock and legs. At first I told myself that I would wait until the clocks struck 2300, then I would stand for a while. I soon changed my mind, fearing if I waited I may not be able to stand. Using my rifle for support I slowly worked my way up the wall to a standing position. Just as I arrived, the bells started their eleven gongs for 2300 hrs. Its not easy keeping your balance when standing in total darkness. I began sliding along the wall feeling for the lone window that I knew was nearby. I finally found it and hooked my elbow over the sill. This helped tremendously, not only did it help me to keep my balance but it took some of the weight off my feet.

Standing in darkness with only your imagination to work with, time moves very slowly. There were no distractions with sights or sounds, except the slow rhythmic breathing of Stern. So you work with what you have. You wonder why the sounds of breathing is so different when sleeping, than it is when you are awake. I understand snoring. Why is this deep breathing during sleep so not the same as when you are awake? It's all involuntary. When you are awake, I suppose your breathing works in conjunction with your senses. A beautiful sight may take your breath away, a horrible sight will make you gasp, you will hold your breath when listening intently, you will sniff the air when there are intense odors, and touching a hot iron, you will gasp. The clocks began their striking. I counted off twelve strikes, Midnight. I wasn't expecting it so soon. One can pass away time by thinking illogical. You had better be able to, for there is nothing happening in a war that a nineteen year old would classify as logical, the least of which is the sacrificing of your life. God's greatest gift.

Switching my mind from the fantasy of logic to reality I realized that my feet had gotten so cold that the feeling in them was almost gone. I wondered if I should shake Stern awake and to cut my tour back to three hours. Then the thought came to me. I will slide down the wall to a sitting position. I will remove my boots and slowly slide my feet beneath the blankets up close to Stern without touching him, and see if his body heat would warm them. After all, wouldn't I be keeping him out of trouble by helping him obey the directive that came down to us at Lucky Strike, about not letting your Buddy's feet freeze. It worked! By the time the one bong came from the clocks outside, my feet were warm.

I shook Stern awake. He groaned, then asked me if it was this dark in here or did he go blind while he was asleep. I could hear him getting his boots on. Then he asked me if I thought it would blow the place if he lit a cigarette. I told him hell yes. He asked me if it was hard staying awake four hours in total darkness. I told him hell no, not with your snoring. He told me that he did not snore. I finally agreed with him and told him he would have to solve his own stay awake problem. What works for me might not work for him. I did tell him about sitting and standing, showed him where the window was, and informed him about the clocks striking. He told me he believed he could figure that one out all by himself. I called him a wise guy and said I was going to sleep, and don't let me wake up and catch him asleep, if I do I will tell Cunningham. Stern informed me that he did not give a damn, that I could tell General Patton. Maybe Patton could lock him up in some place that had a damn light in it. We had a good laugh. Then I told him that his feet were going to get cold and if it became unbearable to slip your boots off and slide your feet beneath the blankets. They would warm up but not to touch me with them. I told him goodnight and not let some Krout slip up and throw a match in on us, and don't forget to wake me at 0500. I fell asleep with Stern mumbling something about if I can't see them how in the hell can they see me.

I was awakened by Stern pushing his foot into my side. I asked him if it was 0500 yet. He answered in the affirmative, said that he had made it fine, and asked if he had woke me when he opened the door. I asked why he had opened the door and he said that 0300 he had to piss. That word made my bladder contract and I started crawling around looking for the door. Being in total darkness is no fun. You turn around once and you become completely disoriented. We crawled around the room and finally found the telephone. I don't know what would have happened if it had been needed during the night. Now that we had located it, we decided to hold it in our hands. While we were fumbling around looking for the phone, the clocks struck 0600. We decided to stay awake and shoot the breeze until daylight. I asked Stern if he thought he could walk all day after having only four hours sleep. He said no and since I was holding the phone, call the motorpool and have them to send a jeep around to pick us up, that we didn't sleep enough last night. I told Stern that I thought the darkness was causing him to hallucinate, had he forgotten that we ate our last K last evening and we only have about one canteen cup of water between us. Stern answered that was another reason to ask for a jeep. We are too hungry to walk. Then he added that he thought a good smoke would bring an end to all his present problems.

The clocks outside struck seven times. I glanced up and I could see a faint light outside the window. The line from Romeo and Juliett immediately popped into my mind. I wanted to repeat the line, but could not think of the exact words. I laughed out loud, Stern wanted to know what I found so funny, I still could not think of the passage, so I just said to Stern that it was getting light outside. Stern said he hoped so, that he was getting tired of feeling his eyelids to see if they were open or closed.

We opened the door and stepped outside. Due to the cloud cover daylight was slow in coming, but as we looked around we saw those little fires start popping up around us. Coffee was being brewed. Not having our K-ration boxes to start a fire, Stern and I looked around for kindling to start a fire. No luck, everything was wet. We began to curse our luck, when Stern remembered he had a can of sterno in his bedroll. He retrieved it and, using a trench knife, we managed to pry the lid off. We sat it between two of the thousands of brick that were scattered around, and lit it with a trusty Zippo. It caught and burned that little blue alcoholic flame. Stern remarked that he had heard that people drank this stuff because of the high alcohol content. I told him that there was no need to drink it in this part of the world, every home has a cellar filled with wine, and besides it has a warning on the label about it containing wood alcohol. Stern said that didn't matter, a drunk can't read but one word, "alcohol." I read the name on it out loud and asked Stern if his family made this stuff. He answered hell no. Why? I told him that his family name was on it. You are the only one that lugs it around promoting it and besides its like you, slow as hell. This cup of water has been sitting over this fire for ten minutes and I am still able to hold my finger in the water. He told me to keep my damn dirty finger out of the coffee water. I told him I was just trying to give it a little color.

The water finally boiled. Stern and I had combined our last water from our canteens into one cup. We each produced a crumpled pack of coffee from our pockets and emptied them into the water. Stern then poured half the coffee into my cup. I told him that I did not think he had poured me half of it. He replied that he had given me more than my share. I told him I was sorry, that I would trade cups with him. He told me to go to hell. I asked Stern if he had anything "squirreled away" that we could have with our coffee since we had run out of rations. He said no and did I have anything? I told him I had a can of pork and beans in my bed roll. He again told me to go to hell. I replied that there was no pleasing him this morning, and that he must have had a bad night. He started with the same come back, thought better of it, smiled and said "Windy you are full of shit do you now that?"

We rummaged around in our gear and finally found an old chocolate bar and a pack of crackers, which we split, drank our coffee and pulled up a few bricks. We sat and had a good smoke and wondered what kind of confusion was going to take place today. I heard Stern say "speaking of confusion, here comes your buddy." I looked up and saw Cunningham coming toward us. Stern went on talking, saying that me and Cunningham sure had gotten thick here lately, and that he was getting jealous. Especially since he had not seen much of me since Saarlutern. I told him that since Cunningham was the man now, a little brown nosing didn't hurt anything, and maybe I could do both of us a little good. Stern said he sure appreciated that good deal I had gotten for us last night and if I got any more of them to leave him out. Cunningham walked up and asked us what we were doing standing out in the cold. Stern answered that we were smoking, and didn't he remember telling us not to smoke inside, that we might blow the damn place up. Besides, it's colder in the building than it is outside. Cunningham told us that we had better build a fire and try to stay warm, that it looked as if we may be hanging around a couple of hours. The kitchen and supply trucks finally broke free of the traffic jam and should be in a couple of hours with our meal rations and water, so we had better make a fire and wait. Stern replied that there was nothing to make a fire, that everything was wet. Cunningham told him he was sure if he got cold enough he would find something to burn. Cunningham walked away telling us he would check on us in a little while. Stern yelled after him to tell someone to bring us some water, that we needed more coffee. Cunningham yelled back that we had a telephone that we could call the Chaplain and he would bring Holy water and punch our T.S card. Stern turned to me and told me that he thought my man was getting to be a real smart-ass since he was promoted. I asked him had he rather not have Cunningham leading the platoon than to have some Shavetail come in and take over. Stern said that I should have known that he was kidding, that all the men in the platoon loved and respected Sgt. Cunningham, and if they tried to replace him, he was sure there would be mutiny in the platoon.

Stern and I had the fire going good when the Communications Sgt. and his helper came by taking up the telephone wire and to retrieve the telephone. He backed up to the fire to warm. We told him that it would cost him to use our fire. He wanted to know how much. We told him a cup of water is all we charged. He asked if we were out of water and we told him that we only had enough this morning to make a half cup of coffee. He told us to hold our cups out and he poured us all that he had in his canteen, saying they had a couple of jerry cans full at Company Headquarters. It did not take long for Stern and me to brew up another cup of coffee, sit back, light up, and enjoy.

It was not long before Sgt. Cunningham showed up again telling us to get our gear together and follow him. We followed about a half block, turned the corner, and there was the rest of the platoon standing in the street. Cunningham called the platoon together and told us that the kitchen truck had made it and was parked at Company Headquarters and that they had rations and water. We were waiting for our turn to go by the truck, draw our rations, and water. We will then take a short break to eat our breakfast ration, then we are going to start walking. We will be headed for a town called Mabach. We should arrive there about the middle of the afternoon. We will stay in this town until it is our turn to cross the Rhine River, which maybe a couple of days. This morning you will only draw two rations, breakfast and lunch. They will have a hot dinner for us tonight. This brought a cheer from the men.

It took about an hour to draw our ration and eat breakfast. The Company was formed up in the street, then Capt. Batts informed us that we would be walking the rest of the day, and that we would reach the town of Mabach late this afternoon. There, we would stay until it would come our turn to cross the Rhine River. We probably would have a couple of days to rest with hot meals and they say they have running water in the town. If so, maybe some of you that need a bath can take one, and if the supply truck doesn't get caught up in a traffic jam, we may be able to change clothes. Don't bet on it since it has only been five days since we have changed. The same warning, don't forget that we are still in a war zone and anything can happen. Capt. Batts went on to warn us that we would be walking on narrow secondary roads with motorized traffic and some of those drivers have not had much sleep. Just what we needed another danger to worry about.

Before we left some of the town's inhabitants began wandering back into town. Some went into houses and some stayed out in the streets, picking up bricks and stacking them. As good a day as any to start the rebuilding process. The one thing we noticed about the German people was that they started the cleaning up and rebuilding process before the dust settled. Unlike the French who would sit around and sip wine, seeming to be waiting for the ones that tore it down, to return, and clean it up.

It was 1000 March 27, 1945 when we started our walk toward Mabach. The villages and people looked the same as the ones we had passed through the last few days. They stand stoically and watched or ignored us altogether. Once, while having a ten minute break near a small village, a group of young boys, eight to ten years old, drummed up enough courage to come close enough to speak to us. Not understanding them, we called Weik, a member of our Platoon that spoke German, over to find out what they were saying. Weik said they wanted to know where we were going. Someone spoke up and said that "Hell we don't know where the hell we are". Someone wanted to know where the German soldiers were? The boys answered that they had crossed the river. Weik asked the boys where their dad was. The boys all answered that their dads were all in the east fighting the

Russians. "Fighting the Russians," was always the stock answer given when you ask any German about where any male member of their family was. I never heard one say that they were fighting the Americans.

Walking on the secondary roads with motorized traffic going both ways was turning into a nightmare for us foot soldiers. We were constantly being forced to walk on the shoulders, which were solid mud and was caused by the thawing snow and constant rain. Around 1300 we were directed onto a road that led onto the runway of an abandoned airport. We were informed that we would have an hour's lunch break. Man did it feel good to sit down on the cement runway after getting very little sleep last night and fighting the mud all morning. All I wanted was a few minutes sleep. I decided to gobble my crackers and cheese down and lie back and get about forty five minutes sleep. My plan was working fine. I had just laid back and closed my eyes, when a shot rang out about two hundred yards to my left and then the call for medic followed. Several medics in the vicinity jumped up and started running toward where the call had come from. I sat up and looked, just like everyone was doing, and wondering what was going on. Shortly afterwards, a jeep came past, heading for the scene. The jeep was carrying a litter and two litter bearers. It returned a short time later with a G.I. strapped to the litter aboard the jeep. He was covered with a blanket, with the exception of his face, which was pale and drawn. Coy, our Platoon Medic returned a short time later. We asked him what happened, and he told us some kid from L Company had "accidently" fired his rifle and shot one of his toes off. Someone said "the poor bastard is going home with only nine toes". I looked at my watch, the hour was almost up. There goes my sleep plans shot to hell. I laid back on the cement and immediately fell asleep. When the rest stop was called over, I looked at my watch again, 1430. I still got my forty-five minutes of sleep. Guess the excitement extended the lunch hour. I felt so much better. It's great what a few minutes of sleep can do for you.

In a couple of hours we merged into a four lane highway. In the distance we could see church steeples protruding into the overcast skies. Word filtered back that this was Mabach, our destination. That maybe we could get a hot meal and a good night's sleep. As we approached, we could see that it was a rather large town and there were no visible signs of damage to the city. Moving on into the town, we could see the women and old people pulling those little wagons with bedclothes, crying children and barking dogs. We knew that our advanced party had been there telling them where they could go.

There was a reason for the way we acquired our billets inside the cities. First we choose the upscale homes. These were the homes owned by SS officers and high ranking Nazi officials. These people had nothing for us under any circumstances, nor we for them, and it gave us great pleasure to get in a little extra punishment for them. The homes were usually large enough to house an entire platoon. They always had great beds and a very well stocked wine cellar. Above all, we would pick the homes that had women, children and dogs, because these were the ones that were less likely to be booby trapped. So when you check out the good stuff you don't get your hand blown off.

Members of the advanced party led our Company to the section of town where our billets were located, and such fine billets they were. Each house was a mansion consisting of three floors and a cellar. Each of the four platoons was assigned a house. The house that our platoon was assigned had enough bedrooms that we had only three men to each room. Best of all, we had running water, hot and cold, plus we had electricity. But we were severely warned about keeping the blackout curtains in place after dark.

Sgt. Cunningham, Sgt. Smith and I took over the Master bedroom. A huge bedroom with two large beds, an unbelievable bathroom and a clothes closet that ran the entire length of the bedroom, about thirty feet. The closet contained, hers and his clothes. The his part of the closet contained SS officers uniforms for every occasion. The insignia on them suggested the owner as being some kind of Field Marshall. The master bedroom was on the second floor. The first floor contained a foyer, a large living room that could almost pass as a lobby, a large den, a library, a study and a playroom I suppose. It contained pool tables and other games. But best of all for most of the men there was the wine cellar containing wine from most of the countries of the world. Leading out of the living room, through some double doors, was a giant dining room that could seat most of our platoon. Adjoining the dining room was a well equipped kitchen. It did not take long for the men to discover the wine and stemware. They were sitting around the dining room table, sipping wine, and bragging about its quality. Me being from Mississippi, which was a dry state and having never indulged, did not know a bottle of wine from a bottle of vinegar. The only spirit that I had observed, came from a fruit jar.

We were interrupted by a messenger from Company Headquarters, we were going to have a Company formation in ten minutes in the street that runs in front of our billets. Capt. Batts called the Company to attention. He got all the platoons present and accounted for. He asked if everyone was happy with their billets? A loud cheer came from the men. He went on and told us that we would be here at least a couple of days and for us to get as much rest as possible. He was sure that things would change once we crossed the Rhine River. The enemy is not showing any signs of giving up. He said while here we were restricted to the Company area because our orders could change at any minute, take care of your billets as best you can, because after you leave there will be other friendly forces taking our place. Leave a few bottles for them. This brought on a wild negative outburst of "Hell No". Capt. Batts went on to say that we would have hot meals as long as we were here. Starting at dinner this evening, when you are dismissed here go get your mess gear and report to the mess truck. He pointed out the truck, which was only a half block away. He apologized for what we were having this evening, saying that due to the traffic tie ups all the supplies got delayed and that tomorrow the meals will be better. We were dismissed after being told that we would meet and eat at 0800 tomorrow morning. We retrieved our mess gear and went through the chow line. The Capt. was right, it was bad, some sort of goulash with black bread. It looked like something they had borrowed from the German army, but it was hot. We returned to our billets with our food sat down at that long table. The goulash wasn't bad with a glass of French red wine.

After finishing our chow, most of the platoon sat around the table and sipped on the wine. Stern came over and informed me that I was not drinking "white lightning" and me not being use to good wine, it might make me sick if I drank too much of it on a full stomach. I told him if I waited until my stomach got filled up that I don't think I will be sick any time soon. I asked if he was an expert on wines? He replied that they made wine in upstate New York and that he knew a good bit about wine. I told him that down in Mississippi we called people that knew a good bit about wine "a wino".

Having had only about four hours sleep, out of the last thirty six, the bedroom upstairs fast became more inviting than the wine cellar. Especially after spending awhile in the warm shower, which was the first good shower since leaving the States. The three of us split the bedding. I, being junior grade took the covering off the two beds, placed it on the floor, and slept there. Cunningham turned the light out. It was pitch black inside the room with the blackout curtains up. I informed Cunningham that he should turn the lights back on, find the night light in the bathroom, and turn it on so that we can locate the bathroom during the night. Cunningham asked me what was the matter was I afraid of the dark. I told him that it was not the dark that I was afraid of, it was the things in the dark, especially in a war zone, and he knew how jumpy I was, and if I should get stepped on in the dark my M1 would go off and hurt someone. Cunningham found the night light.

It was 0700 on March 28, 1945 when I was awakened by that old "grab your socks" routine. Cunningham was in the bathroom shaving and then started yelling at Smith and me to get out of bed that we were having Company formation in less than an hour. He told us to get up and shave while there was still hot water. I told him I was too young to shave. He said that he had forgotten, and that he would go by the kitchen and get some coffee cream to rub on my face, and to catch one of the many cats roaming around and let it lick the fuzz off my face. Smith and I got out of bed. He shaved and I washed my face. We could hear Cunningham going through the building trying to get the members of the platoon up and into the street where the Company formation was already taking place. There were men still rushing into the ranks, after the command for the "fall in" was given. Even with the confusion, the report showed everyone present and accounted for. After the report 1st Sgt. Harrell, a well known imbiber obviously suffering from post imbibing syndrome, stepped up and gave a ranting rendition about the virtues of punctuality. He ended his speech by saying, that if, at the age of forty-five, he could be on time, he knew damn well that everyone else could. He told us Capt. Batts had a few words to say to us. He then called the Company to attention.

Capt. Batts stepped forward gave us the "at ease". Capt. Batts' tone was almost apologetic when he started his talk to us about being late for formations. He said he knew it was hard getting out of bed this morning, after the adverse conditions that we had slept under the last couple of months. He had barely made it out of bed this morning but we have to realize how important it is to always be on time. He went on to tell us that he was sure that we would be here today and tonight, but after that we could be called to cross the Rhine at any time. He said that we will remain restricted to the Company area and that we should spend this day checking and cleaning our gear and making sure that all firearms are clean and in good working order, because it appeared that in a few days we would be using them. The enemy resistance has stiffened since pulling back across the Rhine River. He told us that meals would be served today in the same location, breakfast at 0800, lunch at 1300 and dinner at 1800. The serving line will only be open for thirty minutes, so make your plans accordingly. All I can promise you about the meals is that they will be better than K-rations. This morning we will start the day with French toast, grape jelly, coffee and eggs. The word eggs brought forth a cheer. After a slight hesitation, Capt. Batts said, "powdered", this brought out the "boos". He told us to get our mess gear and fall in the chow line. After going through the chow line everyone returned to the billets and ate in the dining room.

After breakfast Cunningham instructed the squad leaders to see that their men checked and cleaned their gear. He placed Sgt. Smith in charge of the wine cellar and told him to lock it or place a guard at the door. There would be no drinking until afternoon. This went over like a lead balloon. How long does it take a "grunt" to clean his gear? He doesn't have a tank, truck, or a big gun to clean. He has a rifle and a pair of boots to rub dubbing on about fifteen minutes worth of work. After that we sat and looked at each other. Then we decided we would go through the clothes closets and see what the fashion was in this part of the world. While we were checking out the clothes closets, some came up with the wild idea that we could hold a fashion show in the dining room. With nothing else to do, it would help to pass the time away. All members of our Platoon who wished to participate in the show were asked to go through their bedroom closets and to try on clothes until they found something that fit and that they felt comfortable in. Just to watch some of the men trying on clothes, made you wonder if there was not some cross dressers in Platoon. So many of them seemed to enjoy putting on the women's clothes better than they did the men's, or maybe it had been too long since they had felt silk and satin. By noon everyone had picked out the clothes that they were going to wear in the show. I picked out a tuxedo with full compliment of tails, high hat and monocle. I was going to impersonate Neville Chamberlain and mimic his famous speech "Peace in our time". Everyone placed their costume with their gear and we went to lunch. Most of the men returned to our dining room to eat. There was a lot of griping about not having wine with their lunch.

After lunch Cunningham told us that he had to go to Company Headquarters, that Capt. Batts was having a meeting with the platoon leaders and that he would be back around 1500 and that he had instructed Sgt. Smith to open the wine cellar door at 1400. The ones that wanted to sip the wine could, but don't overdo it. He said that he wanted everyone that was going to participate in the fashion show to be ready when he returned. He wanted to see a dress rehearsal before tonight's show. After Cunningham left, Smith must have needed a drink because he opened the wine cellar door as soon as he was out of sight. The rush was on, and it seemed as if everyone needed a drink. Stern asked me what my preference was, I told him that I didn't have one, that I thought wine meant wine. His answer was to give me a short lesson in wine appreciation, covering the grape, color, vintage, sweet and dry. When I told him that in Mississippi, dry meant no alcohol at all. He gave up on me as being a lost cause and told me to just drink what he drank.

We were all sitting around the dining room table, dressed in our costumes, sipping the wine while waiting for the return of Cunningham. We were just beginning to get a buzz on, when we heard that dreaded word, "Attention" shouted from the foyer. Everyone stopped with glass in midair, then we heard the voice of Capt. Batts say "At ease son". Someone at the table said, "Oh shit!" Then the twin doors were flung open and into the dining room stepped Cunningham and shouted out that dreaded word again. We all jumped to our feet, turning over a few glasses, and came to attention. Capt. Batts, in a calm voice said, "Good afternoon ladies and gentlemen, you may be at ease, you seem to be enjoying yourselves, mind if we join you?" There were a few choking "no sirs" emanating from around the room. Capt. Batts asked Cunningham if he could have someone bring him and his Executive officer a set up and a couple of chairs. Cunningham looked over at Stern, who was dressed as a milk maid with bonnet and all, and said, "Frau Stern would you please get these two gentlemen a couple of clean glasses and a bottle of your best red and see that they enjoy themselves. Cunningham looked at me and addressed me as '"Mr. Chamberlain" and asked if I would find a couple of chairs for our company. I said that I would and that they could have mine and Sterns' chairs while I looked for some. I just wanted to get the hell out of the room. I wandered around trying to find chairs, there weren't any. I ran into Stern with the wine and set up. I wanted to say something funny but decided against it. Stern didn't seem overjoyed at playing the milk maid role anymore. We went back into the dining room. I informed them that there were not any chairs, and that they could have Stern and my chairs, that we would stand.

Cunningham spoke first, he assured us that what was happening was in no way meant to embarrass us. At the meeting with the platoon leaders, Capt. Batts asked the leaders how the men were coping with the time spent waiting to cross the Rhine River. He was worried about getting too much into the bitters. Cunningham said he told the Capt. exactly what we were doing and what our plans were. He became interested. When I told him that we were having a dress rehearsal at 1500, he said that he would like to attend. So here he is and I think he wants to say a few things to you. Capt. Batts stood and addressed us with "ladies and Gentlemen". He said that he had some concerns before about what would happen to us after the war but not anymore! He saw some real talent sitting around the table, but he had one word of caution for you, who are dressed in those SS uniforms "don't step outside with those uniforms on. If you do, your dreams may never be realized".

Capt. Batts told us one reason he had come by to talk to us, was after Cunningham told him of what we were planning, that he decided to play a practical joke on Sgt. Harrell. After the admonition he gave you at last evening's formation, he is going to expect great results at this evening's assembly. We want to see his reaction when you do not showup at all. What I want you to do is to remain inside while the rest of the company falls into place at our 1700 formation. At 1700, Sgt. Harrell is going to be looking at his watch and I am going to ask, him what happened to that wayward platoon that you spent so much time straightening out last evening. I am then going to send a messenger here to see what is the hold up. When he enters the building, I want all of you to come rushing out, dressed as you are now, with the exception of the SS uniforms. You people find a dress to put on. I want you to fall into formation. By this time, Ole Sarge will know that he had, been had! We want to see what his reaction will be. Capt. Batts said, that before he left that he wanted to say a few things about Sgt. Harrell. He told us that we all knew that Sgt. Harrell is a Regular Army man his contribution to what this Company has become, is immeasurable! He is the primary reason that a group of high school kids, a few young fathers, a few people from the ASTP program, a few ninety-day wonders, old school teachers and me, who spent a few months at OCS. Most all of whom, three years ago never had a thought about Army life. In one month he will have spent twenty-five years of his life in the service of his country. He then plans to retire, so until then I want every one of you to show your appreciation for what he has done for us. We will start at tomorrow morning's company formation, I want every man standing in place when Sgt. Harrell shows up at the assembly area. At which time we will all give him a big hand.

As 1700 hrs. approached, we of the Third Platoon stood nervously watching from the windows as the rest of the Company formed up, out in the street. At approximately 1655, we could see Capt. Batts, Lt. Irwin and Sgt. Harrell approach their positions in front of the Company. After a couple of minutes Sgt. Harrell began checking his watch. When the time of 1700 hrs. rolled around, Sgt. Harrell strode over to Capt. Batts, saluted and they talked for a few seconds. Then I saw Capt. Batts point toward the ranks and one man came forward and saluted the Capt. Capt. Batts had a few words with him then pointed toward our billet. The man started walking our way. Cunningham told us to get ready. We had already planned our strategy for making our exit from the building. All the non-corns would exit first in full uniform. That was Platoon leader, Cunningham, Platoon guide Sgt. Smith, the three squad leaders and the three assistant squad leaders. This was to assure the rest of the Company did not think that our Platoon had not been taken over by civilians when they saw the rest of the Platoon come out dressed as civilians. Second came the men dressed as women. This was double insurance, surely the men would not attack women. Last was the ones dressed in men's garb. We all took our positions in the formation. Sgt. Harrell threw up his hands, turned and walked over to Capt. Batts, saluted and asked the Capt. if he could be excused, that he wanted no part of these shenanigans. Capt. Batts said he could. Sgt. Harrell walked straight to the Headquarters building and never looked back. Capt. Batts took charge of the Company and remarking, "so much for jokes and jokers". He said that it was time to get serious. That tomorrow the 29th of March we are scheduled to cross the Rhine, the exact time has not been set yet. So starting at 2400 this day, we will all be ready to go at a minutes notice. He said it had not been a picnic east of the Rhine, the Germans were putting up strong resistance, and that we were expected to make contact within three days. We have been lucky since leaving the Saar, seems long ago but is only been one week. Let us all start getting mentally ready for what probably will be happening in a couple of days. From now until we leave or until orders are changed, you are confined to the Company area. Our next formation will be at 0700 tomorrow morning. I want everyone standing in their place at that time. Let us go to chow now. All you men out of uniform do not have to get dressed I have made arrangements for you go through the chow line.

Returning to the dining room to sip our wine and eat our dinner, you could see the mood of the men changing. Having not made contact with the enemy in a week and with all the rumors that the Germans were ready to surrender, combined with the large number of prisoners being taken, we had began to feel that the war may be over before we made contact with the enemy again. The news coming back from the front indicated the opposite being true.

The changing mood of the men turned our little show into a flop. All the things that seemed so comical before, now bordered on the ridiculous. My Neville Chamberlain speech, about how he thought Hitler meant "peace" when he said "piece", was a big dud. Most of the men excused themselves saying they needed to write letters home. Me, I kept sipping the wine until I got sleepy. I removed my Chamberlain suit, threw it in the closet and went to bed.

I must have been drinking the cheap wine. When Cunningham yelled, grab your socks at 0500, my head felt as if it had been separated from my body. My eyelids wouldn't work. So I could not see who was pounding on my head. I looked at my watch and asked Cunningham why in the hell were we getting up at 0500 when the formation wasn't until 0700. He reminded me of our promise to Capt. Batts about not being late. Besides, if we don't straighten up our act in this Third Platoon you are going to find yourself sleeping with some shavetail that finished his ninety days at OCS and will be taking my place. How would I like having a new platoon leader? I told Cunningham that if he was fresh out of OCS, would he be known as a virgin? If so, I wouldn't mind. Cunningham then came out of the bathroom and gave me the towel popping routine, which increased my headache two fold. I asked Cunningham if he had an aspirin for my head? He asked me if I saw a Red Cross on his sleeve, but that he would refer me to Dr. Coy, who resides on the second floor. I told Cunningham to call me when he and Smith finished in the bathroom, that it would not take me long to get ready since I did not have to shave. Cunningham asked me if I was the platoon runner, and if I was, to run my skinny ass up and down the stairs until I made sure that all the squad leaders were awake and getting their men up for the 0700 formation. Remind them that today is the big day. We cross the Rhine today. I managed to find and wake all the squad leaders and while doing so found Medic Coy and managed to get a couple of aspirin from him after he threatened to give me a shot of morphine for waking him so early.

At 0655 on March 29th, 1945 every man of "I" Company was waiting in formation for the appearance of Sgt. Harrell whom took his position at that exact time. He checked his watch at intervals and at exactly 0700 he called the Company to attention, took the platoons report and reported to Capt. Batts that everyone was present and accounted for. Capt. Batts gave us the "at ease" and began by telling us that he had good news. It was being reported that units of the Third Army had taken the city of Frankfort on the Main and now on the move, northeast. He went on to say that Frankfort was about fifty miles from where we are now standing. Remember that no one is to leave the Company area. We could get a call at any minute to load up and head for the Rhine crossing. So stay ready. Before dismissing us for breakfast, he told us this would be our last hot meal for awhile. That when we went through the chow line this morning we were to draw K-rations for twenty-four hours.

After breakfast the speculation and bull session was on. Where all the rumors and information was coming from was hard to fathom. We had not seen or talked to anyone except the men in our Company since arriving here. The military secrets were out. We were being trucked straight to the front, relieving the men at the front by this time tomorrow. The other version was that the men at the front were moving ahead so fast, that by the time we reached Frankfort the front would still be fifty miles ahead of us. I liked that version. But my hopes were dashed when someone else said they heard the Germans were counterattacking toward the Rhine, and we may not be able to cross, and so it went. I knew only one thing for certain, being in the Infantry I would damn well know when we arrived at the front.

Noon came and no word about leaving had been heard. Everyone reverted to the K-ration and coffee diet. After lunch someone asked Cunningham what time was he going to open the wine cellar? He replied that he did not think that he should open it since we would be leaving at any time. Someone spoke and said a little wine would not hurt us. Then some wise guy spoke up and said that we should take a vote on whether to open the wine cellar or not. Cunningham asked him if he had not learned yet that the Army was not a democracy. Just what in the hell did he think all those stripes, bars, leaves, birds and stars were for, decoration. You don't get a vote here, you follow orders. Cunningham said that he would compromise if everyone promised to cooperate. Everyone promised! Cunningham said that he would open the cellar door and the men that drank could get one bottle. The ones that did not drink could have no wine. This was to prevent them from passing it on to their drinking friends which could cause problems. We all agreed. Then line up at the cellar door. I asked my good buddy, Stern if he would help his wine ignorant friend from Mississippi pick out a bottle of good wine. He replied that he sure would, that nothing could make him any happier than helping a buddy. We wandered around inside the cellar for a few minutes. Finally Stern reached into a case sitting in a corner and pulled out a bottle that had "Schnapps" written on it. He handed it to me and said that was just what I would like. That it was like "Mississippi Moonshine" only milder. It was made from potatoes. I thanked him and asked if he meant "sweet taters or Irish tators?" He replied "both" and to remember that, it was a sipping wine and not a drinking one. I went upstairs to my room, sat down on my bed and debated with myself whether to take a sip now or wait until we loaded on the trucks. I could wait and start sipping to help keep me warm, since it seems to be getting colder outside. I decided to wait. So I rolled the bottle up in my bedroll, laid down on the bed and went to sleep.

I awoke about 1800. I was hungry so I retrieved my K-ration from my bedroll and opened it. Sure enough, it contained cheese. I was cursing the cheese, when I spotted the bottle of "wine". I had been told that "wine and cheese" went together. So I picked up my bottle and cheese and headed for the dining room and joined the bull session where the Army's "hurry up and wait" policy was being discussed. I found a wine glass, poured me a small amount, and took a sip. I blinked hard and thought to myself that this must be the double dry stuff. I took a bite of cheese and then another sip, still tough to swallow. After a short while it began tasting better, and then good without the cheese.

It must have been around 2100 when Stern came into the dining room. He came over to where I was and asked how I was doing. I told him that I never felt better in my life and I wanted to thank him for the fine wine he had picked for me. The only problem was that I am seeing two of everything. Stern picked up the bottle I had been drinking from, he looked at it, and told me I was drinking too fast. That what I was drinking was stronger than ordinary wine, and I had already drank too much. Then he said he was taking me to my room and putting me to bed and that maybe I would be able to sleep it off before we left to cross the Rhine, which could be at any time now. I tried to rise to my feet but my legs would not hold me up. Stern sat me back into the chair and told me to wait, that he was going to get Cunningham to help get me to my room.

It all seemed like a dream. I could hear Cunningham asking what the hell was going on, and couldn't a man sip a little wine without passing out. Then I heard Stern tell Cunningham it was all his fault that he had told me the bottle he picked out for me was not wine but Schnapps. That he intended it to be a joke, that he figured when I took my first sip I would know that it was not wine. I could hear Cunningham telling Stern that he expected too much out of a dumb shit from Mississippi that had never drank anything except well water. Then he told Stern to help him get me into the living room and onto the couch. I then recognized the voice of Sgt. Hasemeir, one of our Platoons Assistant squad leaders. He was a former football player, he was telling Cunningham and Stern to move and let him have me. I felt myself being lifted and carried out of the dining room and placed on the couch. I could hear Cunningham telling Stern to go upstairs and get my rifle and bedroll and bring them downstairs. Then place the bedroll on the couch and since he was the instigator of this little joke, he would be responsible for taking care of my rifle until I was sober. Stern answered that Cunningham should know that he was going to take care of his best buddy. To which Cunningham answered, that he had better or he would help me take care of him when I became sober. I could hear

Cunningham telling Hasemeir that he had heard from Capt. Batts and that the trucks that were taking us across the river; were on their way. They should be here in a couple of hours and when they arrive he wanted Hasemeir to put me on the truck with him, along with my bedroll. He also wanted Stern on the same truck and that they were to place me on the floor of the truck beneath the two of them. They were to see that I would not roll around and get injured. Sgt. Hasemeir sounded as if he was standing in a hole, when I heard him tell Cunningham, "I will do that Sarge". I then fell asleep.

I did not know what time it was when I felt myself being lifted and placed onto the tailgate of a truck. I felt myself being dragged along the floor and being placed beneath the seats of the truck in the right front corner. I heard Cunningham saying to Stern and Hasemeir, to not let me roll out from under the seat. Then telling Stern to take care of my rifle until I awoke. Stern kneeled down, placed my steel helmet next to me, and placed my bedroll beneath my head. I again fell asleep. I was awakened sometime later by the excited voices of the men as we pulled onto the Oppenheim pontoon bridge across the Rhine River. The men were "oohing and aahing" as we moved across. I could feel the sway of the bridge, I wanted so much to take a look but was too embarrassed over my conduct of the last few hours to make a move. Finally, I could not stand it any longer, I pulled on Stern's pants leg. He bent over and asked if I was alive. I told him I was barely alive and if he would move his feet. I would like to take a look at the Rhine. He helped me to get from under the seats of the truck. I struggled to my feet and looked out just at the moment we were leaving the bridge. I looked back and all that I could see was the early morning haze hanging above the river. It would be six months later, on furlough to Paris, before I would lay eyes on the Great Rhine River. I sat down on the floor of the truck with my back toward the cab. I apologized to Stern and Hasemeir for the trouble I had caused them. Stern said it was mostly his fault that it happened. Hasemeir who was all of twenty-four years said the two of us needed to grow up. Stern then asked Hasemeir, what he thought our chances of growing up are under our present circumstances? He didn't receive an answer. Stern handed me my rifle, telling me that I had better take it, it might help me to "grow up".

It was around 1000 when we pulled onto the German autobahn. The roadside read "Frankfort 17 km." Pulling onto the autobahn, I was awe-stricken by the sight that was in front of us. I had witnessed this before, but never to this degree. The Autobaun appeared to be one giant U.S. Army parking lot. As for as the eye could see, in both directions, covering two lanes, both shoulders and the neutral zone, was parked Army vehicles of every description. Traffic was moving only in two lanes, one going east and going west. We were in the east bound slowly making our way east. Our movement was slow due to the fact that the Germans were using the scorched earth policy. They were destroying most of the bridges and overpasses on the autobaun. The engineers were working feverishly day and night building bridges and cutting out detours in order to keep troops and supplies moving. It would be impossible to say enough good things about Army engineers. We passed on the outskirts of Frankfort around noon and crossed the Mainz River on one of our Army Engineers, "masterpieces", as they moved on to the east. With all the detours, the going was painfully slow but at times it worked to our advantage. One could jump off the truck, stretch, relieve himself and still catch up before it got a hundred yards down the road. There were no rest stops. You ate and made coffee as the trucks stopped and started. Sometimes this kept the troops, at the head of the convoy, busy starting fire to heat water. The slow progress did not bother me. The rumor was that we were only about thirty miles from the front.

Our destination, after leaving Frankfort was an assembly area in the vicinity of Malsfeld,. This is where we were to join up with parts of the 6th Armored and the 3rd Cavalry group, before crossing the Fulda River. We were to assemble there the morning of March 31st.

The night of March 30th was total confusion. Part of our Battalion that was riding on artillery trucks got lost and we spent the rest of the night searching for them. The scary thing about the night was that everyone we met seemed lost, even the Military Police. When they were asked for directions, each one would point in a different direction. It was after daylight before we got the Battalion together again and moved on toward Malsfeld. Before reaching Malsfeld, we were met by Armored vehicles from the Third Calvary and the Sixth Armored division. We followed them down an unpaved road into a wooded area, to the positions the Third Battalion had been assigned, in preparation to cross the Fulda River on Easter Sunday April 1, 1945. Our position was along a wooded ridge, roughly running north and south, a couple of miles west of the Fulda. We started digging in to spend the night in preparation for the next day's attack across the Fulda. I am thinking, just what we need, is to be beneath a tree if the Germans decided to throw a few 88's at us. The Germans love to bracket the wooded areas. They knew the natural instinct for the G.I. was to get out of the open, and into cover. Of course there was no good place to be when they opened up with the 88's. Some places were just worse than others.

As runner, my assignment was with Capt. Batts and the small Company Headquarters group which consisted of Capt. Batts, First Sgt. Harrell, the radio man and another runner from the weapons platoon. Our Company's position covered about three hundred yards along the dirt road that we had entered the forest on. The 2nd and 3rd platoons were dug in along the east side of the road, our Company Headquarters group was dug in between the 2nd and 3rd platoons. The 1st and the weapons platoons was in reserve on the west side of the road directly behind us. On our right, M Company was set up covering a treeless meadow that was about two hundred feet wide before becoming forested again. To the left of our Company's position, an anti-tank group was dug in.

By late afternoon most of the men had finished digging in and was munching on K-rations and having that last cigarette before dark. I had picked a spot about fifteen yards from Capt. Batts and Sgt. Harrell's positions. It was beside a stack of fresh cut firewood. I dug a trench about twelve inches deep and about six feet long which I spread my shelter half and blanket using my spare clothes for a pillow. I wrapped up in the shelter half and blanket with my trusty M1 and pulled the banned wool knit cap over my ears and went to sleep.

It was around 0400 when all hell broke loose. Small arms fire first erupted from across the road, coming from the vicinity of the first and weapons platoons. There was a lot of incoherent yelling going on except I recognized the word comrade being said a couple of times. On our left the men from the anti-tank outfit started firing small arms plus what sounded like a few 57mm shots mixed in, and at the same time the heavy machine guns of M Company started firing on our right. The shooting lasted a couple of minutes, then silence. I sat up to look around and I heard Sgt. Harrell say "there is one" then I heard Capt. Batts say "no, that is Windham". I lay back abruptly, remembering that I had the wool knit cap with the bib on it that we were told not to wear without the helmet. I quickly pulled my helmet down into the trench and slipped my head into it vowing not to make that mistake again. For the next two and one half hours I lay in the trench on my back, waiting for a silhouette to appear between me and dimly lit sky above. There was nothing, not even a sound. Then around 0630 I could hear Capt. Batts speaking very low, either on the field phone or the radio. Finally it started breaking daylight, the yelling started up again across the road. Capt. Batts was speaking much louder now, on the telephone. He stood up and told his little headquarters group to follow him, that we were going across the road to see what the hell was going on. As we approached the weapons platoon we could see a group of German soldiers standing with their hands on their heads surrounded by members of the weapons platoon with their sidearms drawn and pointing at the Germans. As we walked up M Company opened up with their heavy machine guns, we looked to our right front and could see two figures running across the meadow toward the distant woods. One man fell before reaching the woods but the other one continued on into the forest. As we approached the group at the weapons platoon, we could see a couple of German soldiers lying on the ground apparently dead. One was no older than 14 years of age. He had been shot through the head with a 45 cal. by one of the machine gunners as he walked by the machine gun emplacement silhouetted against the sky. The other dead one had been shot several times, probably from several sources. The story the Germans told was that they had been cut off from their outfit and were trying to make it back to the front lines to rejoin their company. They were walking up the road and saw the vehicles of the Third Calvary parked along the road. They figured that they could cut through the woods and go around them. Big mistake!! When walking back to our positions Sgt. Harrell put his arm around my shoulder and told me the next time he caught me with that knit cap on without the helmet that he was going to shoot me just out of meanness, day or night. I thought about making some lame excuse but remembering our first meeting back at Camp Shelby I only said "yes Sir".

I returned to my position beside the wood pile and started heating water for coffee and looking through my cache of K ration cans, that did not have the word "cheese" written on it. I found one with eggs and ham in bold lettering. When I saw the word "eggs" I remembered that today was Easter Sunday. With all the excitement going on I had completely forgotten. My thoughts went back to not so many years ago, although under the present conditions seemed like a hundred years, back in Mississippi at about this time of the morning, my Mother would be pointing out to me and my brothers and sisters the boundaries within our yard that the Easter Bunny had hidden his eggs. I thought about the young German soldier lying dead across the road, born into a world gone mad, robbed of his age of innocence at a time that he should be searching for the symbols of Easter instead of an enemy to destroy.

The next couple of hours I watched from my position by the wood pile as groups of men from the company searched the woods around us. They found a few more Germans who had tried to hide by lying on the ground and covering themselves with brush. Some of the men from the Anti-Tank outfit on our left came over and told us they had killed a couple of Germans. One of them had stepped up in front of a camouflaged 57mm and the gunner saw him, reached over and pulled the lanyard and the German disappeared.

Around noon we learned that the 261st and the 6th Armored had crossed the Fulda River and were advancing to the east. Around mid-afternoon we of the 260th, and the 259th in conjunction with the 3rd Calvary were to attack toward and across the Fulda River. The move out was slow and torturous. The weather was changing. It began to rain and sleet, everyone was retrieving and putting on their raincoats and parkas. We were told that vehicles would be by shortly to pick us up. Sure enough about three hours later, trucks loaded with all type of supplies began showing up. We of "I" Company were told to find space among the supplies and get comfortable. Not wishing to have spare parts and wooden crates sticking in my ribs, I chose the right front fender of a six by to ride on. I also figured that the heat from the engine would help to keep me warm. We knew by our mode of transportation that our battalion had been placed in reserve behind the 1st and 2nd battalions who were up front traveling with the Armor. This made us more acceptable of our mode of travel knowing that we were traveling with the rear echelon.

My hopes were dashed early that the truck engine would keep me warm as we moved along. The movement was so slow the engine was never running long enough to warm up. I spent the night breaking the ice loose from my raincoat that was being formed on the truck fender.

It was breaking day when we arrived at the Fulda River in the vicinity of Bebra. The 1st and 2nd battalions had already crossed to the east bank of the Fulda without opposition on a bridge that the enemy had failed to destroy. We disembarked from the trucks. It took quite a while to get the feeling back into my buttock after being frozen to the truck fender for so long. We walked across the bridge to the east bank of the Fulda. When reaching the east bank we of the 3rd Battalion of the 260th, were informed that we were to pass through the 1st and 2nd Battalions and take over the point in conjunction with armor units of the 3rd Calvary. Then make our way toward the Werra River with our objective being the capture of the city of Mulhausen, which was about ten miles east of the Werra.

The countryside beyond the Fulda was farming country with small farming villages. Intelligence reports were that the enemy had pulled back across the Werra River where they planned to make a stand. The men of the 3rd Calvary told us they had orders that if one rifle shot came from any of the small villages, they were to back off and fire white phosphorus onto the village and burn it to the ground. The villagers knew about this order and every village we pulled up to, the occupants would come out shouting "no soldiers".

Our first contact with the enemy came around mid morning. We were observing a lone farmhouse which was about three hundred yards away, when a lone German stepped outside the door and began waving a white flag. Capt. Batts sent Lt. Irwin with a half dozen riflemen forward toward the house, while the rest of the company, along with a Sherman tank and a tank destroyer from the Third Calvary took up fire positions about two hundred yards away. We watched as Lt. Irwin and his group approached the house. When they were about one hundred yards away four more German soldiers stepped out each waving individual white flags. Irwin made the men lie down, sent three of his men into the house to search it, meanwhile the three men outside were searching the German soldiers. We observed one of the G.I.s take something from one of the Germans and hand it to Irwin as he did the German started waving his hands and was visibly upset. The group then walked over to where we were standing along with Capt. Batts. The object of attention was a G.I. towel which was taken from the German's knapsack. Irwin had put the German in fear of his life, by questioning about how and where he had obtained the towel. The possessor of the towel could not speak English, so one of his buddies, who could, tried to explain it away by saying that due to shortages the German army often issued captured soft goods. Capt. Batts, knowing that the majority of his men had German Army souvenirs on their person, only smiled and sent the prisoners to the rear. They left saluting and voicing their "danka-shanes". We moved on.

The going was tough, the area we were traveling had mostly dirt roads. It had been raining and the roads were muddy, especially after the tanks had passed over them. We foot soldiers rode the tanks some and walked some. Walking behind the tanks was a mess, keeping out of the mud was next to impossible. The mud stuck to your boots and they would become so heavy that you would have to stop constantly and clean them. You were always on the run trying to keep up with the tanks.

During the day we had searched a number of small farm villages and had not found any enemy military personnel. The villagers were all cooperative, they would run out to meet us yelling "no soldiers". Our burn policy had proceeded us.

As the day wore on we were getting reports that the units on our right and left had met with some light resistance from a few fanatical SS and Hitler Youth groups. We of the 3rd Battalion had not made any contact with the enemy since the incident at the farm house. This all changed around 1400. I was riding on the point tank along with Capt. Batts, the 300 radio operator and Sgt. Rakosi, a squad leader from the third platoon. The members of Rakosi's squad were following, walking behind the tank. We came upon this rather large farm village consisting of about a dozen farm houses. The village started at the mouth of a narrow valley and continued down for about a quarter of a mile. There was a rather steep hill forming the right of the valley. This hill was sparsely covered with trees and the observation among them was good. The hill that formed the left side of the valley was of a gradual incline and for about 200 yards was bare, from there to out of sight the hill was covered with thick evergreen. A dirt road wound its way along the valley floor, next to the hill on the left. The farm houses were all between the road on the left and the hill to the right. As we neared the village a portly elderly man stepped from the first house waving a white flag. We stepped down from the tank and Capt. Batts motioned for the man to come forward. He came up to us and could speak rather good English. He introduced himself and said that he was the burgomaster of the village. He assured us that there was no German Military around, that they had all pulled out during the night and were headed across the Werra River. Then he invited the Capt. into his house for a glass of wine. Capt. Batts, who was known to enjoy a drink, said "what the hell." Then he motioned to a Jr. Officer from the 3rd Calvary to come with him. He then told Sgt. Rakosi, one other G.I. and me to follow him. We followed the German inside the house. He took us into a large room that was a kitchen/dining combination. The first thing I noticed was the warmth, God, how long had it been since I felt heat like this! At one end of the room was a huge wood burning fireplace with a built-in brick lined oven into which we peeked and could see several round loaves of black bread being baked. The smell emanating from the oven made me want to dive right into it. The German motioned toward a large table that was positioned in the middle of the room and asked us to please sit down, which we did with the exception of the one G.I. which Capt. Batts told to stand guard by the door. Our host told us he was going to get his wife to bring the wine. Then he started to walk toward a door that led to another part of the house. Capt. Batts motioned for the guard to follow him. The German opened the door and spoke to someone inside the other part of the house. Then he returned to the table and sat down with us, saying that the wine would be here shortly. He then began to tell us how glad he would be when the war was over and how miserable life had been since Hitler came into power. Only a few minutes had passed when an elderly lady came into the room carrying a large tray. On it was a large bottle of wine, a loaf of black bread, some cheese and wine glasses. She sat the tray down and poured our host a glass of wine. He took a sip and then she proceeded around the table pouring the rest of us a glass of the white stuff. As I watched, my thoughts went back to the last time that I had a drink before crossing the Rhine, when Stern had given me the good stuff. I was hoping this wasn't some of the same. It did not take us long to devour the goodies except a small piece of cheese and bread which we gave to the G.I. guarding the door. We said our thanks to our host and made our way back to the Sherman tank that we had left from. There was no hint that we were about to experience one of the most bizarre happenings we would experience throughout the entire war.

    The tank started forward along the dirt road with Capt. Batts, Sgt. Rakosi and me following close behind. To the rear of us was the tank destroyer followed by the rest of the third platoon. The first building that we were approaching to the right of the road, was a hay barn that was part of our host's compound. We were about thirty yards from the barn when the tank destroyer pulled along the left side of us in order to take the lead. Suddenly, two German soldiers stepped from behind the barn with a panzerfaust (their version of our Bazooka), and aimed it at the tank in front of us, taking everyone by surprise. I don't know what happened. The weapon either misfired or they lost their nerve at the last minute. The two Germans turned to run away. The man operating the 50 caliber on the tank destroyer was the first to react. He started firing as soon as they dropped their weapon. The man running behind looked back. I saw spray come from the back of his head, the one running ahead pitched forward into a heap. The man who had been our host came running out of his house shouting something about not knowing. Someone yelled "shoot the son of a bitch". Capt. Batts said "no" and motioned the man over to where he was standing, and asked him if he knew what was about to happen to the town. The man started pleading and fell to his knees and started to pray. Capt. Batts told him it was out of his hands and that he must start telling the townspeople to start evacuating the village. We were going to burn it down around their ears.

    Capt. Batts called Cunningham forward and told him to take Weik (our interpreter), and two squads of his platoon and search every house in the village. Warn all the occupants that the village is about to be burned to the ground and they had exactly one hour to evacuate. He then told Cunningham that we would meet up with him at the other end of town. We then walked over to where the two German soldiers lay dead. We turned them over on their backs. They were just kids, no more than 13 or 14 years of age. The one that had turned to look back had a hole over one eye the size of a fifty caliber, and the back of his head was gone, along with all the contents. When Capt. Batts, the former high school principal turned away, I heard him say, "what a waste".

We again started forward along the road passing the village. We had the tank destroyer in front followed by Capt. Batts and the radio operator who were walking. Next in line was a Sherman tank followed by me, who was trying to always step in the tracks of the tank in case mines had been laid in the road. Suddenly a horse with two riders bolted from the evergreen trees that were growing over hill to our left. The rider in front had some sort of machine pistol and the rear rider was carrying a rifle. They were firing in our direction without much success since the horse was still moving. Everyone started firing at them, including the tankers with the 50's. The horse bolted and came straight down the hill toward us. The men on the horse were holding on for dear life. About twenty yards before reaching the road the horse either stumbled or was shot. The three of them rolled down the hill landing in the road between the tank destroyer and the tank that I was following. One of the riders was thrown to the side. It was apparent that he was dead. The other rider landed in the roadway pinned beneath the dead horse. He was still alive. I could see him waving and hear his screams above the roar of the motor as the driver steered the tank for him. I was walking directly behind the left track of the tank. I had to jump over the mass of horse and human flesh as it exited from beneath the left track of the tank. To this day I can close my eyes and see the milk white of the man's large neck vertebrae as it popped from beneath the left track of the tank. In the next two seconds my horror was intensified by the breaking of the left track of the tank. The same track that passed over the German soldier. I could not help wondering if this was, "A Message". I walked around the tank, caught up to Capt. Batts and the radio operator walking behind the tank destroyer and never looked back.

When we reached the last house of the village we stopped. The column of men and tanks was behind us they had bypassed the broken down tank and left it for the ordinance crew that was following. There was no sign of Cunningham and his search group. We waited for several minutes and then they came into view searching the last house. Cunningham came up to Capt. Batts and reported that the mission was accomplished and that they had not discovered any enemy military personnel.

While stopped Capt. Batts was approached by a member of the 3rd Calvary. I heard Capt. Batts address him as "Major". Up front, familiarity is about the only way you can identify an officer. They either cover their rank insignia or take them off altogether. This was because the snipers always went after the officers first. This is one reason the replacement system did not work too well. A new replacement never was sure of who was giving him orders.

Capt. Batts and the Major had a short conversation then they got on the radio and talking to someone. Presumably from either Battalion or Regiment Headquarters. After the conversation, a few words were passed between Capt. Batts and the major. The Capt. then got on the walkie-talkie and instructed all of "I" Company Platoon leaders to come forward. When they arrived he informed them that they were going down the road a mile or so taking part of the 3rd Calvary armor with us. We were going to dig in along the roadside and wait until morning to make any further advance. Part of the 3rd Calvary was to remain here and torch the village with phosphorus and they will arrive a little later at the bivouac area. Then we marched off into the gathering darkness.

We had gone only one-half mile when Capt. Batts brought the company to a halt telling us that due to the approaching darkness, we had better find a good position and start digging in. Then he informed us that we would not be in any rush tomorrow morning, which was April the 3rd. We were to let K and L Companies pass through and we were to fall in reserve again. This brought a loud cheer from the men. We began digging in along the hillside to the left of the road. We had only been digging a few minutes when we heard the shelling begin in the direction of the village. It was the boys of the 3rd Calvary putting the torch to the village. In a few minutes the flames began to rise above the trees from the direction we had come. The reaction from the men were mixed. Some cheered while others stared and said nothing. Me? I only remember the knot in my stomach growing larger and wishing we were closer to the fire, as it was already near freezing. I asked Cunningham as we dug in the frozen root infested ground, if he was part of the decision making process that favored digging and sleeping in the frozen earth over sleeping in warm houses? Or didn't he think that we could burn the village tomorrow morning after a warm night's sleep. Cunningham stopped digging, looked up and told me that they tell me what to do, I don't tell them. I told Cunningham that next time suggest it. That he knew that they didn't teach common sense at OCS only about following orders.

The fire from the burning village lit up the whole countryside. Cunningham and I decided to break out some K rations and have a bite to eat while we could read the label on the cans. It was no fun opening cans in the dark and not being able to recognize what was in it by taste or smell. Reading the label helped trick the old taste buds.

Cunningham and I dug until our trench looked like the top twelve inches of a grave. Then we broke a few evergreen branches and threw them in and placed a shelter half and a blanket over the branches. Then we crawled into the trench, stomach to back, pulled the other blanket and shelter half down over us and tried to get warm. I asked Cunningham if he had set up the guard system before coming to bed. I mentioned to him that I thought this was the first time him and I had slept together since Saarlautern and I thought he had lost a little weight. He came back with, he thought I should eat more K rations and gain a little weight. That he was getting tired of furnishing all the heat when we slept together and for me to stay alert. When he turned I was to turn and if I didn't he might mash my skinny ass. It had been a long hard day when I finally relaxed. My mind would not focus on the day's events and I fell asleep.

I believe we use the word sleep when under extreme conditions because of the lack of a word for the medium that I believe exist somewhere between sleep and coma. I know for a fact that a man can rest his brain while being aware of what is going on around him. It is possible to get rest in extreme temperature and even when walking. I believe this is a throwback from early man. Without it man would not have evolved. There are few conditions more stressful than what a foot soldier endures when they are in extended battle situations.

After hundreds of turns to thaw out the frozen side, it started to break day. Cunningham and I sat on the side of our foxhole and smoked a cigarette and prepared to make coffee. I asked Cunningham if he had extra water, that I was almost out. He said that he had, that he filled his canteen while searching the village yesterday. I asked him if he had used the right pump, that they had pumps they used to pump waste from outhouses and their barns. He replied that of course he knew and did I think he was stupid. I then asked him if he had heard that the boys in the South Pacific were suffering through a heat wave. Cunningham said if I didn't shut up he was going to get me transferred. I asked him where did they transfer an Infantry soldier to, to have him punished? His reply was "the graveyard". We drank our coffee while having a breakfast of crackers, ham and eggs and smoked a cigarette. Then Cunningham suggested that we go and see what the Captain had in store for us today.

As Cunningham and I walked toward the Company Command Post we could see those little fires springing up throughout the hillside. The boys were making coffee and heating the ham and eggs.

When we arrived at the Command Post Sgt. Harrell was instructing a detail of men where he wanted straddle trenches dug and for them to hurry. He was about to have coffee and he wanted it finished by the time he finished his coffee. Capt. Batts instructed Cunningham to tell his men that we would most likely be here until around noon. That K and L Companies were to pass through us soon, taking over the point and were to follow them until we crossed the Werra River, around midnight tonight, April 4th. We were then to join up with the 6th Armored Division and attack the city of Muhlhausen along with the rest of the 260th. At the same time the 259th will be attacking the city of Langensalza ten miles to our right. Capt. Batts told us to inform the men that we would be riding with the Artillery Boys this afternoon and probably throughout the night.

The one thing I disliked about being in reserve was having to ride those Artillery trucks at times. I preferred walking to the cramped spot that they wanted you to occupy. Spending all the night in freezing weather unable to straighten out your legs is like being placed on the rack. One would think that those Artillery boys bought and paid for the trucks themselves. When you would crawl up onto a truck after being assigned, it was up to you to find a place to ride. All the Artillery men would be stretched out as if they were asleep, clutching their loot that they were waiting for the chance to mail back to the States. Finally you would find a small space to wiggle into with your knees up under your chin. There you would sit until someone had to make a piss call, then you could maybe gain a few inches of space. The men that had the better bladder control ended up with the most space. Some of our older men, the ones that had already began to shave, could step onto the truck, pat his M1 and say he had his ticket to ride and to make room, which they usually did. They would give me a look of disdain, made me wonder who the hell the enemy was.

Around mid morning the vehicles of the 3rd Calvary started pulling out. Soon Land K Company's began passing through. Of course there was the usual "you will be sorry" from us on the side lines. Which was answered with the good natured raising of the middle finger from the passing troops. Following Land K Company's was some engineer outfit and behind them was our Company's kitchen and supply trucks. We drew ordnance and a day's supply of K rations. The trucks moved on. We were told to take it easy and stay around the area. That the Artillery trucks would be along soon.

Cunningham and I made more coffee and opened our lunch K ration. No surprises. After we ate Cunningham said that he was going around and talk to the men of our platoon and ask if I would like to come along. I told him that I was going to wrap myself up in my blanket roll over into our foxhole and take a nap, which I did. I was awakened a couple of hours later by rain hitting me in the face. A cold drizzle had began to fall. I think about the miserable night facing us on the trucks. Cold and rain, I am wondering if winter ever comes to an end in this part of the world. Back on the farm in Mississippi at this time of the year, we are turning the soil preparing to plant cotton. It was hard for me to fathom that it had only been two years ago on this date that I would be getting out of bed at four a.m. doing my chores before going to school. Then coming home in the afternoon, go work in the fields until dark, do your homework and be in bed before eight p.m. I wondered then if there could be anything in life worse than scraping out a livelihood on a Mississippi hill farm with my mother and dad and eight siblings. Yes there is! And I was living it. Finally around mid afternoon the artillery showed up. With them was a couple of empty six bys which was taken over by the weapons platoon and their equipment. The rest of the company managed to squeeze into, and on the artillery trucks. The trucks moved along at a fair pace until we caught up with some of 3rd Calvary armor. Then things slowed down. Darkness came and the pace really slowed. Finally around 2100 we stopped altogether. Word came down that K and L Company were in the process of crossing the Werra River Which was a couple of miles ahead. There were no sounds of battle coming from that direction, so we figured they were not meeting any resistance. Sometime in the wee hours we begin to move forward. We crossed the Werra sometime before daylight, by then I was in that zone between sleep and coma and I don't remember if we crossed a captured bridge or one built by our engineers.

Finally daylight came, April 4, 1945 we were told to disembark from the trucks that we were going to walk from here, which suited me fine. I had began to loose all feelings in my feet and legs. After sitting for hours with a rifle between your legs, holding it pointed upward and your knees drawn up beneath your chin unable to move, one does not only lose circulation of blood to your extremities but you began to loose all perspective. These two conditions are not conducive to a fast exit when confronted with extreme conditions, such as being suddenly attacked by a strafing plane.

There was a lot of grumbling, groaning and cursing of Hitler and his mama, plus a few choice words for some of our own leaders. We managed to crawl off the trucks. The Artillery Boys pulled away yelling to us to give them hell when we reached Muhlhausen and that they were behind us all the way. Our response was a lot of middle fingers pointing skyward. After the trucks pulled away we busied ourselves making fires and preparing for some hot coffee and cold K-rations. While we were feasting, word came down from the higher-up that our orders had been changed. We were not moving on to Muhlhausen just yet. We were to wait for the 6th Armored Division to move through ahead of us. That brought a big sigh of relief from our boys of "I" Company. After breakfast, we were told that we were going to be moving about three miles east to a small village that the rest of our Battalion had occupied. We would be waiting there until orders came down to move on Muhlhausen. The three mile walk to the next village was not too bad. It gave us a chance to work the kinks out of our backs and legs that we had obtained while crammed into the Artillery trucks. The ceiling was low and we didn't have to worry about those German planes appearing suddenly from out of seemingly nowhere causing a lot of skinned knees and hands and a few men wanting Purple Hearts because the enemy has drawn blood. When the medic gives them that doubtful look, they want to know why there is a difference in being hit on the knee with a flying brick and hitting your flying knee on a brick.

Around 0900 we came to a small farm village which had apparently been abandoned by the townspeople. Only a few G.I.s were visible along with a few 6th Armored Division tanks parked along the road. This made me feel better,. Obviously there were no enemy 88's around or they would not be so bold. We of "I" Company were told that this would be our home until further orders. The platoon leaders were told to select the billets for their men and be sure and see that guards were posted at strategic points and maintained at all times. Cunningham chose a hay barn for him and me, and a squad of our men led by Sgt. Rakosi. My good friend Howard Stern, being in Rakosi's squad was with us. It was great having him around to banter with again. Cunningham said he had chosen the hay barn because it was more open and he could keep better check on his men, without roaming around outside. I agreed with Cunningham and said I liked it because it had more exits than the homes. Stern said he knew why I liked it. That the smell of the cow manure pile outside the door made me feel like I was back home again in Mississippi. I informed him that there was a hell of a lot of truth in what he had said. I looked around and observed Tony Castagliola placing a cigarette in his mouth. I informed Cunningham that Tony was about to burn the barn down. Cunningham yelled at Tony, "if he knew anything about hay" and Tony's reply was that they did not grow hay in Brooklyn. He was informed that if he and any more of the city slickers wanted to smoke, they had to take it outside. Hay was as flammable as gasoline. I informed Stern that the same went for his sterno can. We would not be making coffee inside. Stern smiled and said that he would not be making coffee this afternoon but he had a bottle of that Rhine wine, that I thought so much of, wrapped up in his bedroll, just waiting for us to get together again. I told him to save it for V-Day, then both of us will go crazy together. We then broke out our K-rations, mixed our citrus powder with water in our canteen cups then using it to wash down the popular crackers and cheese.

After lunch some of the men wanted to wash up and shave. They got water from a well pump that was outside the barn. They had filled their helmets with water, brought them back inside the barn and was in the process of shaving when Tony decided he wanted to shave. He asked where they got the water. He was told that it came from a pump outside. Tony took his helmet, went outside, came back a few minutes later threatening to kick everyone's ass for tricking him. When asked what the problem was, he replied that it was not water he had pumped into his helmet, that it smelled like cow shit. We gathered around to take a look. Someone spoke up telling Tony that he had used the wrong pump, that he had used the "honey hole" pump. Tony wanted to know what the hell was a honey hole. Jasperson, who was from Minnesota and knew about such things, informed Tony that it was an underground tank where water was stored that had been used to wash out the farm animal stables. It was pumped into "honey wagons" to be taken to the fields to fertilize the vegetables. Stern told Tony to rub a little on his face and he might not have to shave. This brought the Italian expletives out of Tony. Cunningham told us that we best get some sleep, that orders could come to move out at any time. It did not take much encouragement for the men to wrap themselves in their blankets and "hit the hay".

Sleeping was fine until around 1700 when the movement of Armored vehicles along the road next to the barn brought everyone to a sitting position. Few things raise the hackle of a Grunt quicker than that particular rattling sound of a track vehicle approaching from an unobserved position. The guard at the door yelled out "Friendly Forces". Everyone lay back as if on cue. Cunningham came in a few minutes later telling us that he had some good news. He informed us that the 26th Regiment had reached Muhlhausen and the Germans had pulled out. The 261st along with units of the 6th Armored was already east of the city. He told us that the vehicles we heard passing was units of the 6th Armored moving into Muhlhausen and tomorrow morning we would be following. This good news sure helped everyone to get a good night's sleep. Daylight came, April 5th 1945. Without the sun it was cold and cloudy, but the good news about the enemy pulling out of Mulhausen, left everyone in an upbeat mood. It was rumored that Muhlhausen would be a tough nut to crack.

We sat around awaiting orders to move out. Of course it was as always, hurry and wait. Cunningham told us that the 65th had been assigned to the Eight Corps which was the left flank of the Third Army and after Muhlhausen we were to take the cities of Erfurt and Weimar. Both were reported to be heavily defended. There, we would be closer to Berlin than any allied troops. After Weimar, we would probably head for Berlin. It does not take much grist to get that rumor mill going up near the front.

It was around noon when Cunningham informed us that the kitchen and supply trucks were parked down the street. We should go down and draw our meal rations and ammo if we needed it. I needed meal rations, but I didn't think that I needed any ammunition. I had fired my rifle only twice since leaving Saarlautern. I checked my rifle ammo, the brass was turning green from being out in the weather and the hand grenades in my field jacket button holes were beginning to show rust. I asked Cunningham if I should get new ammo. He told me, "hell no! That the green made them more effective". If I only wounded the enemy with one of those green rounds he would probably die from ptomaine. I asked him about the rust on the hand grenades? He looked at me for a second and asked me if after the incident at Saarlautern, did I think that he should be giving instructions on the nomenclature and use of the fragmentation grenade. I told him that I knew of no one that had been up so close and personal with one as he had. That make him well qualified as a Grenade instructor. Cunningham informed me that his best qualification was in teaching wise asses in when to keep their mouth's closed.

Shortly after noon enough empty trucks showed up to transport the whole company into Muhlhausen.

It was mid-afternoon when we pulled up in front of a large modern four story building. It turned out to be a dormitory for the German military. It had been abandoned when the enemy pulled out of Muhlhausen. Everything in the building was intact and all the utilities worked. At one end of the first floor was a kitchen and a large dining room. The other end contained, what appeared to be, officers quarters and offices. The second and third floors contained what was obvious, the enlisted men's sleeping quarters. The rooms all contained four to six beds. There were bathroom facilities at each end of the floors. The top floor appeared to be all classrooms which was well lighted with lots of windows and skylights. When we arrived, units of the 4th Armored and units of the 6th Armored were already assigned quarters on the second floor. We of the 3rd Battalion 260th Regiment were assigned quarters on the third floor. Senior grade officers of both the Armored units and of the 3rd Battalion 260th occupied the first floor. All junior grade officers were billeted near their command. Capt. Batts set up "I" Company's command center on the 4th floor in one of the classrooms. The telephones and radio in the command center was manned by the company radio operator and the four company platoon runners, monitoring incoming messages and keeping in touch with Capt. Batts at all times. Shortly after our arrival in Muhlhausen, words filtered down that the 259th Regiment was meeting strong resistance in the city of Langensalza, which was located about ten miles southwest of Muhlhausen. Meanwhile the 261st had taken up positions on the northern flank of the 65th Division around the city of Struth. The 65th Division was now holding a line roughly twenty miles long, running from Struth on to the northeast of Muhlhausen to Langensalza, and to the southwest that was supported by units of the 6th Armored.

Capt. Batts spent most of his time on the first floor, where the 260th Regiment and Battalion command post were located. Being in reserve, the 260th was monitoring the situation in Langensalza closely, in case they needed help. Also the intelligence reports coming in from the northern flank showed an unusual amount of enemy troops in the vicinity of Struth, which was only about seven miles north of Muhlhausen.

Late in the evening the reports from the battle around Lagensalza, indicated that the 259th with the support of the 691st Tank Destroyer and the 748th Tank Battalion had caused the enemy to retreat from the city under the cover of darkness. While the news from the west and south was improving, the reports coming from our northern flank indicated the Germans were planning a counter-attack to try and retake the city of Muhlhausen. We of the 260th and other troops occupying the area in and around Muhlhausen were placed on the highest alert and being ready to move at a moment's notice.

All day the 6th of April, troop movements were ordered and most cancelled. The situation seemed to change every few minutes. The Company radio room was fast becoming a mad-house. The 300 radios going and the telephones that were always in constant contact with Capt. Batts. Plus every Platoon leader talking on the walkie-talkies at the same time. Total confusion reined. To regain control everyone was confined to their quarters and all walkie-talkies were to be shut off. All communications were to be limited to the telephones and the 300 radio and the Platoon runners. All communications were to go from the Company Commander, to the Platoon leaders, and through the Platoon runners. This left only six men in the radio room which improved the situation considerably.

As the afternoon passed the weather became worse. Cold and rainy, but the situation around Struth with the 3rd Battalion of the 261st seemed to be improving. The reports of L and K Company's obtaining billets for the night was coming through with no words of any enemy activity. We runners of "I" Company, knowing that we would have to spend the night in the communication room, retrieved our bedrolls from our quarters and spread them out on the floor of the communications room, then tried to get a little sleep.

Shortly after midnight, things started happening. The 300 radio came alive. Hell was going on somewhere. Lt. Irwin was on the phone speaking to Capt. Batts. Mostly what I was hearing him say was "Yes Sir right away". Then he gave us runners the message to awake every man in the Company and to be ready to move out at a minutes notice. Around 0200 it was reported that the 260th was sending two Company's to reinforce the 261st at Struth. The Company's were B from the 1st Battalion and L from our Battalion, the 3rd. The rest of the Battalion was to remain on high alert. Around 0300, radio contact was cut off. The only news that we were getting from Struth was coming by telephone from the Battalion. It was around 0700 when Capt. Batts called and told Erwin that our boys at Struth seemed to have taken control of the situation there. He also informed Erwin that we were going to have a hot breakfast this morning and to get "I" Company down to the first floor at about 0800 but to leave one man to answer the telephone in the communications room. I was elected.

I looked at my watch. It was 0815, I was alone in the communications room. I never liked being alone under any battle zone condition. I always got that funny feeling that I remembered getting when I was a child and was afraid of the dark. I walked over to the windows, which were facing toward the east, that was the direction of Struth. I pulled back the blackout curtains and it was almost daylight, the sun was coming up in the southeast. Quite a contrast to the day before when it had rained all day. It was days like today that made us Grunts feel good, especially since our fly boys seemed to have taken over the skies. I know that our men at Struth were glad to see the sun come up.

I opened the curtains and let the sun bathe the entire communications room. I sat down and leaned back in the chair and was almost asleep when the phone rang. It was Sgt. Cunningham. He told me that radio silence had been lifted and that I could turn the radios on and maybe I could learn something. I turned the 300 radio on there was nothing. The same was true of the walkie talkies. I listened for a few minutes, then I started fiddling with the walkie talkies. I reached a frequency where voices started coming through. I soon discovered I was tuned into the Fly Boys who were over Struth taking out the German tanks that were trying to retreat from Struth. The voices coming from the planes were really excited. They seemed to be flying the P47's equipped with rockets which seemed to be something new for them. They were really excited over the accuracy and effectiveness of the rockets. As I looked out of the window toward the east, and Struth being only 7 miles away, I could see the planes as they turned and made their passes at the enemy. To me, it was almost as exciting as it was to the pilots. It was if I was watching a movie. At the end the debate between the fly boys was how many tanks were destroyed and how many got away. The argument whether it was 11 out of 12 destroyed or 14 out of 15. They finally settled on 11 out of 12. Soon after I had lost contact with the Fighter Pilots, Cunningham and the radio operator came into the communications room and told me to go and get some chow. The word from Struth was good and our boys had the Krauts on the run. I then told him what I had heard from the Flyboys. He replied that he had heard about the planes but since I had gotten it first hand that I probably knew more about what was going on at Struth than he did.

I mention the flyboys incident because of the unusual circumstances of Grunt being able to observe any part of the war from a distance. His war was usually confined to a few hundred square yards in front of him. He never knew what was going on beyond those few yards. He had no time to observe, review or reflect on what happened, nor was there any procrastinating. There was always that next hill. Today was no different, as soon as the outcome of the battle at Struth was determined we were told to get our gear together and be ready to move out at a moment's notice. "Moments notice". Another catch word for "hurry up and wait". Sure enough the words came down around noon and we started our walk out of Muhlhausen around 1500. Our destination was unknown. The rumor was that we were going to a town nearby to regroup and were then to revert back to the 20th Corps. I never understood why we always had to go some other place to rest and regroup. Why couldn't we do these things at our present position?

It was while walking out of Muhlhausen that I observed my first jet aircraft. It was a couple of German ME 163. They came over at about 500 feet elevation making a sound that I had never heard before. It was a far different sound than that rattling sound of "Bed Check Charlie's" plane, which some of our men identified as being a Focke Wulf. The jets flew over us heading toward Muhlhausen. We could hear the chatter of their machine guns as they flew over the city. I wondered that maybe we were lucky getting out of town when we did. Our former billets could have been their targets. We found out later that whatever their target was, they missed it. They ended up hitting their own people and causing casualties among them. Nevertheless, the sight of the jets did not give a boost to my morale. Just what we didn't need to see, a new weapon of the enemy.

We had not walked but a short distance outside the city of Muhlhausen when we were loaded onto trucks and were told that we were going to the town of Waltershasen. A distance of about 20 miles where we would be billeted for a few days to regroup. Our billets at Waltershausen was once again former German Army barracks. Not bad, but not as good as the ones we occupied at Muhlhausen. The barracks had been formerly occupied by members of our 87th Division. They had just moved out earlier in the day onto the front lines. When we arrived our Company kitchen trucks had already arrived. They were set up and warming up some 10 to 1 rations, which was the better of the Army's field rations.

The building that our Company was assigned was two story. It had plenty of rooms but only about three quarters of enough beds. After Cunningham made the bed assignment for our Platoon, five men plus Cunningham and I were left to sleep on the concrete floor, wrapped up in our shelter half's and blankets. The nights in this part of Germany during April, still get below freezing and body heat never warms cold concrete. In order to get any sleep under these conditions, one must sleep with a buddy and keep turning. I asked Cunningham, "why was it that he and I always ended up with the worst sleeping conditions?" He told me that he had to take care of his men. I asked him if I was not one of "his men?" He replied that I was his Runner and that I was obligated to stay by his warm side at all times. I replied that I hoped that it was "damn warm tonight".

After sleeping arrangements had been made, we were told to form up outside in front of the building. Once outside Capt. Batts informed us that a forced labor camp had been discovered nearby a couple of days ago. The place was called "Ohrdruf Nord". Capt. Batts went on to describe how horrible the conditions were there and that orders had come down from 3rd Army that every American Soldier in the vicinity was to tour the place so that they could always bear witness to the Nazi's inhumane treatment of people who they considered enemies of the state. Capt. Batts told us that tomorrow morning after breakfast, which would be at 0700, that we would immediately report back outside in battle gear leaving our bedrolls, ready to load into trucks to be taken to the labor camps. Afterwards we would be returning here to rest up and regroup. Then we would be returning to the 20th Corps for a new assignment. We were told that there was no electricity in the buildings, that we should eat chow and get bedded down before dark and that all blackout rules would be observed.

The night passed like so many nights before, always cold, lying next to your buddy, trying to extract some heat from his body. The position of having your back against your buddy seemed to produce the best results. I suppose it was the warming of the nerves along the spinal cord to all parts of your body that made the difference. Even then you never were fully asleep. The ears were always awake. Another thing that was obvious to me, was when we were on the front lines, dug in and taking turns trying to sleep. You very seldom heard a cough from any of your buddies, but when you were in reserve and in a relaxed state, there was always coughing going on around you. I suppose fear acts as a cough suppressor.

Finally, after another night that was too long, it started breaking day. Luckily we had running water in the building. Unlike so many places we had stayed before, where we had to use straddle trenches and hold your hands up so the wind could blow the grime away.

Shortly after breakfast the trucks showed up. All of "I" Company, except the kitchen crew, loaded onto the vehicles. After a short trip of less than fifteen minutes the trucks turned off the main highway onto a secondary road that led into a wooded area. After a short distance, we came to a long one story building that turned out to be the office and guard quarters for the slave labor of Ohrdruf Nord. This camp was located south of the city of Gotha near the small city of Ohrdruf. The trucks pulled into the driveway in front of the building. There was a scattering of American troops outside. Some were MP's who waved the trucks to a halt. An Army Major came out of the building and met Capt. Batts who had stepped down from the first truck. They spoke for a few minutes and then Capt. Batts called the platoon leaders over and spoke to them. After the meeting the platoon leaders told us we were to break up into eighteen men groups and that there would be G.I. guides to take us through the camp. Each platoon was broken into two groups. We were led away, entering the camp through two gates. As we entered the gates, we could see several long low profile wooden buildings that was surrounded by a twelve foot high net wire fence, and topped with several strands of barbed wire.

As we approached the buildings we could see what appeared to be human bodies scattered over the area. They were human alright, but they had long since lost all appearance of a normal human. There was nothing there except skin and bones. Although they had been dead for several days there was no bloating, unlike the tissue laden bodies that we observed on the battlefield. After a couple of days they would be swelled twice their original size. Most of the bodies were dressed in the dirty grey and black vertical prison stripes, some were dressed in black pants and a jacket, and a few were totally naked. Upon close observation you could see that each one had been shot through the back of the head. The guide told us that the 4th Armored Division had come upon the camp April 4th and it now looks just the way it did the day of the discovery. Nothing has been changed. They had orders not to change anything until the "High Brass" came to inspect it and also to bring in News Correspondents to record the story. Especially since it was the first such camp that had been discovered inside Germany. The guide went on to tell us that the reason the prisoners were shot was that they were unable to walk. He said that when word came to the Germans that the Americans were closing in, the camp commander was given orders to move the prisoners to another camp deeper inside Germany. The only way they had to move was walk, and if there was any that were unable to walk, they were to be executed inside the camp. They did not want anyone left inside the camp to tell the story or take a chance on anyone escaping and taking revenge on the Germans that might live nearby. As we went further through the prison yard, we came upon a large pit that was criss-crossed with railroad rails, which had some half burned body parts on them. The guide told us that this was the crematory where the Germans cremated the bodies of the prisoners which was quite a few every day. At the bottom of the pit there was unburned parts of bodies, like arms and legs that had fallen through the cracks in the rail grid. An attempt to cut down on the stench was made by the Germans, by pouring lime over the body parts. With little success I might add. There were a couple of bodies that were hanging on the fence that surrounded the yard. They were shot as the tried to escape by climbing over the fence and then becoming lodged as their feet caught on the way down where they hung upside down. Next, we were led into a long low wooden building, approximately 150 ft. x 30 ft. At each end of the building was large double doors that opened into a runway that ran the full length of the building. The runway was wide enough to accommodate an average size vehicle. In the center of the building along the ceiling ran a single electric wire, from which hung a shaded light fixture with a single bulb. There was a total of 5 fixtures in the runway. There was no other artificial lighting in the building. The only other light in the building was coming from a few small barred windows that was at the top of the walls. There was no sign of any heating or cooling system.

Along the runway on both sides of the building was a platform that was about 3 ft. high that ran the full length of the building and was about 9 ft. wide. On top of the platforms next to the walls were 3 ft. x 6 ft. cubicles containing a straw mattress. On the inside of the platform, next to the runway was a bannistered walkway that ran the full length of the building. To the inside bannister, next to the sleeping cubicles was attached a chained shackle that could be used on either the leg or the arm of the person sleeping in the cubicles.

After entering the building through the double doors our group was split up. A column to the left and one to the right. We were told to take the short stair steps up to the walkway that ran along the platform next to the runway. As we moved along the runway and our eyes adjusted to the dim lighting. We could see that most every cubicle was occupied by a person. As our eyes became more adjusted to the light we could see that each person was obviously dead. Each person had a small hole in the middle of their forehead. They had been shot while their arm was still shackled to the railing. The bodies were in such emasculated condition that only a couple of drops of blood came from the bullet hole in their forehead. We walked the full length of the building and almost every cubicle contained the same macabre sight. One body still chained to the railing with a single bullet hole in his forehead, dressed in grey black prison garb, and lying on a straw mattress half covered with one dirty grey blanket. After walking out through the door at the other end of the building, our guide told us that this building had contained the incorrigible and mentally deranged. They were scheduled for execution and were waiting their turn before the Americans arrived. When word came that the Americans were closing in, the executions were carried out, but there was no time to burn the bodies on their "Funeral Pyre."

After we had finished our tour of the labor camp we returned to the parking lot where the trucks were unloading other G.I.s that were to tour the camp. Before loading onto the trucks for our return to our billets at Waltershausen. Capt. Batts asked if any one of us wanted to take a walking tour of the town of Ohrdruf, which was only a mile away. There were about two dozen men that volunteered to go. Cunningham and I were two of them. Cunningham sought out Pvt. Weik and persuaded him to come with us and be our interpreter. Cunningham was mad and he said he wanted to know why people that lived so close allowed things like this to happen.

Our little group, led by Capt. Batts, set out walking the half mile to the main road. After entering the main road we walked about another half mile when we came to a gate that was in an ancient looking wall. Over the gate in wrought iron letters was written "Ohrdruf." The M.P.'s at the gate waved us through. After walking down a slight incline for a couple of hundred yards, we entered a beautiful small city untouched by the war. There was a scattering of M.P.'s and a few curious civilians along the streets. Our group came to a halt about the center of town and Capt. Batts told us we would break up in small groups and take a walking tour of the town. We could ask the townspeople any questions that we wanted to. Capt. Batts had his own interpreter, whose name I can't recall. We of the 3rd platoon formed our own little group. It consisted of 12 men: Cunningham, Kindol, Rakosi, Jasperson, Castagliola, Blubaugh, Lavine, Hasemier, Stern, Spicer, Weik (our interpreter), and me. We looked around., but there were very few people near that we could ask questions. We walked down the street. After going about a half block, we observed through a window, loaves of bread stacked inside, and standing near the doorway was a middle aged man. About half of our group went inside. Cunningham started conferring with the man, using Weik to interpret. We found out that we were in a butcher shop and not a bakery. Cunningham asked the man if he would step outside, that some of the men had questions the wanted to ask him. He agreed and came out. The first question asked was who and where was the Burgomaster of the town. He gave us some name and told us that at the present time the Burgomaster was being questioned by the American Army officials. The man went on and told us that he was a Burgher in the town and that he would officially answer any questions that we might want answered. He said this with such an air of importance, that I provoked Cunningham to ask "what in the hell is a Burgher?" The man replied that it was a man of importance in the town and that he would answer any questions that we might have. Cunningham told Weik to ask if he was aware of the prison about a mile out of town. The man replied that he was. He was then asked if he was aware of the conditions there. His reply was that he had never been there and was unaware of any of the activities that went on there. Cunningham told him that he did not believe that a man of such importance, as he claimed to be, was unaware of what was going on within a mile of his town. The man answered, what made him a man of importance was that he always attended to his business and not other people's. This answer really burned Cunningham up and he told the man that we were going to change his business. We were going to see that pretty soon he was going to become a "Grave Digger". Cunningham also told him that he should tell all the townspeople to start practicing their Litter Bearing and Grave Digging technique. After speaking with this man, we knew that speaking with any of the other residents was pointless. We also understood more about how the places like The Ohrdruf-Nord Labor Camp could exist. It ran much deeper than "good people saying nothing". We walked back to the gate and waited for the rest of the group to arrive. They all came back shaking their heads in disbelief. It was hard to believe that no one in the town knew what was going on at the camp. Did the wind always blow one way? The trucks came and we loaded up and returned to our billets at Waltershausen. The ride back gave me time to reflect on what I had observed this day. I had heard rumors of these things going on inside Germany. Today I saw with my own eyes, never to be forgotten, man's inhumanity toward other men, and that we must always be cognizant of what goes on inside other governments of the world, even our own. The pages of history are filled with similar exploits that Hitler undertook.

We arrived back at the billets too late for lunch, the men who returned earlier had eaten. The mess sergeant offered to prepare us something since the men who had returned prior to us were not too hungry and some did not eat at all. There was plenty of food left and it would not take him long to heat it. We all agreed that we would wait until dinner. Our appetite had taken a leave of absence.

Returning to our quarters and seeing our bedrolls on the floor, we that had slept on the floor last night, started planning on what steps to take to prevent that from happening again. We decided the best plan would be to go out into the town, scout around and see if the townspeople had extra mattresses. We agreed that we had best check with Capt. Batts before we carried it out. The Capt. agreed that in light of what we had seen today, that he thought it was an excellent idea. Off into the town we went. At first we sought out the generosity of the German people, but it did not take us long to realize that this had to turn into a raid. After witnessing what had happened at the labor camp and the callousness of the people in the town of Ohrdruf, we were in no mood to be deterred by the crying of children, the screaming of old women and the barking of dogs. We formed our mattress brigade and marched through the heart of town and right into our billets. The M.P.'s only smiled at us as we paraded past them. Cunningham and I slept well backed up to each other that night.

After a couple of days rest at Waltershausen, we were given notice that we would be moving out to the south, toward the town of Arnstadt. It was reported that the 87th and 89th Divisions, who were attacking east, had bypassed a rather large contingent of Germans that were not ready to surrender. It seemed that it had fallen the lot of the 259th and the 260th to change their minds.

While at Waltershausen, the rumor mill had been grinding. It seems that on the same day that the 4th Armored had discovered the labor camp at Ohrdruf, the 90th Division had discovered near Merkers, a town, a short distance east of Ohrdruf. It was a salt mine containing most of Germany's gold

Murdered prisoners near the main gate in Ohrdruf-Nord

American Generals view dead bodies left out for a week

Survivors told Eisenhower prisoners were hung with piano wire

Americans view cremation pyre on April 13, 1945

Gen. Eisenhower views bodies burned on railroad tracks

Corpses sprinkled with lime in shed at Ohrdruf-Nord camp

Ohrdruf-Nord survivor shows shallow grave to Generals

reserve that had been moved there from Berlin and other places in Germany, so as not to fall into the hands of the Russians. The cache was reported to contain $3 billion in paper money from every country in Europe that the Germans had invaded. There was also 250 tons of gold, in gold bars, bullion and trunks filled with gold teeth, gold rimmed glasses, gold watches, wedding rings and strings of pearls taken from the extermination camps. Besides the gold and paper money, there was also 400 tons of art, most of which had been looted from the countries of Europe that the Germans had occupied. It was reported to have taken 30 10-ton trucks just to move the gold and paper money.

All this gold and treasure got the attention of all the high brass in the European theater and they all converged on this little spot in Germany. In this group was both General Eisenhower and Bradley. On the 12th of April General Patton met Eisenhower and Bradley at an airport near Merkers. They proceeded to the salt mine to check out the cache. After leaving the salt mine, they came by the Ohrdruf-Nord Labor Camp to observe what had been reported to them about the camp. They said that the horror inside this camp could not be described, it had to be seen. It was reported that General Patton got sick after touring the place. He recovered in time to give instructions on how he wanted the situation handled. He said that he wanted all the civilians in the nearby towns to be brought in to see their handy work. Then he wanted the civilians to help carry the bodies of the victims to a designated burial place, which he would point out, and they would also help bury them.

It was around noon on April 11th when word came down that we would be moving out of Waltershausen toward Arnstadt, town near where it was reported that the first battalion of the 260th was. At the present, was engaged in bitter fighting trying to clear out the pockets of resistance left by the 87th and 89th Divisions as they attacked east through Truringer towards the Republic of Czechoslovakia. After lunch we were told to return to our billets and remain until the trucks came for us, which could be at any time. Sure enough "any time" was about three hours later. Late was alright by me. I wasn't spoiling for a fight. The only bad thing was leaving this late in the afternoon usually meant spending a cold night hunkering down in a cold truck with nothing asleep except for your ass and legs. When the trucks pulled up, there was a cheer from the men. They were Red Ball and we were all thankful we would not be riding cramped up on those Artillery trucks.

The trucks moved out and after a short distance, pulled onto the Autobahn. The traffic on the Autobahn was slow due to the large amount of traffic and the blown bridges that the retreating Germans blew up as they retreated. The engineers were kept busy building detours. The sun was setting when we turned off the Autobahn onto a secondary road, heading southwest. A road sign read "Arnstadt 17 kilometer". The trucks came to a halt and word came down that we would have a rest ,stop and feast on K rations, and have our last smoke for the day before darkness. While we were eating, word came down that the 1st and 2nd Battalions had made contact with the enemy near Arnstadt and it was reported that tiger tanks were involved. Just the news I needed while trying to push the cheese and crackers past the knot that was beginning to grow in the pit of my stomach. No need for worry, the trucks did not travel over 5 miles all night. I was very cold but happy that I was only in earshot of the battle. It was always great to play that reserve role.

Daylight came and word filtered down that the battle was over around Arnstadt. All the enemy had been killed or captured. After the good news everyone was ready to build those little fires and have a cup of coffee and a smoke. Boy those canned ham and eggs never tasted so good. We remained parked on the road outside Arnstadt while an advanced party from our 3rd Battalion went into Arnstadt to check out the results of the fight and to check for billets for the Battalion. The rumor was that we were to spend a couple of days in the vicinity while being reassigned to the Corps and we were to move from the northern flank of the 3rd Army to its southern flank. Our objective was to cut off the escape route of the Germans who were reported to be trying to retreat into the Alps Mountains to set up a Redoubt Area to make a last stand.

It was around noon before the advanced party returned. We were told to retrieve all our gear from the trucks, that we were going to walk the rest of the way. The trucks were then dismissed. They turned around an went back the way we had come.

It was only a couple of hours walk to Arnstadt. We stopped in front of a barracks type building which was rather small. You could hear groaning coming from the men as they kept saying "not again". Space being limited in the barracks, we of the 3rd Platoon of "I" Company took over a couple of private homes located near the barracks. This gave us an opportunity to do what we had not been able to do in the last couple of weeks, check out the wine cellars. This we did and by the time Sgt. Cunningham finished with the briefing by Capt. Batts, we of the 3rd Platoon were well on our way to a high that we had not enjoyed in a while. Cunningham was unhappy about the situation and asked Sgt. Smith why he had let this happen. Smith's only answer was "man, I was thirsty". Cunningham told the men that they had only made it hard on themselves. There would have to be four more men for guard duty tonight to guard the doors to the wine cellars. Stern did not help the situation by telling Cunningham that he thought he could get volunteers for that job. Sgt. informed Stern that he was glad to hear him volunteering for the job.

The next morning April 13th, we were called out for Company formation in the barracks parking lot. Capt. Batts informed us that the day before, on April 12th, our Commander in Chief and the President had died while on vacation in Warm Springs, Georgia. My first thoughts were of the effect that this might have on the duration of the war. Then a feeling of great loss came over me. Being only six years old when Franklin D. Roosevelt was elected president, he was the only president that I could remember having. After the death of the president announcement, Capt. Batts went on to tell us that the 65th Division was receiving a new assignment. We would be reassigned to the 20th Corps which was moving to the southern flank of the Third Army. There, we of the 65th Division, would be given a new zone which is running through Bavaria, across the Danube River through the city of Regensburg and into Austria. There we would be facing the enemy in rugged terrain, the foothills of the Alps Mountains.

The rest of the day was spent checking and cleaning gear and drawing needed ordnance. The Quartermaster trucks showed up in the afternoon, bringing our duffel bags with a change of clothes. Having no running water around, we changed clothes without a bath. We found a few hand pumps scattered nearby and some of the men were able to shave and take spit baths from their helmets. The kitchen truck showed up late and had to rush to get to us the hot meal we were promised. The meal consisted of some sort of goulash, stale bread and coffee. The goulash was so bad that the cook's were accused of using the meat from the dead horses we had seen along the highway.

After breakfast the next morning on April 14th, the trucks showed up and we were told to board them while no destination was given to us. We pulled onto the highway where we joined a long line of other trucks which contained the rest of the 3rd Battalion of the 260th. We moved along the highway for a few miles, where we came to a large open field. The trucks pulled into the field forming a huge circle, reminiscent of circling the wagons in the western movies. Inside the circle was every high brass of the 3rd Battalion and then some. After a short conversation among themselves, they called for all the Company to come forward to where they were. After a few words with them the Company Commanders came over to the trucks and informed all the troops that they were to unload from the trucks bringing all their equipment and form up inside the circle of trucks. "Then wonder of wonders." The powers that be, broke out the "Bull Horns" and proceeded to give instructions on what we were to do. First we were told to unroll our bedrolls, that we were going to have a full field inspection, that we were to display everything that we had in our possession onto the blanket in our bedroll, that included everything that we had in our pockets. After this was done we were then told to take everything that was not G.I. and place it on the ground in front of our bedrolls. This was done and then the inspection began. After a lot of milling and looking by the inspectors, we were told to roll up our bedrolls leaving everything that was not G.I. on the ground. Then some Full Bird Colonel identifying himself as being from 20th Corps Headquarters, got on the horn and began telling us that making us give up our loot was for our own protection because if we were captured our captors might take offense to us having in our possession German Military Hardware or other German goods. The Colonel's words brought a rumbling from the men. Through my mind goes the thought that if you want to protect me, make me your jeep driver. We were ordered to return to the trucks and to be on our way. There were a lot of disgruntled Grunts grumbling as we pulled away. We felt as if we had just been robbed. We had risked limbs and life from the threat of booby traps to secure our booty. But faith springs eternally, the war wasn't over yet.

The next five days were spent heading south in reserve behind front line troops. The going was slow because we kept running into pockets of fanatical German SS and Hitler Youth that were not ready to surrender. Heading south, we were roughly following the route of the southbound Autobahn. Sometimes walking, sometimes riding, and always having to take detours because of the German's scorched earth policy. They blew up every bridge on the Autobahn as they retreated, trying to slow our advance.

On the evening of April 18th, we moved into Bamberg where we secured billets. Our first night not spent on trucks since leaving Arnstadt. While at Bamberg, the rumor mill was grinding it out. The 65th was nearing their assigned sector at the southern flank of the Third Army and would be moving up to make an assault across the Danube. Bamberg wasn't too far from the city of Nurnberg, which was a large city, and that the units of the 7th Army had just taken it and moved on south. The Germans had retreated out of Nurnberg, and gone east toward the Danube River where we of the 65th would be making contact with them in a couple of days. The next day we boarded the 65th Artillery trucks and moved southeast to the town of Altdorf.

While at Altdorf, the battle plan for the 65th began to emerge. Our objective was to capture Regensburg. A city on the south side of the Danube, and situated in a large bend in the river. The 65th's battle plan was to cross the Danube, above the city and come in through the back door. Roughly, the plan was for the 65th to cross the Danube west of Regensburg, swing down river to join forces with the 71st Division, who was crossing the river east of Regensburg. This would be cutting off the escape route of the enemy and capturing the city.

The positioning of the 65th was to have the 260th on the left, the 259th in the middle, and the 261st on the right. From Altdorf the three regiments would move abreast toward the river positioning themselves for the assault across the river. Early on the morning of the 26th of April, the 260th and the 261st would cross the river abreast in assault boats while the 259th remained in reserve.

We moved out of Altdorf on the 20th of April, slowly making our way toward the town of Duerling, where we were to assemble and prepare for the crossing. Our progress was slowed by the strong resistance the 259th was encountering at the city of Neumarket, which was located on the main highway that led from Nurnberg to Regensburg. The resistance was probably coming from German troops that had been driven from Nurnberg earlier by units of the 7th Army. The enemy's purpose here was to slow down our advance toward Regensburg. We of the 260th, on the left of the 259th and the 261st on the right, pushed by the 259th, figuring the Germans would retreat from Neumarket for fear of getting cut off from retreating across the Danube but they hung tough until the 22nd of April. By then they had all been killed or captured.

The three days were spent traveling south toward the town of Duerling which was located near the Danube River near the planned crossing site of the 260th Regiment. The seventy miles from Altdorf to Duerling took almost five days. The men on the point kept running into pockets of resistance and by the time units were organized to meet the resistance, the Germans would pull back. After these small skirmishes, it usually would take us from two to three hours to get moving again. We were digging in at night, not wanting to get too far ahead of the 259th, who was meeting strong resistance on our right in the city of Neumarket. During the five days the weather was good and the Jabos controlled the skies. The only plane that the Germans put up during this period was "Bed Check Charlie" who would show up as usual, right after dark.

On the afternoon of April 23rd, between the towns of Velberg and Duerling one of our artillery spotter planes observed a small detachment of German army troops moving out of a rather large fenced in area which was located on a wooded hillside, about 300 yards to our left. The Germans were spotted leaving through a back gate about a quarter mile away being transported by light armor. "I" Company drew the assignment to search the fenced facility. We of the third platoon drew the assignment to go inside the fence and check it out, while the remainder of the Company remained outside the fence to cover us. Inside we found quansethut type buildings, some built into the hillside. The first buildings we searched contained Nazi propaganda material. There were hundreds of bales of leaflets that were of the type dropped from planes. They were in several languages and millions of small paper flags with the swastika insignia on each side. Other huts contained straw mattresses and old grey blankets of the type I remembered seeing at the prison at Ohrdruf. The buried and half buried huts contained munitions, some had concrete cellars containing more munitions. We found the place abandoned and as we met with the Battalion officers outside the gate to inform them of our findings, everyone was wondering why the place had escaped the wrath of our Air Force. Someone pointed out the similarity of the site to the slave labor camps that dotted the area. From the air it could have been mistaken for one of these camps by reconnaissance planes.

After a short meeting of the Battalion brains, it was decided that since the Battalion was going to bivouac in the area for the night, we of the 3rd Platoon would dig in along the fence and place guards at the gate to the dump. The rest of the Company left us and dug in along the roadside about a half mile away. Sgt. Cunningham had the men dig in along the fence line. Then he decided that he and I and the three Assistant squad leaders would spend the night in the guard house that was beside the gate. The five of us would take turns pulling guard duty and let the men get a good night's sleep. This plan was alright with me since it put us inside, out of the weather, and each of us would only have to pull a couple of hours guard duty.

It was shortly after dark, some of the men were still working on their foxholes, when we heard the distinct sputtering of Bed Check Charley's Focke wulf motor approaching. Someone shouted "Here Comes Charlie right on time!" I don't know how many Bed Check Charlie's there were, but he flew the battle line every evening right after dark. I suppose to see how much the battle line had changed in the last 24 hours. The sound of Charlie's plane suddenly changed. He was turning and was in a dive, seemingly headed straight at our position. At that moment I think all the men were wishing that the depressions that they had dug to sleep in were just a little deeper. We heard the release of the bomb as it whistled its way toward us. It fell about 300 yds. from us inside the compound. The plane turned and came back over us but this time he never released a bomb, but flew on by. We were mystified by Charlie's sudden change of behavior and wondered if it was Charlie at all. We found out the next morning that the bomb had missed an ammo dump by about 30 yds. Later it was rumored that the dump contained chemical bombs. We all felt lucky that Charlie's aim was bad.

The next morning on April 24th, we were relieved of our guard duty at the ammunition dump by a unit of the 13th Armored Division. We joined our Company, were served a breakfast of rehashed 10 in 1 rations by our Company cooks, whom had caught up with us during the night and spent most of the night preparing a hot meal for us. It was much appreciated by all.

By evening of the 24th, the 260th was assembling near the town of Duerling in preparation for the assault on the city of Regensburg, which was rumored to begin sometime in the early hours of April 26th.

Most of the evening and night of the 24th was spent in what appeared to me as total confusion. There were discussions of billeting going on and areas of assignments being questioned. Nothing was accomplished. The troops sat on the trucks or lay beside the roads until daylight of the 25th. That's when things started to get organized. The only ones that seemed to accomplish anything during the night was the cooks. They had set up the kitchen trucks and had those 10 in 1's ready by daylight. It was great just holding your canteen cup out and having it filled with hot coffee without all the jousting of a half dozen cups trying to heat water over a small fire, giving up and drinking it lukewarm.

After drawing rations for the 26th and being issued ordnance, the battle plan began to emerge. Basically the plan was for the 260th and the 261st to cross the Danube River in assault boats abreast about seven miles west of Regensburg. The 260th was on the left nearest to the city, and the 261st was on the right. The 260th was to establish a bridgehead out to about a thousand yards deep, then wait for the 261st to pull alongside the 260th's right flank, there they would attack to the north entering Regensburg through the back door.

We spent most of the 25th reviewing battle plans and studying maps. About mid afternoon we were told that the cooks had prepared a hot meal for us, that we would eat and then prepare to start moving toward the river to get into position for the crossing, which would begin shortly after midnight. I could not eat, that knot in my stomach had enlarged and moved up into my throat. I managed to swallow a little of that lemonade made from powder. That last meal scenario kept going through my mind as I looked around at some of my buddies and wondered, "Who this time?"

After chow, we began moving towards the river. It was a slow process getting a regiment in position according to plans. As we of the Infantry moved toward the river, we passed through armored vehicles with the artillery already in position, and the engineers with all types of equipment from assault boats to all types of bridge building materials. Seeing the engineers always gave us Grunts a morale boost. These guys knew what it was all about, "hold the ground and they will get you help" and lots of times they helped with the holding of the ground. The Army Combat Engineers were amazing! They did their work under some of the worst possible conditions and to watch them was an inspiration to all of us grunts.

It was around 2200 when our slow advance toward the Danube was halted and we began to get our last orders and briefings. I as the third Platoon Runner was again assigned to the Company Headquarters group and was to cross the river in the assault boat with Captain Batts, Sgt. Harrell, the man operating the 300, and a couple of more runners from the other platoons. Slowly the battle plan for the crossing of the river by the 260th began to emerge. The second Battalion would be the first to cross in assault boats. After reaching the other side they would fan out and advance down river, sweeping along the river bank. The third Battalion would follow, led by "I" Company. We of "I" Company were to cross the river, go east about 500 yards then turn north for a couple hundred yards. K and L Companys were to pass to our rear, then pull up on our right flank. Then the 260th was to work slowly towards Regensburg which was located about eight miles down river in a steep bend. The reason for us to go slow was to wait for the 261st to come up along our right flank. The plan was to be in Regensburg by sundown. These were the best laid plans.

0130 came, we were alerted to get ready to move up in position behind the second Battalion, who had already began loading onto the assault boats. Word came down that the decision had been made to not do any saturation shelling by our artillery across the river. Maybe we could catch them by surprise. The no shelling order brought forth a lot of grumbling from the men. Through my mind runs the thought that we may outnumber them but we sure as hell are not going to surprise them. Especially with the moonlight that we had tonight.

0200 came and all was quiet. Then suddenly all hell broke loose upriver in the vicinity of where the 261st was crossing. At first, it was only small arms fire with an occasional mortar round. There certainly wasn't any surprising going on upriver. Meanwhile, there was not a sound coming from across the river where the second Battalion had landed. Finally around 0400 the last of the second Battalion had loaded onto the boats and was preparing to cross. Captain Batts whispered to us that we were next. By this time the river banks had turned into a quagmire and we were struggling to keep our balance in the mud. Finally the engineers started showing back up on our side of the river. After a short conference with some of the higher brass, it was decided that the battalion patrol would be the first of the third Battalion to cross. The patrol moved by us and started loading into the assault boats. I recognized some of the group, but had not seen them since Saarlautern, and had heard of their exploits. They were a small group and it only took a couple of boats for them. As they pulled away I heard someone complaining about not having a boat paddle. Someone answered telling him to use his rifle as a paddle.

Finally our time came, as our little "I" Company Headquarters group stepped up to board the boats. A 2nd Lt. stepped up and said that he was crossing with us, that he was a forward observer for the Artillery, and that he would be moving with us for a while. He told us that we had better protect him or we would not get any protection from the Artillery. We Grunts understood that. There might have been some resentment when we were riding on their trucks, but we sure did appreciate them when we ran into trouble. They could lay the big stuff out where we needed it with pinpoint accuracy when they had that Forward Observer in place.

About fifteen minutes later we came to the other side of the river. There still was not a sound coming from in front of us, while hell was still raging upriver where the 261st were crossing. The silence in our zone made me wonder if we were not doing something wrong. When reaching the other side of the river we moved up a slight bank into a growth of small trees and then into an open meadow. We were being followed by the second Platoon which was led by Lt. Collins.

At this point Capt. Batts called for the scouts from the second Platoon to come forward. He instructed them to move ahead, following a direct southeast azimuth, slowly to about 500 yards and wait. Meanwhile the first Platoon was to cross the river, cut across our rear, then pulling along our right flank. The third Platoon was to cross and take up positions as Company reserves. The 1st Battalion of 260th was to cross last and take up positions in Regimental reserve. As we moved slowly along, we were meeting no resistance. In fact, there were no sounds of any kind coming from the 260th's zone of operation. The sounds coming from up river were telling a different story about the 261st zone.

It was around 0530 when we reached the rallying point with the second Platoon scouts. Captain Batts was on the radio speaking with Battalion headquarters. After the conversation with headquarters, Capt. Batts got on the walkie-talkie to the Platoon leaders, informing them that we were to advance north about 300 yards and dig in and wait because the 261st was meeting strong resistance and would not pull along our right flank at the planned time.

It was breaking day when we reached our assembling point. We were in an open field. There was a wooded ridge to our left front, starting out at about 300 yards and disappearing into a forested area about a half mile away. To our right and front was rough terrain covered with mixed forest. After daylight we could see a building of some sort, partially hidden by trees, about 500 yards on the ridge to our left front.

The reports coming in over the radio was that the engineers were having a hard time bridging the river and ferrying supplies across because of the shelling by the Germans. It was also reported that our second Battalion had captured some German prisoners to our left along the river, but could not take them to the rear because the river crossing was not completed yet. The prisoners were reported to have been turned over to the Battalion Patrol. We were told to hold our position until further orders.

It was around 0900 when word came down that the river had been bridged and supplies and heavy equipment was being moved across. At this time we of third Battalion received orders to move forward, to clear the highway leading from Matting to the junction of highway leading from Abbach to Regensburg. We had moved about 100 yards when suddenly the sound of shelling and small arms fire was coming from our right flank, which was K Company's zone. At about the same time we began receiving machine fire onto our position. It was ascertained that the fire was coming from the building that we had spotted earlier to our left front. Someone on our left opened up with aBAR, firing toward the building. The rest of the 2nd Platoon joined in. The machine gun fire slowed down for a minute. That is when the Artillery Observer, who was with us, went into action. He was on the radio immediately to the Artillery determining the position of the enemy's machine gun. A few seconds later a couple of artillery rounds landed near the building where the machine gun was located. The Observer never stopped talking. The third round slammed into the building. I heard the observer tell the gunners to "fire for effect". In seconds the building was a blazing inferno. Expecting the 88's to come raining down on us at any second, we immediately began moving forward as fast as possible, before being bracketed in. Sure enough, as soon as we were about 200 yards away our original position was being pulverized by German 88's.

We moved toward the tree lined ridge where the machine fire had come from. We entered a draw to the left of the ridge. Entering the draw, we and the second Platoon was in a staggered column as we drew near the building where the machine gun had been, which was on our right at this time. Capt. Batts halted the column and had several men from the second Platoon to check out what was left of the burning building. Finding no life, the men returned and we continued on up the draw. Sounds of strong shelling was coming to us from over the ridge to our right. This was the vicinity where K Company was advancing. We kept moving slowly up the draw following a couple of scouts from the second Platoon. Strung out behind our little headquarters group, followed the second Platoon with Sgt. Craig in front, a couple of steps behind me. Lt. Collins the second Platoon leader was at the rear of the Platoon. All of a sudden we started getting tree burst from German artillery. A shell slammed into an evergreen that was standing about ten feet to our right. It struck about thirty feet up, severing it. The top part of the tree came down and stuck into the ground only a few feet to our right. We of the headquarters group and several men of the second Platoon were knocked off their feet by the concussion. There was a loud grunt from the man in front of me, who was carrying the 300 radio, because he hit the ground with the radio on top of him. Lying on the ground, I heard a low moan behind me. As I slowly turned around I spotted a steel helmet laying beside me with a jagged hole in the top of it. Turning further I could see Sgt. Craig a few feet away on his back, ashen faced, with blood coming from the top of his head. Sgt. Harrell, who was lying nearby, crawled over, laid his hand upon Craig and mouthed the words, "He is breathing." He then called out for the medic who was at the rear of the Platoon. The medic came forward along with Lt. Collins. They kneeled down and started administering to Craig. The shelling stopped as abruptly as it had began. We were preparing to move on when Sgt. Harrell felt pain in his stomach. He looked down and blood was coming through his shirt above the belt line. He opened his shirt and there was a gash about three inches long across his stomach. Evidently a piece of shell fragment had struck him and in the ensuing excitement, he had failed to feel the pain. We moved on, leaving Craig, Harrell, the Aid man, and a second Platoon Rifleman to wait on the litter bearers, who had been called and were on their way. We again started to move toward our objective, which was a couple of farm houses at the edge of the Village of Matting. It had been reported that there was a detachment of German soldiers dug in nearby, ready to defend the road leading to Regensburg.

When we were within about a half mile of our objective, a patrol of eight men were sent out to see if they could make contact with the enemy. The patrol reported back about an hour later, saying that the only Germans that they had encountered were being held prisoner by members of our Battalion patrol in a hay barn near the buildings we were to secure. They said that they had entered the two farm houses in question and had searched the premises, but had not seen any signs of the enemy. The patrol also reported that the Battalion Patrol told them the Germans had pulled out for fear that they would be cut off by K Company, which was moving up on our right. As we approached our objective, members of the patrol pointed out the barn where the Battalion Patrol were holding the prisoners. Standing outside were a couple of G.I.'s. As we drew near a 1st Lieutenant came out of the building. He came over to us and reported to Capt. Batts. He said that he was holding nine prisoners inside the barn and one of them was mortally wounded, that he was shot through the "gut." He went on to say that he had been in touch with the Battalion. They were sending men to pick up the prisoners, but that three hours had passed and no one has shown up yet. He asked if the men were with us, or if we had seen them? Capt. Batts told him we had not. The Lieutenant then asked Capt. Batts if he could spare a couple of men to take the prisoners back across the river. Capt. Batts answer seemed to agitate the officer. He saluted, turned and walked, mumbling something about, he guessed that he would have to take care of the problem himself, that he was getting fed up with all the moaning and being questioned about when are the medics going to show up. He went on to say the Battalion Patrol had not been organized to shuttle P.O.W.'s. Capt. Batts told him that he would have to take that up with Battalion Headquarters.

We moved up and took control of our objective which consists of two farmhouses and the surrounding area. The house had been abandoned, all the furniture was in place and the farm animal quarters showed signs of recent occupancy. It was around 1300 hrs. when we finished taking up our positions and my appetite had long ago returned. It had been twenty-four hours since I had thought of eating. I had already learned, through experience and observation, that fear knots and K Rations were not compatible.

After eating the breakfast and lunch portions of the day's rations, the men of the second Platoon were scattered around trying to get some badly needed sleep. I was still with Capt. Batts and the Company Headquarters group. We sat in the kitchen of one of the houses and sipped coffee made from water heated on an old wood stove, that we had managed to get a fire built in, not only for the coffee, but for the heat. After relaxing we had began to feel the bitter cold that seemed to be never ending in this part of the world.

Capt. Batts was on the radio. The news he was receiving was not too good. It seemed the bridge that was reported completed, was knocked out shortly afterward, and was not yet completed again. They were still ferrying supplies across, but was unable to get the heavier equipment across. The 261st was still bogged down at Abbach and it appeared they would need help in securing the road leading from Lengfeld to Regensburg, which was vital to our success in taking Regensburg. After communicating with the Battalion, Capt. Batts called in all "I" Company Platoon leaders. Cunningham, who was on the right, having his men dig in along the roadway, arrived with a few of my buddies who were tagging along. One of them was my old buddy Stern. He was wanting to see the P.O.W.'s that were in the barn, just a couple of hundred yards to our rear. I told him I would go with him, I was curious also. As we approached the door of the barn, we recognized one of the guards by the door. He was one of our former Platoon members before joining the Battalion Patrol. When we stepped inside the barn, we could see the prisoners to our right. Most were sitting against the wall, one was lying in front of them on a bed of hay, obviously wounded. He was accompanied by another prisoner who was holding the wounded man's hand and applying a wet cloth to his forehead. Standing in the middle of the barn was a German Army officer conversing with the Battalion Patrol Officer. When we walked in, the German officer spoke up in a loud voice, using perfect English, "maybe these men have a Medic with them." The Battalion officer replied that he had already checked with our Company commander and that our medic was still at the rear, treating the wounded. Stern and I stepped back outside and was talking with our old Platoon mate, Harlumpus. When the Patrol Officers came out murmuring something about, "He is not going to need a medic where he is going". He then started giving instructions to our friend, telling him to take two members of the patrol, and the three of them would take the P.O.W.'s back to the river crossing and turn them over to the M.P.'s. The three of them must be back by 1600, because that was when their mission started. Stern and I returned to the Company Headquarters. We never found out what happened to the P.O.W.'s or what the Battalion Patrol's mission was.

After returning to Company Headquarters we learned that we were to dig in, along the road for the night. The 1st Battalion of the 260th was to go to the aid of the 261st at Abbach and help clear the highway leading to Regensburg. I returned to my Platoon and again I had to spend the night in a foxhole keeping Cunningham warm.

Lying in our shallow trench Cunningham and I tried to remember the last night that we slept in a foxhole. We could not remember the last few days, they all ran together. Although it had only been a short time, some of the happenings seemed to have occurred long ago. I suppose this was due to the semblance of the villages, always having bad weather conditions and the repeat nature of our missions, would cause one to lose all perspective.

Daybreak, the 27th of April, it finally arrived. The little fires of the coffee makers started to appear up and down the road. The night had been a quiet one in the 260th's zone, but the sounds of war raged all night, upriver in the 261st's zone. I could not help thinking about the adage "The luck of the draw". Breakfast was skimpy this morning. Almost everyone had finished off their rations the day before, and the conditions that existed along the river prevented us from being resupplied. Everyone was emptying out their pockets, dipping into their reserves, and trying to borrow from their frugal friends. Some were searching the area around the farm houses, just in case the owners failed to catch one of their chickens or farm animals as they evacuated the farm.

As I watched the men having breakfast, it was amazing to observe how the camaraderie among the men had grown since coming on the line. It was not that we were not close before. It had grown from, "you buy me a beer, I buy you a beer", at Jack Dempsey's, to "I have an extra candy bar and I will sell you one", at Camp Lucky Strike. Today it was, "If I have two bites, the two of us have a bite each" and it grew from there to, "Eat it, I am not hungry". I did not know at the time, that this feeling for each other, of the men who stood toe to toe with the enemy, would last a lifetime.

The weather today, was like most days we had seen since landing in Europe. Cold, cloudy, low ceiling with pretty good vision along the surface. We could expect little help from the boys upstairs unless the weather improved.

It was around 0900 when the good news started filtering down. It was reported that with the help from the 1st Battalion of the 260th, that the 261st had captured Abbach and had opened up the highway from Lengfeld to Regensburg. Also the 13th Armored Division had crossed the river and were moving up through the bridgehead to join us in our attack on Regensburg. It appeared the enemy had all been captured, or had pulled back toward Regensburg.

Around 1100 we were told to form up along the roadway, that we were to walk about two miles to the juncture of the highway leading from Lengfeld to Regensburg, once there we would draw supplies and rations. We then would board trucks and follow Recon units from the 65th and 13th Armored toward Regensburg. The plan was for the 260th to enter the city first, led by the third Battalion. We arrived at the junction shortly after noon. The trucks had already arrived. When we saw the trucks, we could hardly believe our eyes, no artillery trucks. Just empty trucks with Red Ball drivers. Everyone would have a seat, with no haggling. We were told to hurry and grab our supplies, go and directly load onto the trucks, that we could eat our K-rations while aboard them.

Things were pretty well organized and it was not long before we were moving along toward Regensburg. Someone asked Cunningham, why the trucks? That it could not be too far to Regensburg. Cunningham replied that he wanted his ass rested when he arrived. That he might have a job for him, and if he would shut his mouth, that some of us probably could catch a few minutes of sleep. The pace of the trucks gave credence to Cunningham's statement about us being rested on our arrival. We could have walked faster than the trucks were traveling.

About mid-afternoon the trucks topped a rise in the road, and from this point we could see for miles to our left and to our front. To our left, was rolling farm land that extended for a couple of miles to the bans of the Danube River. It was a beautiful view, but no one broke out humming the "Blue Danube". To our left front we could see, through the haze, the city of Regensburg, to our right along the road, was a strip of forest about fifty yards wide, and beyond the trees, the land broke abruptly downward, almost ravine like.

The trucks came to a halt along the high point of the ridge. We could see, about a mile in front of us the recon vehicles, as they were slowly winding their way toward Regensburg. Suddenly, about a mile to our left, in what appeared to be a plot of fresh plowed ground, shells started exploding. Someone said that it must be outgoing mail. Almost simultaneously shells began landing and exploding all around us. Some one yelled for us to get off the trucks and take cover. At the same time, some person that was in charge of the trucks was giving orders to the drivers to get the trucks turned around and get the hell out of here, and that those shells were not rubber. As the trucks made their hasty turn the men taking cover in the ditches had two types of missiles to dodge. As the shelling continued, some of us decided to seek shelter in the ravine past the trees. As we ran through the trees, we were getting tree bursts right and left, but we got lucky and suffered no casualties. As we broke over the edge of the ravine we ran smack into a German Officer that was set up with a radio. He turned out to be the forward observer for the German guns that was doing the shelling. As soon as we captured him the shelling stopped. We returned to the road where we had departed the trucks. Not one truck was in sight. They had all gotten away without a hit. We took our prize to Capt. Batts. He made a call over the radio, and some M.P.'s showed up shortly, and took control of the prisoner.

We finally got the Company back together. No one was hurt. There was only one casualty and that was a man from M Company who was following close behind us. His injury was only a slight cut from a shell fragment. While we were being formed up, Capt. Batts gave us some good news. He said that it had been reported that the Officer that was in charge of defending Regensburg had pulled out last evening to keep the city from being destroyed. Our question was, if the enemy had pulled out last evening, who was shelling us a few minutes ago? His answer was, what we already knew. Those fanatics, the Waffen SS and the Hitler Youth. He went on to tell us that nothing has changed and unless we wanted to be the last to die in this war, we must continue to take the fight to them, paying no attention to rumors. To remember the way the fanatics operate, we face grave dangers behind the battle lines and that the primary reason for us being in this area is to prevent these fanatics from reaching the Alphine Redoubt and extending the war beyond any logical conclusion.

After the pep talk by Capt. Batts, we of "I" Company 260th led the march on Regensburg, followed by M Company and the rest of the 3rd Battalion. The only enemy we encountered were the ones coming out of hiding with their white flags, wanting to surrender. The only threat of violence we encountered was when a German Officer refused to surrender his sidearm to a machine gunner from M Company saying that he would only surrender his firearm to his Commanding Officer. The German lost the argument and the G.I. gained a souvenir.

It was getting late by the time we moved into the main part of Regensburg. Our Company took control of about a two block area. Capt. Batts called the Platoon leaders together and instructed them to start clearing the homes in the vicinity to be used to billet the troops. Cunningham returned to the Platoon and informed us of the situation. As luck would have it, we were standing in front of a large nice home that seemed almost large enough to accommodate the entire Platoon, and it was only a couple of doors down from a large modern hospital. Regensburg showed far less damage than most of the mid-sized cities that we had occupied lately. It could have been the area that we were in. The hospitals usually had that huge white cross painted on top of them so that they could easily be identified from the air.

The streets were almost deserted. Our Platoon was dispersed, covering one side of a city block. The Recon outfits light armor were parked at the street intersections. Sgt. Cunningham selected Sgt.'s. Rakosi and Kindoll, our interpreter Weik, and me to go with him to the door of the house we had selected for our billet. We knew the home was occupied. We had observed someone peeking from behind the blackout curtains. We could also hear a dog's bark coming from inside. After a few loud raps on the door, an elderly lady opened the door. Standing behind her was an elderly grey haired man, with a quizzical look on his face. In the center of the room stood a much younger lady. She was holding a rather large dog by a leash, and crying. The old man stepped up in front of the women and stammered out something that sounded to me as if he was asking if we were lost. I was about to answer "Hell yes I'm lost" when Weik started speaking to him in German. I found out he was saying "Vos es los" which means, what is wrong? The young lady was trying to subdue the dog, but couldn't. Cunningham walked over and extended his hand toward the dog. The dog licked his hand, wagged his tail and stopped barking. This seemed to calm everyone down. Cunningham began telling the old man, through our interpreter Weik, that we were taking over their home, and that they would have to find another place to live until we left. At first, the old man said that they would stay in the cellar and not get in the way. After Cunningham explained that this would not be acceptable, the old man started telling about his bad heart condition. He was on medication and he had to stay close in case he needed the doctor in an emergency situation. Cunningham countered this by telling him that we would take him and his wife and check them in the hospital, which was only a few doors down the street. The old man did not give in. He immediately answered that the hospital would not allow dogs to enter. Cunningham told the old man and his wife to get their coats and whatever else they would need. They were heading for the hospital to spend the night and that we would see that one of the neighbors would take care of their daughter and the dog. The decision had been made. Cunningham, Weik and I took the old couple to the hospital. Rakosi and Kendoll took the daughter and the dog around the corner to an apartment building where she said a friend of hers lived. The person at the hospital welcomed the old man and woman like long lost friends and immediately took them to rooms. Weik told us as we were walking away, that the hospital personnel were addressing the old man as some sort of commander. We dismissed the comment. At the time we had other things on our mind. After returning from the hospital, we of the 3rd Platoon took over the old man's home. It was too small to accommodate the entire Platoon, but since half the Platoon would be on patrol at any given time, the accommodations worked out well.

After the outpost and patrol assignments had been made, the rest of the Platoon returned to the house to get rest and work out a schedule for the relief of the outpost and patrols. After returning to our billet, as always, our curiosity got the best of us and we searched the closets, dresser drawers, the kitchen cabinets and any other places the enemy could be hiding or maybe hiding something important from us. Like a new camera holding evidence or maybe even a Luger left laying around. That could be dangerous if some Grunt unfamiliar with German equipment came across it.

Downstairs in the house was a large office. Cunningham and Weik started going through the drawers of a large desk that sat in the middle of the office. After reading a few letters, Weik determined that the old man that we had taken to the hospital was some sort of German Army General, probably retired. As we searched through the closets, we came across several officer uniforms.

It was getting late when Cunningham said that he wanted to check the men on the outpost before it got dark. We walked out onto the street. We could see a flurry of activity going on down the street in front of the hospital where we had left the old man. Since the outpost in front of the hospital was our responsibility, we started walking toward the hospital. After we had only gone a short distance, we met Sgt. Rakosi and the six men who were maintaining the hospital outpost. Cunningham asked Rakosi what was going on. Rakosi replied that a company of M.P.'s had shown up with half the brass of the 65th Division. They informed us that they were taking over the hospital and for us to return to our outfit. Rakosi said that when he asked them why? They informed them that a very important prisoner was being held there. Shortly after we arrived back at our billet, two jeeps pulled up. One filled with M.P.'s and the other held a full bird Colonel, a civilian, and jeep driver. The officer with the M.P.'s came and informed Cunningham that they were going to search the office of the owner of the building, which they did. Taking papers and other paraphernalia from the building. They left without saying a word. After the Colonel and his men left, Cunningham informed the men of our Platoon, that were not on guard duty, that they had better get some sleep. They would have to relieve the men on the outpost at midnight and would remain there until 0600. Sgt.'s. Kendoll and Rakosi took over the bedroom that Cunningham and I had selected. Cunningham told them they were to sleep there until midnight, that he and I would remain with the men on the outpost until 2300. At which time we would get them up to take charge of the second shift and remain with them on the outpost until 0600 the next morning, the 28th of April.

The men being relieved on the outpost returned around midnight. It had been a long day, and it did not take them long to settle down. Cunningham and I crawled into the bed that Kindoll and Rakosi had vacated and for a few seconds we tried to recall the last time we had slept in a bed. We could not. The next thing that we knew, Kindoll and Rakosi were entering the room telling us to wake up, that the kitchen truck had caught up and had a hot breakfast for us. Nothing jolts a Grunt awake quicker than the words "Hot Breakfast". After several days of freezing weather and eating from K-ration boxes, the breakfast consisted of rehashed 10 in 1 rations. The cooks had some how managed to obtain the boxes containing the cans of bacon, which made everyone happy, except Stern and his cohorts, who had to settle for an extra spoon of powdered eggs. The cooks had managed to somehow get hold of fresh baked bread, which made everything else more palatable, especially the coffee, since we did not have to build those little fires to heat the water.

It took a couple of hours for all the men of "I" Company to be served breakfast. After we had eaten, Capt. Batts called the Platoon leaders together and told them that he had to report to the hospital. There was a retired German Army General who had taken control of Regensburg after the General, who was in charge of defending the city, fled the morning of the 26th, then taking his troops with him. He was ready to formally surrender the city to the Americans. As Capt. Batts walked away, someone joked that it was maybe the old man that we had stuck in the hospital. These words turned out to be prophetic.

Later in the morning Capt. Batts came to our billet, then came into the room where Cunningham Kendoll, Rakosi, Weik and I were staying. He stated that he wanted to congratulate us. While we were wondering why, he began telling the story about the old man that we had taken to the hospital the evening before. The old man turned out to be the retired general who was left in charge of the city and Capt. repeated the story that the old man had told to his captors, as he signed the surrender of Regensburg. He said that he had feared for his life when we approached his home the evening before, and that he had considered suicide before we had arrived. Once he had let us inside he could see in our faces that we meant to do him or his family no harm, and on the way to the hospital he had come to the decision to notify the people in charge of the hospital to make contact with the proper American Officers and inform them of his decision. Capt. Batts thanked us for a job well done. Although we received no medals, we still felt good about the situation.

The 28th of April passed without further incidents. The troops of the 13th Armored that we had been working with, pulled out and it was reported that they were to continue the attack to the southeast. We would be following soon.

The next morning after breakfast we were informed to draw our K-rations and ammo, to be ready to move out at a moment's notice. The phrase, "a moment's notice" seemed to have replaced, "moving out soon" in recent days. My theory on this wording change, was to make the men believe that there was not enough time to check out the wine cellars, which recently seemed to contain more Schnapps than wine. This strong alcoholic drink could render an inexperienced drinker, incapacitated for hours. I can give a testimonial to that. The day wore on. We maintained our patrols and outposts. The kitchen trucks remained parked and set up on the street, furnishing hot coffee throughout the day. Word came down that we would be served hot meals at lunch and dinner. After dinner we would be relieved by some M.P. outfit. Then we would prepare to move out by trucks. The weather was turning bad. It had begun to rain and sleet. Cold and wet, that always seemed to be our cue to load onto those open trucks.

The Infantry's first class transportation was the Red Balls "deuce-and-a-half". When equipped for hauling personnel, it could comfortably carry about twenty personnel in street clothes. Under combat conditions, the least number that was loaded, were two squads and all their equipment. The only redeeming value here, was that you could sleep without falling over. The important thing was that you slept with your head erect, so that the ice water dripping from your steel helmet doesn't run down your shirt collar and along your spine. After that, it didn't matter about the feelings you had left in your rear end, that left a long time ago. My next favorite way to be transported was on the T.D.'s, and then the tanks. Although the variant sounds emanating from these track vehicles were at times maddening. After that, came the artillery trucks and the engineers. Riding these vehicles there was always some piece of equipment protruding into your ribs.

It was almost 2300 when word came down that we could relax and get some sleep. It appeared that we would not be moving out until around 0700 the next morning on May 1st. There was alot of bitching coming from the men. Not that they were anxious to join the fray, but they felt that they were deliberately put on alert to keep them out of the wine cellars. This was not a bad move by the Brass at this time. The rumors were flying that the war was coming to a close, and the men seemed ready to explode into an impromptu celebration at a moment's notice. The Brass enforced their point by increasing their reports about the stiff resistance the enemy was putting up, and that we must stay focused unless we wanted to be the last to die in this war. The next five days, action proved them right.

We were surprised to wake up around 0700, and find that our mess truck was still in place, and serving breakfast. The weather was cold and rainy. Breakfast went slowly due to the rain. No one seemed to eager to stand in the chow line. So they showed up one at a time to be served.

It was around 1000 when the Red Ball Express showed up. Everyone was in a good mood because we had just been informed that the front line had moved fifty miles in front of us and was approaching the Inns River. The 260th assignment was to follow behind the 261st in reserve, until we reached the Inns. Our jubilation was short lived. About mid afternoon, we of the third Battalion were informed that we were to make a short detour to check out the village of Natternberg. This is where it was reported to be some diehard enemy troops holed up. After arriving, a search party was sent into the village. After a couple of hours they returned and reported that they had found no military. The townspeople had reported that they had moved out the night before, across the Danube, toward the city of Deggendorf. By the time the search party returned, it was getting late. The rain and sleet were still falling, darkness was closing in, along with the fog from the Danube and Isar Rivers, whose convergence was only a short distance from where we sat.

After Natternberg, our assignment was to proceed to the city of Plattling. This is where we were to cross the Isar River on a pontoon bridge built by the 13th Armored Division. Although Plattling was only 12 miles away, it was midnight before we arrived at the crossing. The crossing was slow because of other traffic being funneled into one of the few crossings of the Asar at that time.

Leaving Plattling, we were to follow the 261st along the southern bank of the Danube to the city of Passau. Passau was a rather large river port located where the Danube and the Inns Rivers converged. It was reported to be well defended by the enemy. Movement was very slow after crossing the Isar. Military seemed to be going in all directions, the weather was bad and visibility was limited to about a quarter mile. It was daylight when our convoy stopped, and we were told to get all our gear and disembark from the trucks, that we would be walking for awhile. At this point these were welcome words. After unloading, we were standing between the highway and railroad tracks that ran parallel to the highway. Through the haze I could make out a few buildings scattered about. Across the railroad tracks I could make out a building that appeared to be a train station. A sign across the top read "MOOS". It is funny how some things are forever inscribed in your memory. As I read the sign, I wondered what the word meant in German, or if it had a meaning. I know at the time I was relating it to a farm in Mississippi.

After making our little fires to heat water for coffee, we had a fine breakfast of K-rations. I remembered we had not had a breakfast of K-rations since the morning after crossing the Danube in the attack on Regensburg, which seemed so long ago. After about an hour we were motioned onto the highway and started walking. It felt good to be able to stretch your legs and get the blood moving again. The weather was still very cold, but after walking awhile it wasn't noticeable. With a low ceiling and no sun, I was completely turned around. I asked Stern if he knew what direction we were going. He whipped out his compass and informed me that we were traveling southeast. Then he asked me if I had lost my compass or was it my mind. I did not answer as I was wondering the same thing. I felt into my jacket pocket and found the compass in the place it should be.

As the day wore on, there were times when the clouds would partly clear away, and we could get a view of the countryside. It was breath taking. We were walking along the foothills of the Alps Mountains, looking out over the Danube River basin. There were patches of evergreen forest covering the countryside. The ones along the highter were covered with a dusting of snow that we had encountered the last couple of days. I was struck by the sharp contrast of what we were seeing and why we were here.

It was getting late in the afternoon as we moved toward the city of Osterhofen, which lay on the edge of the Danube Basin. As we moved through the Basin there seemed to be a village every few hundred yards, all with strange sounding names, ending with Dorfs, muhl, Gaus, sings, Marks, Dings, some upper and some under. We even came across another Moos near Osterhoffen. Made one wonder if he were not going around in circles.

We were on the outskirts of Osterhofen when we were loaded onto trucks. Most of the trucks were from the artillery outfits. It was still raining and cold. I felt real lucky as I was directed onto a canvas covered six-by. I felt luckier still when I discovered it was our own "I" Company kitchen truck. I suppose a lot of other men felt lucky. They kept coming until the truck was like the proverbial sardine can. Things went pretty well for a while as we inched our way along slippery roads. Most of the time we spent just sitting. I was amazed at how the truck drivers were able to keep awake, watching that little black out light on the truck in front, and moving when he moved. Sometimes it happened, the driver would doze off and miss the light movement ahead, and we would become lost and all the trucks behind would be lost. Come daylight, it would be round up time with lots of bitching and arm waving by the Brass. We Grunts could care less as long as we did not go beyond the front line, and end up in enemy territory. Hell, I had been lost since I left Mississippi.

I awoke sometime during the night and was having a panic attack. There were arms and legs all over me. My legs and knees were cramping and I was unable to straighten out my legs. I dug my way out, through the bodies, toward the tailgate using the excuse, that I needed a piss call. I was not alone. A few more men bailed out with me. Luckily the truck was just sitting at the time. It was still raining and sleeting. After doing our thing the other men crawled back upon the truck. I went up to the drivers side of the truck, he had heard us scrambling around, and had stepped outside to see what was going on. I told him we were having a little piss call. I asked him how many men did he have in the cab with him. He said that he had the assistant driver and some second louie. I asked him if it would be alright if I rode on the truck fender for a while. He told me yes, but not to go to sleep and fall my young ass off and get run over. Draped over the truck hood, I figured that I would get a little heat from the truck's engine. I was wrong, we did not move enough to keep the engine warm. It was still raining and sleeting but it was better than being cooped up in the back of the truck. Daylight came, the folds in my raincoat were filled with ice. My fingers and toes were numb but I still felt better than when I awoke in the back of the truck. Besides it was time to make those little fires and start heating water for coffee and having that long awaited cigarette.

After a breakfast of K-rations, it was walking time again. The rain had stopped and the rumors about the war nearing its end picked up. The rumors that the 3rd and 7th Army's were the only ones still fighting, that their thinking was that the Germans were still trying to retreat into the redoubt area. It was located in the Alps Mountains. I suppose the Brass's thinking was being influenced by the history of WW1 when the Austrians, Hungarians and Italians suffered through the horrible winters of fighting in the Alps.

It was a slow go from one small village to another. I believe the 261st had bypassed every German soldier. At every village the Wehrmacht were coming out waving those white flags to surrender. It was during this time that I finally got possession of a German Luger. A German officer attempted to hide it in the grass as he exited a building to surrender and I was watching. At one village, which we were about to enter over a bridge that crossed a small river leading directly into the town square. We observed a number of enemy soldiers milling around the square, all fully armed. Before we could react some German officers exited a door on the town square carrying with them a white flag. Capt. Batts got on the radio to Battalion and in a short time some Major from Battalion Headquarters showed up in a jeep and joined Capt. Batts. The Major departed the jeep carrying his white flag. He and Capt. Batts walked to the middle of the bridge where the German Officers were waiting for them. There was lots of discussing and arm waving going on with the group as they met. After about fifteen minutes the group separated, the Germans returned to the village and the Major and Capt. Batts returned to where we were waiting. The Captain was smiling and we knew it must be good news. Capt. Batts told us the first words out of that son-of-a-bitch's mouth were, "we are ready to surrender" that they had us surrounded. Captain went on to tell us that he and the Major told that son-of-bitch, if he didn't have all the soldiers in that village disarmed and standing at the end of the bridge in fifteen minutes, that the village would be nothing but a grease spot. We already had our artillery set up and ready to level the town. He had nowhere to go, that we already had men across the Inns River. He said the German officer smiled and said he would do. Capt. said that he figured the officer was only trying to save face with his bluster. A few minutes later the soldiers came marching out to the end of the bridge, being led by the officer. They halted at the end of the bridge and the German Officer motioned for Capt. Batts to meet him on the bridge. Capt. obliged. Capt. returned and told us that the officer wondered if the men could surrender with dignity, without their hands over their heads. Capt. had told him why not. The men formed up and came marching across the bridge in formation and in step with their hobnails counting cadence. There were jeers from our men, but there was also a rippling of applause.

It was shortly after the incident at the bridge, when we officially received word, which had been a rumor, that Hitler was dead. He had been dead since April 30th. A victim of his own hands. The news made everyone feel as if the war was surely about to end. It did not take long for reality to set in. The war was still going on. There were reports of the fierce fighting by the 261st in the city of Passau, just a few miles ahead. As we moved slowly behind the 261st, doing the mopping up of the bypassed enemy troops, the pattern of the holdouts changed from putting up of their resistance in the villages, to resisting from the growing number of wooded areas. I suppose the reason for their change in tactics was because of the pressure put on them by the citizens. When they realized that we were making good on our promise to destroy every village that we met any resistance from. The idea of defending from the woods turned out to be not so brilliant for them. After a few shells from our Artillery boys the Wehrmacht would usually come forth waving their white flags. The Waffen SS and most of the Hitler Youth were different. They usually kept their pledge of death before surrender. At this stage of the war it was not hard for them to find someone to oblige them.

The trek toward Passau was a slow one. Although the report was, that the 261st had already taken the city, and had crossed the Inns River, then had entered Austria. We were being slowed down by the increasing number of P.O.W.'s. A few diehards thought they wanted to fight until confronted. Also the traffic of the 65th and support groups were being funneled toward the only two bridge crossings in the vicinity of Passau. This was causing terrible traffic jams.

Here it was May 3rd and the weather here in Bavaria, Germany was the same as it was in the Saar Valley in March, snow, ice and bitter cold. The reason they said, was the higher elevation and the wind blowing down from the Alps Mountains. I couldn't help thinking that this time of the year in Mississippi they would be plowing corn that was already waist high.

Around mid morning we were standing around waiting for something to happen. Word came down that Sgt. Harrell, who was bringing up the rear of the Company, had become sick. We were not surprised. Harrell our First Sergeant, was in his mid fifties and this was his second war to fight in Europe. He had landed in LeHavre, France 27 years earlier and had fought in WW1 in France. Sgt. Harrell was the men of "I" Company's mentor, as well as their tormentor. He did his job well and he was tough. He had made every step we young men made and suffered the same indignities as the rest of us Grunts and complained less. I believe the greatest compliment I could pay him is, "If we had more men his age participating in War there would be less Wars". The jeep with driver and Aid Man pulled up to where Sgt. Harrell was sitting beside the road. He stepped up into the jeep without help. The jeep drove the full length of the Company with Sgt. Harrell holding a salute the entire way. It stopped once and First Sergeant said in a strong voice, "Men, if we have another War I want you with me". As the jeep drove away I was thinking at least he is not a battle casualty, but my heart was giving a lie to this thought.

Another incident happened on the afternoon of the third that held us up, was the capture of our Battalion executive officer Major Thayer, along with his jeep driver Capt. Albanese and Cpl. Morris. I have heard several versions of the Major's capture and cannot deny or guarantee any of them. I can only give my version which I will not guarantee is correct. The reason being, that I was a Company messenger. The first lesson learned was, an oral message repeated through five different people, at the end, bears no resemblance to the original message. The second lesson learned was, observing something at a distance of five hundred yards or more without assistance, can never be reported as factual.

It seems that Major Thayer, his jeep driver and one other person (whose name is unknown to me) had driven out of sight of Headquarters Company which was leading the Battalion in our advance. As the jeep moved through a wooded area they were captured by a couple of enemy soldiers. They ordered the jeep driver to drive where they thought their unit would be. When they arrived their unit had pulled out and at this time Major Thayer talked the Germans into surrendering. It was about two hours later, when I observed the jeep returning to the head of the column with five men, reported to be Major Thayer, his two men, and the two German prisoners. The report came back to us that the prisoners were searched, interrogated, then turned over to a machine gunner from M Company, whose squad was attached to Battalion at that time. The machine gunner was a Georgia boy that had experience in handling P.O.W.'s. This action I observed at a distance of five hundred yards and the information was passed on to me through no less than five mouths.

It was late afternoon May 3rd, when the Third Battalion started loading on trucks of various descriptions, slowly moving toward the Inns River to be in position when it became our turn to cross into Austria. There we continue our advance on toward our next objective, which was Linz. Austria's second largest city. The battle plan for the 65th to take Linz, was for the 260th to cross the Inns River, turn north until we reached the left flank of the 261st. The two regiments would attack southeast with their objective being the capture of the city of Linz, Austria.

As we moved slowly toward the Inns River it was reported that we would be crossing the river in boats. About 0700 May 4, word came down that the 65th engineers had almost completed its repairs to the Neuhaus Scharding Bridge. We of the third Battalion probably would be crossing the Inns on the trucks we were presently riding on. This made everyone happy. Sure enough at 0900 the 4th of May, 1945 we rode across the Inns River into Austria. The birth place of Adolf Hitler.

After crossing the Inns River we turned north along the river until we reached the left flank of the 65th Division's battle line. Then we turned southeast toward Linz. At that point we were about 45 miles from Linz. As we moved out of Scharding the sun came out for the first time in several days. As the sun broke through it revealed one of the most beautiful sights that I had ever seen. On our right, in the distance, was the snow covered Alps Mountains. To me, a nineteen year old farm boy from Mississippi, the sight was breathtaking. Having never been west of the Mississippi River I had not seen a real mountain before this day. The thoughts of my childhood days, when in grammar school studying geography and reading library books about the Alps, came to me. Not ever in my wildest dreams did I ever think I would see the Alps. Surely not the first mountains I would see.

The 1st and 2nd Battalions had crossed the Inns River ahead of the 3rd Battalion. That placed the 3rd Battalion in reserve, as we moved toward Linz. Around noon we were told that it was break time. That we would have lunch, then would be walking for awhile. The mixture of trucks we were riding had other assignments. As we walked along, the rumors were flying about how near the end of the war was. Everyone was upbeat. We were seeing the sun for the first time in several days, the scenery was great, and the war was coming to a close. The word came down that they had finished the bridge across the Inns and that equipment was pouring across. We would be picked up by Red Ball later in the afternoon and that we were going to ride into Linz.

It was late in the afternoon when we were informed that the trucks would be picking us up shortly. We were going to have a rest period, eat our K-Ration dinner and wait. It was after dark when the Red Ball trucks arrived. By then our bubble had been burst. Word was coming down that our Intelligence and Reconnaissance Platoon had run into trouble at the town of Erferfing. Some of them had been captured and that the first Battalion was running into strong resistance trying to enter the town. We were about five miles from the action and were able to hear the action and see the flames. Around midnight the Brass made the decision that we would spend the night where we were in case we had to help out at Erferfing.

A perimeter was set up along each side of the road. The men maintaining the perimeter were placed in place with instructions that they would be there until daylight with only one man sleeping at a time and not to move around. Everything that moved starting at 0100 would be shot. After the perimeter was set up, there was plenty of room left on the trucks for the men that remained to stretch out and sleep. It had been several days since I had more than a nap and I took full advantage of the next few hours.

Daylight came on May 5th, the weather was cold and it was threatening rain again. One day of sunshine since leaving Regensburg. The little fires started popping up along the roadway as usual. There were no sounds of war coming from any direction. The only sounds were coming from men on walkie-talkies. The reports were coming in that we were in control of Erferding, but had suffered quite a few casualties. The Germans and Hungarians who were defending the city, suffered a large number of casualties, plus several thousand were taken prisoner. After breakfast, the decision for the 3rd Battalion had been made for it to bypass Erferding and move on to Linz.

As we moved slowly eastward toward Linz, Austria it was stunning to see the number of people moving toward the west. There were Germans and Hungarians carrying their white flags with a scattering of women and children among them. There were large groups of civilians, some saying that they were from labor camps and some were citizens that were abandoning their homes out of their fear of the Russians. All were saying that the Americans would treat them well and protect them from the Russians. Some were in vehicles. Mostly of the coke burning variety. Most were carrying their belongings or pulling them in some sort of small wagon.

We met little resistance as we moved toward our objective. Occasionally we would be slowed when our recon group would meet some token resistance, or by the gathering up of P.O.W.'s. As we drew near the city, the news came down that Linz had been declared an open city. This meant there would be no fighting, that the 260th would move in and occupy the city. This bit of news brought loud cheers from the men. On the outskirts of Linz our column came to a halt. Word of Linz being an open city was again repeated and also the war appeared to be over for us. For a few seconds there seemed to be a huge sigh emanating from the troops. Maybe not. The sound could have been coming from the deflating of that huge knot that I had been carrying around in the pit of my stomach for the last few months. As we returned to the trucks we were told to stay alert, that there might still be some crazies out there waiting to do you harm. As it turned out it was not the crazies that drew last blood but the carelessness that drew the last blood.

As we moved slowly through the streets of Linz, Jasperson and I were sitting on the tailgate of the truck. Our assignment was to watch the roofs of the buildings to our rear for snipers. I was watching left and Jasperson was watching to the right. There were a few people standing along the street waving, most seemed to be workers from the labor camps. As Jasperson raised his hand to wave, his rifle slipped from the tailgate onto the pavement, butt first. When it struck the pavement it discharged. The muzzle blast was horrific. It felt as if it had gone off in my face. When I opened my eyes I could see blood spatter on the right sleeve of my jacket. Above the ringing in my ears I could hear someone calling for the medic. When I opened my eyes, Jasperson was standing in the street behind the truck, holding his left wrist with his right hand with blood dripping from his arm onto the street. By the time I realized that I was not injured and the blood spatter on my jacket had come from Jasperson's arm as the bullet passed through, our Platoon medic Coy, was with Jasperson with one arm around his shoulders and the other hand holding up Jasperson's damaged arm. They walked across the street to my left, walked up a few steps, entered the building and disappeared. The truck moved on. As we moved all my thoughts and feelings were about my buddy who had just gotten a "million dollar" wound too late. As I sat on the tailgate alone, I heard this voice come from behind me. It was coming from my good friend Howard "Murphy" Stern. He was telling me that I should be more careful about who I hung out with. I told him I would and asked him if he would like to join me on the tailgate. He did.

Night was approaching when the trucks started pulling into what appeared to be some sort of industrial park. There were factory type buildings surrounded by military type barracks. We were instructed to unload from the trucks. This would be the place that we were going to spend this night. I am thinking what a place to celebrate the end of the war. A work camp. The powers that be must have been reading my mind. The first thing out of their mouths were "Men the war is not over yet so remain alert. They went on to tell us that we would remain here until further assignment, which should come soon. We were then assigned to our billets. The billets we were assigned were long barrack type buildings. Two Platoons of men were assigned to each building. We moved inside. The barracks was devoid of any furnishings. Another night of sleeping on cement floors, wrapped in a shelter half and blanket. The only saving grace was at one end of the building there were restrooms and shower facilities that worked.

Early morning of the 6th of May we were aroused by someone walking through the building, yelling for us to get up, that the kitchen truck had caught up with us and was ready to serve us a hot breakfast. After washing up we went outside. Sure enough, there were those powdered egg specialists lined up beneath a square of canvas, trying to prevent the misty rain from blowing onto their fixings. There it was all laid out. Lumps of powered eggs, cold greasy bacon, and cold toast. Just looking at it brought to me flashbacks of Camp Lucky Strike. I ate the powdered egg lumps the only way a grunt knew how, with his hands. It was hard to balance those lumps on a fork or spoon, especially when you were shivering in the cold. Breakfast turned out better than expected. I suppose it was, because it was not competing with that fear knot that had disappeared for the last couple of days.

After breakfast everyone was instructed to fallout in front of the two barracks that "I" Company was occupying in full battle dress with the exception of bed roll, that we would be returning later in the day and probably would spend another night here. We were then instructed to get our gear and go by the kitchen truck and draw a lunch K-ration. Then meet with your platoon leaders, that they would give us our assignments. Cunningham called the Platoon together, he had been given a rough drawn map of the area in Linz that our platoon was to search for weapons and any military that might be hiding out. We were to prevent any looting by the displaced persons that were moving into the city by the thousands. Most claiming they were running from the Russians who were occupying the area just a few miles east of Linz. As we moved about the streets it seemed as if everyone had memorized those four words of English "Americans good, Russians bad".

As we moved through our assigned area, searching the homes and buildings for military personal and any person that their demeanor cast suspicion onto himself, would be turned over to the Military Police. As we moved through our sector, most of the people were very cooperative. A few showed their resentment and a very few even questioned our authority. There was one such lady that did this, telling us we were insulting her husband's memory, who had given his life for his country, fighting on the Russian front. After we searched her closet and found those SS officer uniforms hanging there, we threw them out onto the floor. Then I discovered a German Officers dress knife and placed it in my shirt. Her Nazi upbringing began to manifest itself, as she screamed at us in two languages every curse word known to man. The knife was placed among my souvenirs.

It was while we were having our noon break that Cunningham told us our assignment had changed. It seemed that a problem was developing with the displaced persons looting the shops that were trying to open for business. Several of us drew the assignment of guarding a ladies dress and hosiery shop. It turned out to be a fun place. It seemed that every lady in eastern Europe had worn out their hose running from the Russians. All the G.I.s were delighted to assist them in their purchase. It was late afternoon when we reluctantly relinquished our assignment to the men from the 259th and returned to our billets to get ready for those rehashed 10-in-1's.

After chow Capt. Batts gathered "I" Company around him, not in formation but in a semi-circle. Capt. Batts held both hands above his head and said in a loud clear voice, "Men of "I" Company, I am saying to you, not officially but with a reasonable assurance, that the war in Europe is over". This brought a cheer from the men. Capt. went on to say, "There is one more thing that I am going to say with reasonable assurance. Tonight will be the last night that you will have to sleep on cold cement. We won, surely one of the spoils should be a soft warm bed. Capt. then told us starting tomorrow morning we will begin our peacetime assignment. We will be moving back to Eferding to take over the security at two P.O.W. camps, Hungarian and German and will be there until the interrogators finish their jobs. We have thousands of displaced persons to deal with. Working with us there will be a Company from the 259th, plus some Special Forces units. We want all of you that speak another language besides English, to think about being a volunteer for special assignment when we arrive at Eferding. Also when we arrive at Eferding the Quartermaster will have our duffel bags waiting there for us. For our billets we have selected duplex type apartments with no more than two men assigned to a bedroom. We will be scattered over a large area, so it will not be feasible for our mess facilities to operate. Instead, you will be supplied with 10 in 1 rations and you will do your own heating and cooking in the kitchens of your own billets. We are making arrangements with local barbers to give everyone a free haircut. We were told that the Austrians are pretty adept at using clippers and straight razors. Due to the fact that we are moving out early tomorrow morning directly after breakfast which will be at 0700. I am restricting everyone to their Quarters tonight. So all you men that have those silk stockings in your pockets and your intentions were to use them to barter tonight, "Forget it". We were then dismissed to go to our quarters.

The next morning after breakfast the trucks were waiting. It was only 18 miles from Linz to Eferding. Around 0800 we pulled into Eferding and stopped near a large building that was reported to be a hospital. Next to the hospital was a huge building surrounded by a high stone fence. We found out later, to our pleasure that this was a winery and Schnapps distillery. Only a couple of doors down the street was a large building with an American flag out front. This turned out to be our Company Headquarters building. After the trucks came to a halt we were told to disembark onto the street and to bring all your equipment. After we lined up along the street, our attention was directed toward two canvas covered trucks down the street, a few yards beyond where we were standing. We were told that these trucks contained our duffel bags. The trucks were to pull up near where we were standing and the attendants with the trucks will remove the bags from the trucks, reading the name stenciled on the bag aloud. When your name is called, step forward retrieve your bag, return to formation, placing your bag in front of you. This procedure took about one hour. After the Quartermaster trucks moved away, Capt. Batts again got our attention. He asked if we remembered at last evenings meeting, that he asked for volunteers that spoke any other language other than English, and if they wanted to do so, pick up your duffel bag and equipment and go to the lead truck. You will then be taken to be interviewed for possible temporary assignment. There were several volunteers from the Company, three from our Platoon. They were Sgt. Rakosi who spoke Hungarian, Castagliola who spoke Italian, and Weik who spoke German The next assignment was for two squads from each Platoon to be assigned to Provost Marshall section to be used as guards at the P.O.W. camps. The squads would be selected by the Platoon leader.

After the assignments had been made, there were fourteen men left in our Platoon. They were our Platoon Leader Sgt. Cunningham, the Platoon Guide Sgt. Smith, Squad leader Sgt. Kendoll, Assistant Squad leader Sgt. Poage, our Medic Coy, Pvt.'s. Meeks, Urean, Hughes, Cisco, Stamms, Matus, Joseph, Stern and myself. The fourteen of us were told to get our gear and duffel bags and get onto the truck and it would take us to our Quarters. Quarters, a term I had not heard lately. Maybe the war is really over. After loading, we were escorted by two M.P.'s in a jeep to the southern edge of the city. We came to a stop in front of the last two buildings on the street. The two buildings were almost alike. They turned out to be duplex apartment buildings. Beyond the buildings was farm land and in the distance beyond the farm land you could see the snow covered Alps. We unloaded the M.P.'s unlocked the doors to the apartments, handed Cunningham the keys, then we went in to inspect the place. It was much more than we expected.

The four apartments consisted of a total of sixteen bedrooms, two more than the total number of men left in the Platoon. This observation brought forth a remark from Stern, that since there appeared to be such a housing shortage, that we should be able to make a little extra cash by renting out the extra bedrooms. I told him that he was always the business man, to try and lighten up and have some fun. His reply was that he was thinking about having fun in combination with his room renting plan, but since thinking it over maybe his plan would conflict with the "No Fraternizing" policy.

The floor plans of the four apartments were the same. A kitchen, living, dining and master bedrooms and bath downstairs. Upstairs contained three bedrooms, one bath plus a lavatory in each bedroom. The bedrooms all contained a double bed. All the apartments were stocked with all the supplies that was needed to run a household.

Cunningham called the men together, gave them their room assignment and told us what our duties would be. Our duties were minimal. The only thing that we were required to do, was to keep the apartments clean, and have two guards patrolling the street in front of our apartments during the hours of darkness. I was assigned the bedroom downstairs and Cunningham took the first bedroom at the head of the stairs. Cunningham told me my duties as Platoon Runner would be to see that the kitchen was kept clean and that if anyone failed to clean up their mess after using the kitchen, I was to run upstairs and inform him. If he needed anything from the kitchen day or night, I was to run it up the stairs to him, whenever he yelled for it. I shot him the bird after that last request.

After the assignments had been made everyone was in a festive mood and was ready to celebrate. The war was over and the prospect of some much needed rest seemed close at hand. The mood was there but we needed an enforcer. Having no wine cellar, some of us decided to see if we could make our way back to Company Headquarters. Remembering that it had only been a short ride, this morning to our apartments and also remembering that it was located near a winery.

After consulting with Sgt. Cunningham and getting the okay to go, our little troop, which consisted of about half the men in the apartments, started out led by Sgt. Kendoll. The street we walked down, leading back into town was lined on both sides with large trees. I remember noticing small green buds emerging from the branches and wondering how this was possible when only a couple of days ago it was snowing. Then I remembered it was May, springtime. May 7, 1945.

As we walked along I struck up a conversation with Stern, asking him when he thought we would be going home. His answer was that he thought he and I would have to go through Japan to get home. My reply to Stern was that I did not think so, that we would be going home soon. I was wrong. One year from the exact date that I spoke those words to Stern, May 7, 1946 I walked into a farm house in Mississippi, went into the kitchen and announced to the lady preparing a meal "Mama, I'm back".

We found the winery, but the M.P.'s had taken it over and had placed guards at all entrances. After consultation with the officer in charge, we were informed that we would need a written request from our company commander before we would be able to receive any goods. We walked down the street to Company Headquarters and told Captain Batts what our problem was. Captain asked us how many men we had at the apartments. We told him and he said for us not to worry for us to go back to our apartments. When we finished exploring the city, that he would personally deliver to us all the refreshments we wanted. That he needed to check our quarters. He also informed us that he had worked out a deal with a couple of nearby barber shops for us to get our hair cut. He said that there had not been any currency rate worked out yet, that we would sign our names and what our outfit we belonged to, the army would take care of the cost. Most of us did the hair thing. We also found a camera shop where for the first time I discovered film that would work in the camera that I had liberated from an oven in the vicinity of Bamberg Germany. After hassling over how I was to pay for the film, we finally settled on silver coins that my buddies and I managed to find in our pockets.

When we arrived back at the apartments, Captain Batts had already delivered the goods, Two cases of wine and one case of schapps. It was time for the celebration to begin. Sgt. Cunningham made a short speech about handling our alcohol and remembering the lessons we had learned about it.

The party was rather subdued considering the occasion. With most of our buddies on special assignments and the conversation turning to our buddies that would never attend a victory party, our party was tame, compared to what we saw later on news reels at the movies. I asked Stern if he thought that our survival was a matter of luck. He reminded me of the pact that we had made while under fire at Saarlautern. I asked him if he thought that our pact had anything to do with it. He answered, "Windy, I will always believe that it did". Two men, two different religions, one answer.

The next day May 8, 1945, the war was officially over. I had a slight headache, but the knot in my stomach had been totally eradicated. I was able to take a deep breath again. I walked outside and looked toward the southeast. My eyes caught the reflection of the sun off the snow covered Alps and a sense of peace came over me. The first days following the war were chaotic, mostly due to the number of displaced persons coming from the east in fear of the Russians. The ones coming in were mixing in with the ones that were being released from the labor camps. There were the P.O.W.'s to contend with Germans, Italians and Hungarians. There was the added burden of the Russian P.O.W.'s that were held by the Germans and were being released. They were clashing with the so called White Russians who were reported to be friendly toward the Germans. The logistics alone in dealing with this problem seemed overwhelming. It was amazing to watch as the Military Government took over. They had anticipated the problems and had plans in place when the war ended. Within thirty days the problems at Erferding had eased enough that "I" Company was sent back to Linz to join the rest of the Battalion.

We were in Linz one night. The next day, June 12th we of the third Platoon were given the assignment to board trucks and proceed north, to the Austrian Czechoslovakia border, a distance of about 25 miles. We were to relieve an M.P. unit that was maintaining check points along the border. The Russians occupied the Czech side and we, the Austrian side. The reason for these check points were the territory south of the border was in dispute. The Russians claimed that their zone of occupation was to run south as far as the Danube River. Our association with the Russians was quite an experience. After five weeks the dispute was resolved. It was agreed that the Russians were entitled to the territory south to the Danube. Moving day was a heart breaker. Everyone in the disputed territory wanted to move south with us.

Our Platoon ended up in and around the small town of Mittendorf where we just hung out and enjoyed doing our thing for the next month. During that time I went on leave to Switzerland and visited Berchisgarden, Hitler's retreat. Toured southern Austria, stepped over the border into Italy, so I could say that I had been there. I also rode the trains into Hungary and Yugoslavia, returning displaced persons. It was also during this time that I began to lose my buddies to the point system. They were being transferred to outfits that were being sent back to the states. I was happy for them to be going home, but it was hard for me to watch my buddies leave. Knowing that I may never see them again.

On August 30, 1945 the 65th Division was deactivated. We low point men of the Division were put on trains and were sent to Garmish, Germany to join the 10th Armored Division, which was on its way to the States for furloughs. Then on to war with Japan. While on our way to Garmish, our orders were changed, due to the war had ended with Japan a few days earlier. Our orders were to report to the 9th Division which had been assigned to the Army of Occupation in Germany. I was assigned to the 9th Division, 60th Regiment A Company on September 12, 1945 and stationed at Phoffenhoffen, Germany. One week later I went on Furlough, two weeks later to Paris, France. I returned, made the Battalion basketball team, played basketball until mid December. After that I signed up for the Army Education Program and was accepted. Attended Nutmeg Prep 60th I&E at Frising, Germany until April 1946. Then I was assigned to the 778th Anti-Aircraft Automatic Weapons Battalion who was on their way to the States. We were trained to Bremerhaven, Germany. There we caught the SS Fayetteville and headed home. Landed 11 days later at New York City. To the tune of "There Is Going to Be a Happy Hallelujah Time". Left New York, and went to Ft. Dix,. There I caught a train and arrived at Camp Shelby, Mississippi on May 4th. I was discharged May 6th and arrived home May 7, 1946. I walked into the kitchen and told my Mama "I am back". She kissed me and smiled through the tears. I hugged her tight and thanked her for her prayers that brought me Home.

EPILOGUE

My decision to write about my World War II experience, was made in early 2000, after my son Mike and I had visited the D-Day Museum in New Orleans. Mike asked me a few questions after we had left the Museum. It was then, that I realized I had never discussed the war with him or my involvement in it. In fact, I had hardly discussed it with anyone.

After being discharged from the Army in 1946, I attended school under the G.I. Bill. That is where I met my future wife Mary in 1948. We were married in 1949. Within five years we had three children, after that it was work with no time for memories.

My discussion with Mike made me realize that a very important period in my life would never be known, if I didn't write it down so that my children, grandchildren and great grandchildren would be able to read about my involvement in one of mankind's great achievements.

As I started thinking about writing, names of buddies and the events of the war was no problem remembering. Getting the events in chronological order, and the places they happened ,was impossible without research. After starting my research, I discovered that my Division, the 65th. had formed an association forty-seven years before. I joined the association and began my search for some of my former buddies. I made contact with six former Platoon mates, plus making contact with three family members of deceased Platoon buddies. I also obtained valuable information from the Association's Historian and also got in touch with a German Historian in Deggendorf, Germany. He furnished me with invaluable information and maps.

My objective in writing this book was not so much to tell of battle, which I always found very confusing while in progress, and hard to detail afterwards. Therefore it was the most difficult for me to remember. My objective was to tell of the things that I remember vividly and the things that I learned. The thing that stands out most in my mind was trying to survive the harsh elements. This battle was fought every day twenty-four hours a day, seven days a week. The nights were the worse, when you could not have any fire at all, not even a cigarette. You were huddled together on an open truck, or you were in a foxhole with a buddy, holding on to each other to keep warm, or rubbing and holding your buddies feet next to your body, trying to prevent frostbite. It was under these conditions that I learned about Camaraderie, Tolerance and Equality. There were no questions asked because the answers were obvious.

**MEMORIES OF THE 3rd PLATOON
I COMPANY, 260th INFANTRY
in Eferding, Austria
V-DAY PLUS ONE
Waiting for clean up and to start Celebrating**

STANDING: Meeks, Urean, Hughes
BOTTOM: Kendoll, Cisco

Above: *Top row:* Smith, Cunningham, Thayer
Sitting: Cisco, Meeks, Urean, Mueller

Left: Stern, Windham

Below: Hughes, Meeks, Urean, Matus, Stams,
Sitting: Cisco

TOP: *Standing:* Moncada, ?,?,?
Bottom: Rakosi,?

BOTTOM LEFT:
Standing: Windham, Hendrix, Weik

BOTTOM RIGHT:
Shaw, Spicer, Smith, Cavanaugh, Webb

Joe Windham, Jack Zinnaman and Ellsworth Cunningham
1st Meeting after 58 years in Biloxi, Mississippi in 2002

Harrell, 1st Sergeant of Company "I" 260th Infantry
Veteran of 27 Years Service

Dewayne Simmons, Collins, Frank Blubaugh, Ralph Lavine, Harry C. Rice and Clark, preparing for overseas assignment in New York City, New York on December 1944.